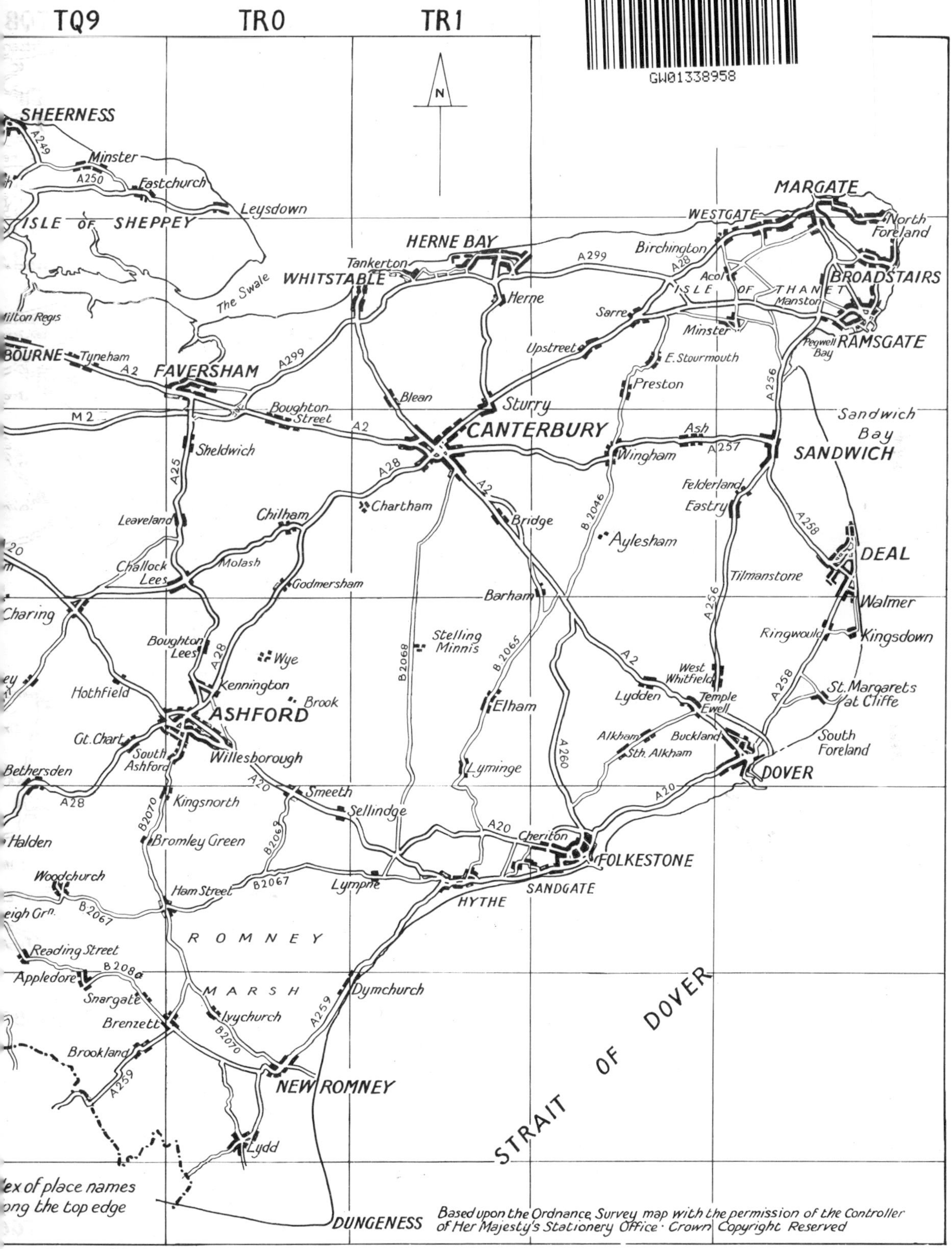

Based upon the Ordnance Survey map with the permission of the Controller of Her Majesty's Stationery Office · Crown Copyright Reserved

KENT: THE GARDEN OF ENGLAND

Jacket illustrations: Hop picking at Spring Grove, Wye; Hamden, near Biddenden; The Pantiles at Tunbridge Wells.

Kent: The Garden of England

PAUL BURNHAM
&
STUART MCRAE

Paul Norbury Publications   Tenterden   Kent

KENT: THE GARDEN OF ENGLAND

©Paul Burnham & Stuart McRae 1978

*All rights reserved.
No part of this publication
may be reproduced or transmitted
in any form or by any means
without permission*

PAUL NORBURY PUBLICATIONS LTD
Caxton House, High Street, Tenterden, Kent, England

First published 1978

ISBN 0904404 234

This book has been set in Times Roman 11 on 13.
Printed by Geerings of Ashford Ltd.

To the Rev Dr S. Graham Brade-Birks and our other predecessors and colleagues at Wye College.

CONTENTS

List of Plates ix
List of Figures x
Acknowledgments xiii
Introduction xiv
Chapter 1 Landscapes of the Past 1
Chapter 2 Geology and Landscape 29
Chapter 3 The Farmer's Landscape 45
Chapter 4 Wildlife in the Landscape 79
Chapter 5 The Industrial Scene 101
Chapter 6 Buildings in the Landscape 111
Chapter 7 Towns and Villages 139
Chapter 8 Kent Now and Tomorrow 161
Bibliography 163
Index of Place Names 169
Index of subjects 175

LIST OF PLATES

Plate 1	Satellite photograph of Kent *(Nigel Press Associates from a NASA original)*	xv
Plate 2	Devil's Kneading Trough and Brook *(Institute of Geological Sciences)*	xiv
Plate 3	The 'Hugin' *(Kent Messenger Group)*	7
Plate 4	The Court of Shepway *(Kent Messenger Group)*	13
Plate 5	Folkestone Warren Landslip *(British Rail Southern Region)*	24
Plate 6	Dover Harbour	27
Plate 7	Apple Orchard with Sheep *(Kent Messenger Group)*	57
Plate 8	Picking Apples	60
Plate 9	Stringing Hop Wirework using Stilts	64
Plate 10	Stringing Hop Wirework using Stringing Pole	64
Plate 11	Cutting Hop Bines	66
Plate 12	Hop Pickers *(Rev. R. W. H. Ackworth)*	70
Plate 13	Tallyman in hop garden *(Rev. R. W. H. Ackworth)*	70
Plate 14	Chestnut Coppice	78
Plate 15	Ragstone Quarry *(Institute of Geological Sciences)*	103
Plate 16	Northfleet Cement Works *(Blue Circle Group)*	105
Plate 17	William Balston *(Whatman Ltd.)*	108
Plate 18	Dungeness *(Aerofilms Ltd.)*	109
Plate 19	Cliffe Church	112
Plate 20	Wealden House near Maidstone	121
Plate 21	Weatherboarded Cottage at Biddenden	125
Plate 22	Early Oasts at Bough Beech	132
Plate 23	Oasts in use at Wye	133
Plate 24	New style Oast House *(S. G. McRae)*	133
Plate 25	Furnace Pond, Cowden	137
Plate 26	Canterbury	144
Plate 27	Pargetting at Maidstone	146
Plate 28	Tenterden	151
Plate 29	Mediaeval Barn at Brook	154
Plate 30	Cricket on Leigh Green *(Kent Messenger Group)*	158

Unless otherwise stated, the photographs were taken by C. P. Burnham

LIST OF FIGURES

Fig. 1	Early Kentish Silver Penny	*xvi*
Fig. 2	The County Arms of Kent	*xvii*
Fig. 3	The Swanscombe Skull	1
Fig. 4	Kits Coty	2
Fig. 5	Oldbury Hill Fort	3
Fig. 6	Roman Pharos	4
Fig. 7	Romano-British Kent	5
Fig. 8	Mediaeval Kent	9
Fig. 9	William the Conqueror	10
Fig. 10	Rochester Castle	11
Fig. 11	Hever Castle	12
Fig. 12	Deal Castle	14
Fig. 13	Georgian Kent	17
Fig. 14	East Farleigh Bridge	18
Fig. 15	Martello Tower No. 3	19
Fig. 16	Kentish Turn-Wrest Plough	21
Fig. 17	Jane Austen's Bower	22
Fig. 18	Victorian Kent	25
Fig. 19	Dickens House	26
Fig. 20	Kingsferry Bridge	28
Fig. 21	Landscape Regions of Kent	31
Fig. 22	Geology of Kent	33
Fig. 23	Fossil ammonite	34
Fig. 24	Iguanodon	35
Fig. 25	Fossil lamellibranch	36
Fig. 26	Fossil belemnite	37
Fig. 27	Pyrite nodule from the Chalk	38
Fig. 28	Fossil sea urchin	39
Fig. 29	Fossil shark's teeth	40
Fig. 30	Gypsum crystal (selenite)	41
Fig. 31	Geological Cross Section	42
Fig. 32	Romney Marsh	44
Fig. 33	Rainfall of Kent	46
Fig. 34	Soils of Kent	49
Fig. 35	Cross-section from Greensand Ridge to North Downs	51
Fig. 36	Rendzina and Brown Calcareous Earth	52
Fig. 37	Brown Earth and Humo-ferric Podzol	53
Fig. 38	Stagnogley and Ground-Water Gley	55
Fig. 39	Fruit in Kent	58
Fig. 40	Hops in Kent	58

Fig. 41	Hops	62
Fig. 42	18th Century Hop Pickers' Token	68
Fig. 43	Early 19th Century Hop Pickers' Token	68
Fig. 44	Late 19th Century Hop Pickers' Token	68
Fig. 45	Vegetables in Kent	73
Fig. 46	Land Use Capability in Kent	73
Fig. 47	Wild White or Kentish Clover *(Trifolium repens)*	74
Fig. 48	Romney Marsh Sheep	77
Fig. 49	Nightingale *(Luscinia megarhynchos)*	80
Fig. 50	Lady Orchid *(Orchis purpurea)*	82
Fig. 51	Bee Orchid *(Ophrys apifera)*	84
Fig. 52	Late Spider Orchid *(Ophrys fuciflora)*	85
Fig. 53	Hoary Cress *(Cardaria draba)*	87
Fig. 54	Hothfield Common	88
Fig. 55	Wall Pennywort *(Umbillicus rupestris)*	89
Fig. 56	Thorn Apple *(Datura stramonium)*	91
Fig. 57	Pollution in the River Stour	92
Fig. 58	Great Crested Grebe *(Podiceps cristatus)*	94
Fig. 59	Salt Marsh Vegetation at Shell Ness, Sheppey	95
Fig. 60	Sea Holly *(Eryngium maritimum)*	96
Fig. 61	Kent: Nature Reserves, National Trust Sites and Forest Walks	98
Fig. 62	Greenshank *(Tringa nebularia)*	100
Fig. 63	Shoreham Church Porch	111
Fig. 64	Cast Iron Fireback: The Old Hall, Wye College	113
Fig. 65	New Romney Church Tower	114
Fig. 66	Goodnestone Church Tower	115
Fig. 67	Brookland Belfry	116
Fig. 68	Canterbury Cathedral	116
Fig. 69	Bexley Church Spire	117
Fig. 70	Typical Wealden House	118
Fig. 71	Plan of Typical Wealden House	119
Fig. 72	Priest's House, Small Hythe	119
Fig. 73	Knole	122
Fig. 74	Gables	123
Fig. 75	Hadlow Castle Tower	124
Fig. 76	Dering 'Lucky' Window	126
Fig. 77	House in Chequers Park, Wye	127
Fig. 78	Garden of Chilham Castle	128
Fig. 79	Construction of barn at Brook	129
Fig. 80	Construction of barn at Teynham	129
Fig. 81	Oast House	131

Fig. 82	Rolvenden Windmill	134
Fig. 83	Cranbrook Windmill	135
Fig. 84	Westwell Watermill	136
Fig. 85	Kent: Population of Towns	138
Fig. 86	Canterbury before 1612 (based on Speed's map)	140
Fig. 87	Chancel of St. Martin's Church	142
Fig. 88	The Murder of Beckett	143
Fig. 89	John Fisher (1469-1535)	147
Fig. 90	A Bathing Machine	148
Fig. 91	The Royal Sea Bathing Hospital, Margate	149
Fig. 92	South Eastern Railway Locomotive	150
Fig. 93	Tenterden Church Tower	152
Fig. 94	Brook Church Tower	153
Fig. 95	Brass of John, Lord Cobham, died 1408	156
Fig. 96	Samuel Morley M.P. (1809-1886)	157
Fig. 97	Methodist Chapel at Lenham Heath	159
Fig. 98	Protection of the Kent Landscape	160

ACKNOWLEDGMENTS

'Kent—The Garden of England' owes much to its predecessor 'The Rural Landscape of Kent' and to those who assisted in the preparation of that volume. In addition, C. Amos, B. H. Green and R. J. Spain have read and made comments on the sections concerning hops, ecology and watermills respectively. Sources of plates are acknowledged in the captions. In particular, however, Plates 2 and 15 (Crown copyright, reproduced by permission of the Controller, Her Majesty's Stationery Office) were supplied by the Institute of Geological Sciences, who also supplied the basic information incorporated in Figs. 22 and 31. Plate 1 was supplied by Nigel Press Associates from a NASA original and Plate 18 by Aerofilms Ltd. Meteorological Office data was used with permission for Fig. 33. The authors pay particular tribute to the skill of C. J. Hodgson of Wye College who drew Figs. 23 to 30 and Figs, 41, 47, 48, 49, 53, 55, 56, 58, 60, 62, 68, 77 and 90. Other contributors of figures were Kent County Council (2), R. R. Sellwood (5, 7), R. D. Green (32), S. J. Fordham (35), B. H. Green (50, 51, 52), R. F. Farrar (81), T. G. Burnham (92). Fig. 96 was taken from E. Hodder's *The Life of Samuel Morley* (1887) by kind permission of Lord Hollenden, and Fig. 16 from J. Boys' *A General View of the Agriculture of the County of Kent* (1796). S. G. McRae drew Figs. 21, 22, 31, 39, 40, 45, 61, while C.P. Burnham was responsible for all the remaining figures. Mrs. V. Maag coped with two contrasting styles of handwriting to produce the typescript and D. Simons gave technical assistance with photographs. A more fundamental debt is owed by the authors to those who fostered their interest in the history and geography of Kent, especially for C. P. Burnham, to his grandfather, E. H. Clark of Maidstone, and for both authors to the tradition of scholarly interest in the environment maintained at Wye College.

INTRODUCTION

Kent is a splendid county, and its inhabitants have every reason to be proud of its rich history and varied geography. A deeper understanding of the landscape of Kent will well reward the interest of visitors and the loyalty of residents.

Kent is fortunate in having a natural integrity. Looking down from a satellite (Plate 1) the distinctive coastline is seen, ranging from chalk cliffs to estuarine marshes and shingle banks, while the woodlands of the High Weald, dark in tone, form a natural southern boundary. From more traditional viewpoints along the crest of the North Downs (Plate 2), each component of the landscape can easily be seen.

Kent has a long history as a political and cultural unit. 'Time has not yet stripped this county of its ancient name' wrote Camden, as he traces it from the Cantii, a Belgic tribe, through the Roman 'Cantium' and the Saxon 'Cant'. Kent, indeed, is not simply a county but a kingdom, which flowered early under Ethelbert (?560–616). He it was who established Kentish supremacy over

Plate 1
Satellite photograph of Kent. Landsat image supplied by Nigel Press Associates from a NASA original dated 11th February 1976. A little cloud in the Thames Estuary and over London. Pale toned arable land, usually on drier soils contrasts with dark pasture on damp marshland and Weald Clay, and reveals the pattern of dry valleys on the North Downs.

Plate 2
View from the North Downs showing a scarp face coombe (The Devil's Kneading Trough) and the village of Brook. Well-wooded Gault vale to left, arable land of the Stour valley to right.

Plate 1

most of England and compiled the earliest code of English law still extant. By welcoming the mission of Augustine, Canterbury established a primacy in Church affairs which has long outlived the political independence lost in the late eighth century, first to Mercia and then to Wessex. The reintroduction of coinage shows the Kingdom of Kent as a cultural innovator. One of the earliest Anglo-Saxon coins is a small seventh century gold piece of very advanced style, bearing the Latin name of Canterbury. About a century later, the first known silver penny was minted at Canterbury and is ascribed to King Heabert (c. 765).

As befits a kingdom, Kent has regional loyalties within itself. The Medway bisects the county, and the 'Kentish men', born to the west of it, are traditionally distinct from the 'men of Kent' to the east. A similar, but not identical, division parts Kent into two Anglican dioceses, Canterbury in the east and Rochester in the west, a feature surviving from the days of Kentish independence. The shadow of this independence and distinct customs, particularly relating to inheritance, have been much prized. It is said, for example, that the inhabitants of Kent were never conquered by William the Conqueror, but that representatives met him near Swanscombe and accepted his rule upon terms. Hence the county motto 'Invicta', which expresses a pride and loyalty still felt by many.

The greatest threat to this regional spirit has been the proximity of London. London was of no importance before Roman times, and was again unknown to history in the 5th and 6th centuries. The emergence of Westminster as the effective capital of a united England dates from the accesssion of Edward the Confessor in 1042, at the earliest. By then London had established a pre-eminence in wealth and population, which has continued to this day. This has ensured that Kentish culture was metropolitan rather than provincial. At the same time, the growth of London has nibbled away much of north west Kent, a process deplored by William Cobbett, who esteemed London 'the Great Wen'. More inhabitants of Kent than might be supposed would support Cobbett's thesis, and certainly even modern antiquarians often maintain its 'historic boundaries' to include consideration of Greenwich and Eltham, lost administratively in 1888, or at least Bexley and Bromley, lost in 1965. In historical contexts this convention is continued here. Kent has long been called the garden of England, and proximity to the 'big house' of London has contributed to the distinctive landscape which makes the term an appropriate title for this book. London markets bene-

Fig. 1
Early Kentish Silver Penny
Minted at Canterbury for Wulfred, Archbishop 805-832. Reads: O–Vulfredi archiepiscop, R–Doroverniae civitatis. Actual diameter 19 mm.

fited commercial horticulture, while the 'seats' of the gentry, especially numerous in West Kent, were often sited to facilitate regular visits to London, as are those of their humbler successors today.

Kent also has the pre-eminently desirable characters in a garden of a favourable climate and good soils. It is dry enough for the cultivation and harvesting of field crops, and enjoys summers as warm as anywhere in Britain. Medium textured soils, avoiding the extremes of sand and clay and possessing good natural fertility, are widespread, especially in the north and east. Maps of land quality pick out Kent as including the largest proportion of superior land for agriculture and horticulture of any of the Home Counties. The high concentration of fruit, hops and vegetable crops contrasts with the woods and heaths on the sandy soils that cover much of Surrey and with the less intensive landscape of the Essex clays.

Attractiveness to the eye is also characteristic of a garden. Strong geological bones show through to make the Kentish landscape pleasingly diverse. The orchards and hop gardens are massed on the better soils, while the poorer are often partly clothed with deciduous woodland. Enclosure, which was early and informal, has given a homely landscape. Apart from Thanet and the marshes, many hedgerows remain.

If Kent were not its attractive and highly productive garden, it could well be named the Gateway of England. It is the nearest part of England to the Continent and offers the traveller the choice of two relatively easy routes to London and beyond. One route lies up the Thames, with Kent offering on the southern shore landing points such as Chatham, Gravesend and Greenwich. The other landlubbers route offers a dry road with no streams to cross other than the rivers of Stour, Medway and Darent. This is the chalk outcrop, with two roads: the prehistoric ridgeway on its southern flank and Watling Street on the northern edge. Nature's road indeed, no metalling was needed for light traffic on large parts of these early routes, as walkers on the North Downs' Way can prove for themselves. Surprised archaeologists made the same discovery when they found that the Roman road across Barham Downs was quite unmetalled, although thick and frequently repaired road beds elsewhere on Watling Street show that a metalled road would have been provided if required.

Kent's major towns are either ports or have grown where roads crossed a river: Canterbury, Rochester and Dartford on the Roman

Fig. 2.
The County Arms of Kent
The white prancing horse on a red background is said to have been the emblem of Horsa, one of the Jutes who took over Thanet in the early fifth century. The mural coronet commemorates the fact that Kent was a kingdom, and is symbolic of the many fortified castles and towns in the county. The three masts and sails and the supporting sea lions emphasise that Kent is a maritime county, connected with the navy, mercantile marine and sea fisheries. Round the neck of one sea lion (on the left) hangs the arms of the Cinque Ports, round the other, part of the arms of the Archbishopric of Canterbury, the primary See of the English Church.

route, Ashford and Maidstone on a modern alternative. Even along the ancient ridgeway Wye, on the Stour, and Aylesford, on the Medway, had their special importance and gave their names to 'lathes', major sub-divisions of Kent dating from Saxon times.

Convenient access from the Continent may be a commercial asset but is a military liability, so Kent has been not only the Gateway but the Guardroom of England. Doubtless the Belgae of the 1st century B.C. were not the first invaders, but it is from this period that the earliest surviving fortifications date. Since then, several actual invaders and a much larger number of potential or threatening invaders have marched across the pages of Kentish history. These fears may often have proved insubstantial, but are recorded by a formidable litter of very solid castles, redoubts and pillboxes. Dover, overlooked by fortresses and underlain by the remains of others, has been Britain's premier janitor.

Nor is this guardian role a matter of ancient history only, for many of Kent's present inhabitants stood in the front line in World War II, and sustained the shock of bomb, shell, flying bomb and rocket. It was essentially in Kentish skies that the Battle of Britain was won, making good once more the proud boast of 'Invicta'.

PAUL BURNHAM, STUART McRAE

Wye, April 1978

Landscapes of the Past

PRE-ROMAN KENT

The landscape of Kent has been affected by human occupation for many centuries, and behind modern features vestiges of the past constantly appear.

The gravel pits of North-West Kent have yielded many thousands of Stone Age implements, such as choppers, scrapers, cleavers, hand-axes and other tools fashioned from flint. One day in 1935 an amateur archaeologist was searching for these in Barnfield Pit, Swanscombe, when he made the far more exciting discovery of a piece of human skull. Two other fragments have since come to light and the remains (fig. 3) have been dated as 250,000 years old, by far the oldest ever found in England so the Swanscombe Man (in fact a young woman) rightly merits the title of the first Englishman. Human occupation of Kent has not been continuous since then, being restricted to relatively mild intervals within the Ice Ages when conditions were favourable for the wild animals and plants on which early man's nomadic hunting and food-gathering existence depended.

Fig. 3.
The Swanscombe Skull (top view)
The lady died in her early twenties. Her brain was almost as large as a modern one.

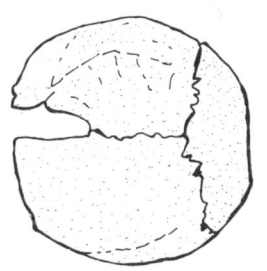

As Britain emerged from the latest glacial period about 12,000 years ago the improving climate encouraged northward migration from the continent of herds of deer, horses and reindeer, roaming across more or less open country. As the climate became milder trees and shrubs such as juniper, beech and pine began to appear, and with this change to a more closed woodland Paleolithic gave way to Mesolithic (Middle Stone Age) man. These were hunters and fishermen from across the sinking land-bridge with northern and western Europe and seemed to prefer sites on or near rivers, particularly the Thames, although they sometimes penetrated the thick forests of the Weald. Rock shelters on Oldbury Hill at Ightham and flint implement workshops there and elsewhere give some indication of their life and work.

Much greater changes resulted from the establishment between 4,000 and 3,000 BC of Neolithic (New Stone Age) settlers in Britain, for these were the first farmers. Land had to be cleared and cultivated for their crops, chiefly wheat and barley, and consequently settlement was concentrated in and near areas of well drained, early worked, chalky soils, as in Thanet, East Kent and along the valleys of the Cray, Darent, Stour and particularly around the Medway where it cuts through the North Downs. In this last area are several megaliths or burial chambers, notably at Trottiscliffe, Addington and Aylesford. Kits Coty near Aylesford (fig. 4) is perhaps the most spectacular of these, representing a ceremonial 'false doorway' to a long barrow the remainder of which has been levelled. A long barrow still exists as Julieberrie's Grave in the Stour Valley near Chilham, while remains of huts, cooking holes and stock pens have been found at Hayes Common, near Bromley.

Fig. 4.
Kits Coty
False doorway of a Neolithic long barrow, once 65 m in length. On Bluebell Hill between Maidstone and Chatham.

About 1700 BC there appeared in Kent tribes from the Rhineland, known from their pottery as the Beaker People. They brought with them bronze tools, but did not apparently know how to manufacture them until several hundred years later. Although they had improved implements, these Bronze Age settlers, like Neolithic Man, avoided the heavily wooded North Downs dipslope and the Weald, preferring the river valleys and chalk country, especially in North East Kent. Remains of small fields and lynchets, natural terraces due to slight soil erosion, are sometimes seen over the chalk. More certain relics of the Bronze Age include about 20 round barrows and several hoards of implements, notably one at Minster in Thanet which yielded 143 items. Even gold ornaments, probably from Ireland, have been found indicating, along with the importation of the copper and tin needed to make the bronze implements, considerable trade with other communities.

From about 500 BC onwards there began piecemeal immigration by small groups of people who knew the secrets of working iron. In spite of this common technological bond there were several quite distinct groups, and open warfare took place between them. Some of the Iron Age hill-forts in Kent may have featured in the battles. About ten hill-forts are known, including Bigberry near Canterbury, Castle Hill Camp near Tonbridge, High Rocks at Tunbridge Wells, Oldbury (fig. 5), at Ightham, Hulberry, near Lullingstone, Squerryes Park Camp at Westerham, and the so-called 'Caesar's Camp' at Keston.

About 75 BC, perhaps due to Roman pressures from the south, the

Belgae from Gaul began to cross the Channel into Kent. They brought with them several technical innovations including wheel-turned pottery, war chariots, and perhaps most important for its effect on the countryside a heavy plough which enabled soils of heavier texture to be cultivated. Thus arable farming became more extensive, and by the Roman invasion the fertile brown earth soils of North Kent and the Maidstone area were densely settled. Some Iron Age finds have been made on the Lower Greensand of West Kent and towards Tonbridge, but otherwise the thick Wealden forests seem to have remained almost uninhabited.

In East Kent the Belgae established a number of hutted settlements, the most important being Durovernum, the modern Canterbury. From here a track ran through Bigberry to join a major trackway which ran along the footslope of the North Downs from Folkestone to the present county boundary at Westerham and on towards Salisbury Plain. The name 'Pilgrim's Way' is inappropriate, although it appears on signposts and maps, since it was in use long before any pilgrims made their way to Canterbury. An equivalent route is now a recognized long distance footpath, the North Downs Way.

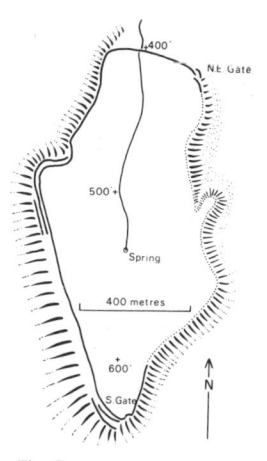

Fig. 5.
Oldbury Hill Fort. *Built about 100 BC and strengthened about the time of the Roman Invasion. Many sling stones have been found on the ramparts, but signs that the NE Gate was burnt suggest that the defence was unsuccessful.*

The Belgae probably spoke a Celtic language and remnants of this survive in the river names of Thames, Stour, Medway, Darent and Cray as well as in the name of the county itself. Caesar referred to the area as Cantium and spoke of it as a prosperous, civilized and densely populated farming area. Trade with Europe was active, including the export of corn, cattle and hides, hunting dogs and even slaves in return for luxury items such as wine, oil, jewellery and glass.

ROMANO-BRITISH KENT

Julius Caesar himself set foot in Kent twice, in 55 and 54 BC, landing both times near Deal. On the first occasion determined resistance by the Belgae and storms which smashed his ships made his stay a brief one. His return the following year was more successful, although storms again damaged his ships, and after marching through Kent he defeated the massed British tribes somewhere north of the Thames before his final departure from these shores.

A hundred years later, in AD 43 the Romans returned in force under Aulus Plautius to conquer Britain on behalf of the Emperor Claudius. At the time the coastline of Kent was somewhat different from today's (fig. 7). Romney Marsh was still a swamp and Thanet still a true island cut off from the mainland by an arm of the sea, subsequently called the Wantsum. The Romans landed on an island in the Wantsum which they called Rutupiae (the modern Richborough). Although the landing was unopposed the Romans subsequently met stiff resistance from the Britons of Kent especially at the Medway crossing near Rochester (Durobrivae), but eventual victory here subdued Kent leaving the Romans free to extend their conquest of lowland Britain over the next few years. The main Roman ports of the Kent coast were Rutupiae, Dubris (Dover) and Lemanis (Lympne), all with substantial forts (fig. 7). The largest was at Rutupiae with a huge monument, probably commemorating the invasion, acting as a land-fall. Another major landmark must have been the pharos (lighthouse) on the Eastern Heights above Dover (fig. 6), and the matching one formerly on the Western Heights, overlooking the fort which was in later Roman times the headquarters of the British Fleet. Part of the fort at Lympne has been destroyed by landslipping, and it now lies several miles from the sea due to the silting up of Romney Marsh. The fourth Roman fort in Kent, at Regulbium (Reculver) to guard the northern entrance to the Wantsum Channel, was threatened by almost total destruction until defences were built in the nineteenth century.

From these coastal forts and ports, well-constructed Roman roads (fig. 7), characteristically straight except in avoiding awkward hills, ran to the local capital Durovernum (the modern Canterbury), and as the subsequently named Watling Street through Durobrivae (Rochester) and Vagniacae (Springhead) to London. Other roads of lesser importance were also built, including some to the Weald where local iron ore was smelted with charcoal as fuel. Some of the roads are still followed by modern roads or parish boundaries.

The impact of Romanization on the landscape of Kent was more sociological than technological. The Romans brought few new techniques, but may have introduced apples, cherries and vines. The peace and stability, at least of the earlier Roman period, encouraged the spread of villas, more or less isolated farmsteads, each with its own estate and a social structure echoed later in the mediaeval system of landlords, tenants, serfs and slaves. About 60 villas are known from Kent. There was also a change from subsistence to surplus farming, for sale in the urban centres, and to the army, especially grain, some of which was even exported. The spread of villa farms was also encouraged by the communications network, and indeed the overall settlement pattern is closely linked with the road and river systems, although still favouring the

Fig. 6.
Roman Pharos
A lighthouse, now within the walls of Dover Castle, built of rubble and hard mortar 19 m high. The top 6 m is mediaeval.

Fig. 7.
Romano-British Kent
Showing probable coastline, and transport and settlement pattern.

Landscapes of the Past

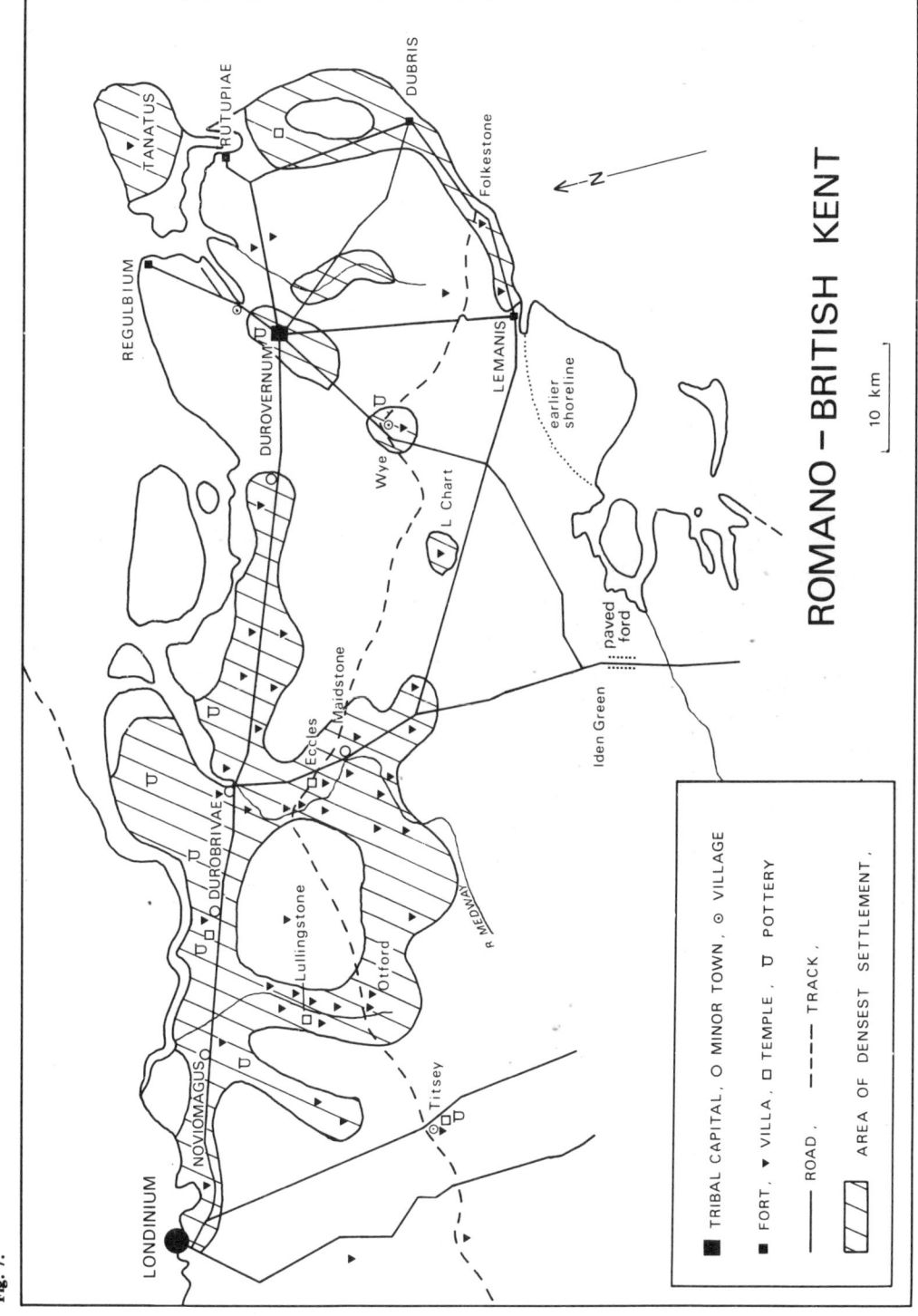

Fig. 7.

relatively easily worked soils (fig 7). The bulk of the rural population lay along Watling Street and in the valleys of the Darent and Medway. East Kent, Thanet and the immediate vicinity of Canterbury were also relatively well populated, with the Weald still a negative area, although with a few iron smelting and charcoal burning settlements.

SAXON KENT

As early as the end of the third century Teutonic tribes were raiding Kent and other parts of eastern England, and with the final withdrawal of Roman rule around AD 400 raiding became invasion and settlement. Romano-British rulers did their best to stem the tide by means of the Roman Forts of the Saxon Shore and enlisting outside help. Tradition has it, for example, that King Vortigern of Kent elicited help from two Jutish leaders Hengist and Horsa, promising them Thanet in return for their services. Whether by means such as this or by overt invasion, so-called Jutish people took over Kent. These people probably came originally from the Rhine Valley and Southern Germany, and were distinguished from the Angles and Saxons who colonized other areas of southern Britain. This piecemeal invasion gave rise to a number of separate Kingdoms, including the Kingdom of Kent and one of the Kentish Kings, Ethelbert (560-616) was for a time the overlord of all other Kingdoms south of the Humber, a precursor of the true English Kings. For the next 200 years Kent was alternately independent or under the rule of another Kingdom, passing finally to the control of Wessex in 825. Ethelbert's rule is significant for another reason, the re-establishment of Christianity in England starting with the landing of St Augustine at Ebbsfleet in Thanet in 596. He became the first Archbishop of Canterbury the following year and established a second diocese at Rochester under royal patronage in 604.

The population of Saxon Kent was almost certainly less than 50,000, or about three per cent of the present population of the county. Archaeological evidence and study of place names has shown that, in early Saxon times, the fertile soils of North Kent still provided the most settled area with very little population in the huge forest of Andredsweald (the Saxon form of the Roman Anderida) south of the Greensand ridge. Hundreds of Kent place-names originate from Saxon times. Names ending in -ing (formerly ingas) mean group of people, for example Bobbing (Bobba's people) and Malling (Meallo's people) and by analogy their place of habitation. These are thought to have been some of the earliest Saxon place

Plate 3
The 'Hugin', now preserved at Pegwell Bay. Fifty young Danes rowed this replica from Frederikssund, Denmark, to Kent in July 1949 in commemoration of the first landing of the Jutes in 449.

names. Other names such as Bridge, Hythe (landing place), Chart (a rough common), Leigh (a woodland glade) are also Saxon words, sometimes compounded with an adjective or noun, e.g. Greenhithe, Sandwich (village on the sand) and Higham (village or homestead, ham, on high ground), or with a personal name, for example Chelsfield (Ceol's field) or Harrietsham (Heregeard's -hamm or meadow). Later names, notably these ending in -den (a woodland swine pasture) or -hurst (a wooded knoll), show the incursion of Saxon settlement into the Wealden forest, to which area such names are almost completely restricted, e.g. Bethersden, Biddenden (plate 21), Goudhurst and Hawkhurst. Some show ownership of these cleared areas by people often originating many miles away, e.g. Tenterden, the den of the people of Thanet.

The siting of the Saxon villages of Kent is strongly related to geological outcrops. In North Kent these villages avoid areas such as the Blean (London Clay) and the highest part of the North Downs plateau, which long remained as woodland. In mid Kent the most striking feature is the long line of about 18 settlements roughly along the spring line at the foot of the North Downs escarpment, generally on the outcrop of the Lower Chalk. These villages have long narrow parishes running transversely to the physical and geological features. Thus each parish had a ready supply of spring water, arable land on the Lower Chalk, downland pasture on the escarpment of the North Downs, woodland on the crest of the Downs and on the Gault Clay, with perhaps further woodland and heath on the Folkestone Beds. A further line of villages is associated with the Hythe Beds escarpment (e.g. Pluckley, Egerton, Ulcombe, East Sutton and Sutton Valence), and here too proximity to springs issuing from the base of the Hythe Beds may have influenced the settlement pattern. In the latter part of the Anglo-Saxon period, Kent was again under attack, this time by the Danes. Sporadic raids were interspersed with more determined efforts to occupy Kent and other parts of the south east during the second half of the ninth century. Campaigns including some in Kent, led by King Alfred of Wessex, successfully confined the Danelaw to northern and eastern England. A relic of this in Kent is the total absence of any place names with Scandinavian origin. For a short time (1016–1036), Kent, in common with the rest of England came under the rule of the Danish King Cnut, but the Anglo-Saxon dynasty returned with Edward the Confessor.

MEDIAEVAL KENT

Following his success at Hastings, William skirted the still dense forests of the Weald, heading for London via Dover and Canterbury. England had undergone its last military invasion and entered the mediaeval age with the feudal system under which Kent was to become as prosperous as any part of Britain.

The essence of feudalism was service of the lower orders to their lords in the form of work in return for protection, law enforcement and rudimentary social services. The system was in operation in late Saxon times and the Normans merely refined and reinforced it. In Kent, as elsewhere in England, the former landowners (the Saxon thanes) were dispossessed and their land redistributed to William's followers. Only the King could 'own' land—he had about a twelfth of the cultivated land in Kent, while other land was 'held' in return for a 'feud' (a fee or service). The major landholder in Kent was William's half-brother, Bishop Odo of Bayeux (fig. 9), who became Earl of Kent and controlled just over a third of the cultivated area, while five other lords had a further tenth between them. The Church, now with Norman archbishop and bishops, held the rest, half by the Sees of Canterbury and Rochester, the remainder mainly by the monasteries of Christ Church and St Augustine's in

Fig. 8.
Mediaeval Kent
Distribution of settlements in mediaeval Kent.

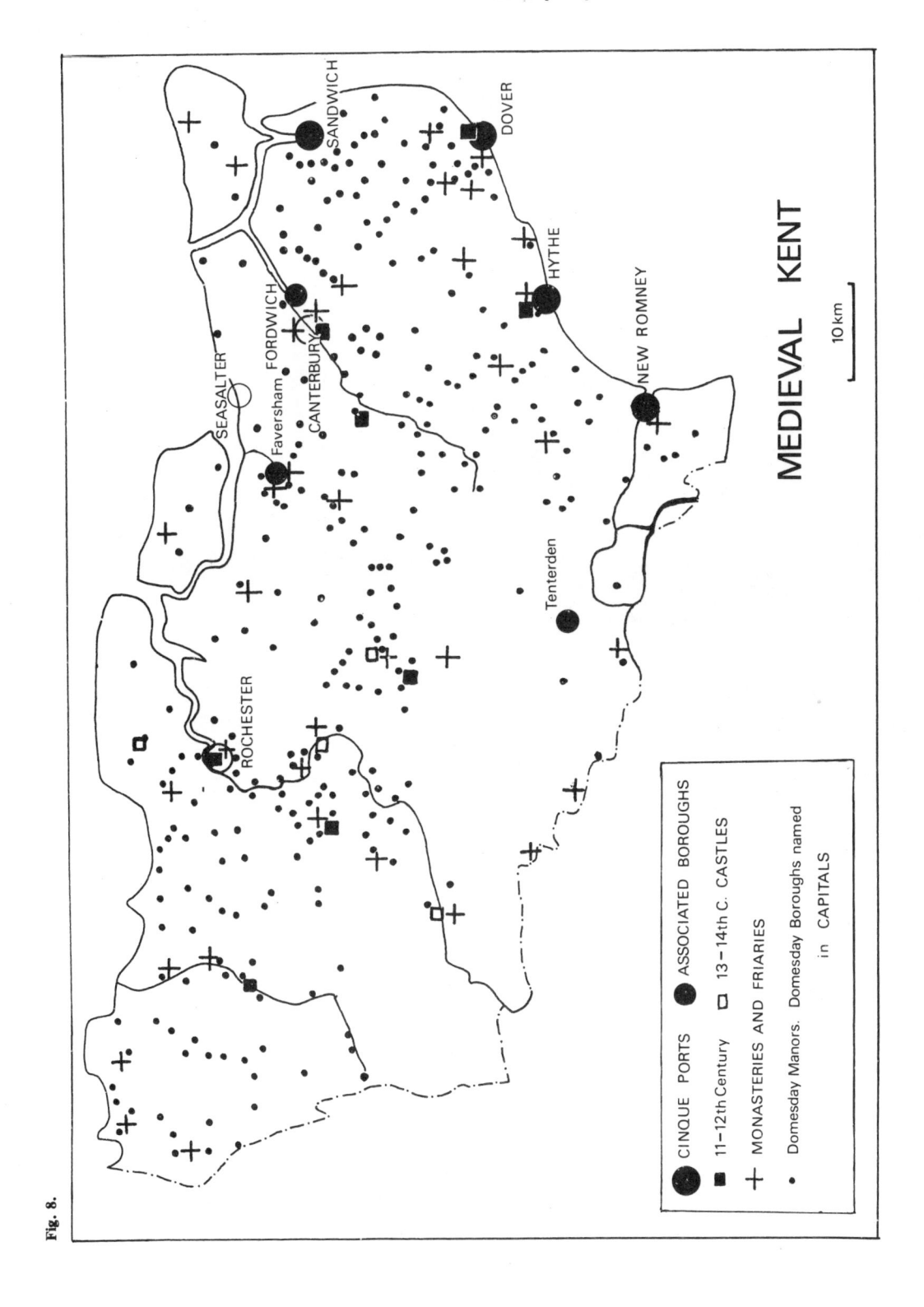

Fig. 8.

Fig. 9.
William the Conqueror
He sits between his two half-brothers, Odo, Bishop of Bayeux, and Robert of Mortain, the latter said to have been 'of little capacity'. From the Bayeux tapestry, thought to have been embroidered at Canterbury for Odo, who is shown with a large hand, and was given huge estates including one third of the cultivated area of Kent.

Canterbury.

Each estate consisted of a number of manors scattered throughout Kent, only the Constable of England, Hugo de Montfort, having holdings more or less in one block in the strategic area of Dover, Folkestone and round his castle at Saltwood. The purpose of the Domesday Survey in 1086 was to record the past and present holders of the manors (of which there were about 300 in Kent—fig. 8), their extent, value, type of land and ancillary activities and subdivision (if any) to other tenants. The lord of the manor kept a portion of the land, the *demesne* to himself, either farming it himself or renting it out to a *firmarius* or *farmer*. The rest of the cultivated land was held by tenants in return for services to the lord, for example helping to cultivate the land in *demesne*, although paid agricultural workers were also necessary.

Most manors also had areas of pasture and woodland. The tenants had certain rights over these and over their own land including rights of inheritance which, in Kent, were of a form peculiar to the county called Gavelkind. In this system, if the father died intestate, the land was not inherited by the eldest son, but was split up amongst all the sons. This led to the creation of small independent farms. 'Assarts', which were areas cleared from woodland, were also individually owned, and overall Kent became characterized by many small individual farms farmed by the forerunners of the 'Yeomen of Kent'. Thus the great enclosures in the eighteenth and nineteenth centuries scarcely affected Kent, since most fields were already enclosed by hedges and in single ownership. The Midlands open-field system was never common in mediaeval Kent although some cases are known, for example in East Kent and around Wrotham.

Kent was prosperous farming country in the Middle Ages, particularly in the thirteenth and early fourteenth centuries, with much of the land under arable cultivation. The main crops were wheat (there was even a surplus to export), oats, and barley used mostly for brewing. With the inherently fertile soils and good husbandry, including liming and manuring, yields were reasonably high. Peas and beans were also common crops, partly for human consumption and partly as fodder for the large numbers of cattle. Sheep were very common, particularly in Thanet and Romney Marsh. They yielded meat, milk for cheese and especially wool, much of which went for export. In the fourteenth century Flemish weavers, encouraged by Edward III, settled in Kent, especially in the Weald around Cranbrook and for over three hundred years there was a flourishing industry, making Cranbrook one of the largest and wealthiest towns in Kent.

Fig. 10.
Rochester Castle
The keep of 1127-39, built mainly of ragstone by William of Corbeuil, Archbishop of Canterbury.

The most populous rural areas, at the time of Domesday, were North East Kent (east of a line from Whitstable to Dover), the hinterland of Folkestone and the Medway valley around Maidstone. In these areas the estimated population was over four per sq. km. In the rest of Kent it was around two to three per sq. km., with the notable exception of the Weald south of the Greensand Ridge where the average was less than one. The total population of the county was about 60,000 at Domesday, but was seriously depleted by the Black Death of 1348-9, especially in West Kent, and overall a third of the population may have died. Discontent, mainly of a social nature as the feudal system started to break down, led in the generation after the Black Death, to the Peasant's Revolt of 1381. Many of the leaders of the Revolt were from Kent, notably Wat Tyler who led a reputed 100,000 rebels to a confrontation with the 14 year old King Richard II, but although the mob was in charge of London for a time, the rebellion came to nothing. Another rebellion starting in Ashford in 1450, but involving mainly men from West Kent and the Weald, was of a more serious nature, with political rather than social overtones, and the rebels led by Jack Cade forced Henry VI to leave the capital for a time. After a short time, this rebellion too collapsed although some reforms specifically relating to Kent were gained.

To deter internal strife or invasion castles were built. Dover and Rochester castles (fig.10) were initiated in the Conqueror's reign and stone keeps added in the 12th century, when other keeps were built at Canterbury, Chilham and West Malling. Enclosures surrounded by stone curtain walls, of which 12th century examples are Eynsford and Saltwood, became the dominant form in the thirteenth century, entered by strongly defended gatehouses of which examples are at Tonbridge and Dover. On the royal castle at Dover £7,000 was spent between 1168 and 1190, almost a year's income of the Crown. At Saltwood on 28 December 1170 four knights met to plot the murder of Archbishop Becket next day. Later the castle was returned to the Archbishops, and has recently been the home of Lord Clark, the historian.

Fig. 11.
Hever Castle
Built about 1385 and home of the Boleyn family from 1462. Anne was educated here. Much enriched by W. W. Astor (1903–7).

Other castles were the homes of notable Kentish families in earlier eras, such as the Wyatts of Allington, the Culpepers at Leeds and the Boleyns, progenitor of Anne, at Hever (fig. 11).

The main mediaeval towns or boroughs were Canterbury, Dover, Rochester, Faversham, Sandwich, Fordwich (the port of Canterbury), Hythe and Romney (fig. 8). Particularly important were the Cinque Ports, a confederation of Hastings (in Sussex), Romney, Hythe, Dover and Sandwich, which two more Sussex ports, Rye and Winchelsea, joined later. In exchange for providing ships to the King, the Cinque Ports secured self-government (plate 4) and exemption from taxation. Dover and Sandwich were pre-eminent as commercial ports, although all shared in the lucrative sidelines of piracy and fishing. Their hey-day was over in 1350 because of the competition from larger ports like London and Bristol, and because all had lost their original harbours by silting up and retreat of the sea. The confederation still exists however, and some of their privileges and traditions are maintained.

During the Middle Ages the Church had a profound influence, not only on men's souls but on the landscape around them. The parish church became a focal point of villages, while numerous monasteries, nunneries, hospitals (i.e. hostels) and latterly friaries were built (fig. 8) some in rural or semi-rural sites but most of all in Canterbury, reaching their zenith in the thirteenth and fourteenth centuries. Well before the Reformation monastic establishments in Kent, as elsewhere in England, were in a poor neglected state and the dissolution of the monasteries and other religious houses must have had little effect on the general populace. Two thirds of the land in Kent held by monasteries remained in ecclesiastical ownership (the Archbishop of Canterbury and the Deans and chapters of Canterbury and Rochester), about a tenth was retained by the Crown and the rest was passed to various laymen.

Plate 4
The Court of Shepway always meets at Dover under the presidency of the Lord Warden, here Sir Winston Churchill (1946). It regulates relations between the Cinque Ports and foreigners, and from its decisions there is no appeal.

TUDOR KENT

The Reformation led to threats of invasion by the Catholic powers, and the ruins of the monasteries were robbed not only to build houses for the new owners of their estates but also to construct castles along the Kent coast. Cannon now had to be contended with, and Henry VIII built castles (1539-40) to a distinctive circular plan (fig. 12) at Sandgate, Walmer, Deal, Sandown and at Camber in Sussex. Other defences were built at Gravesend and Tilbury, while Edward III's castle at Queenborough was rebuilt to a circular pattern. To these Elizabeth, whose early experience of Kent castles was unhappy for she was imprisoned for a time at Leeds Castle, added Upnor Castle. This completed the defences to the important dockyards at Deptford (then in Kent), Woolwich and Chatham. A signalling system, the Armada Beacons, was also set up to warn of possible invasion. One of about 30 beacons was on Tolsford Hill, where today the masts of another beacon—for air traffic

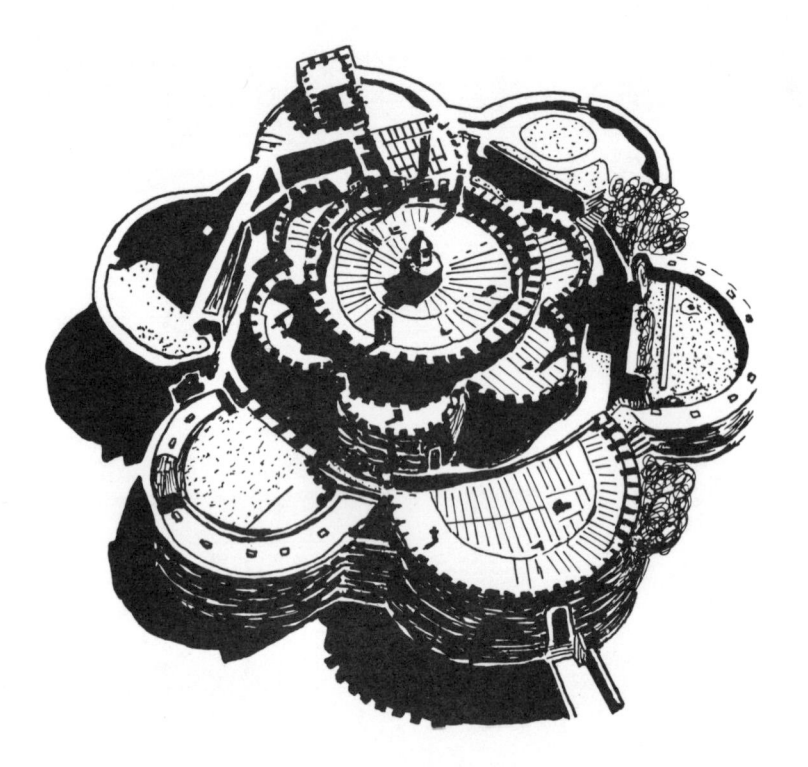

Fig. 12.
Deal Castle
Built in 1539 to protect shipping in the Downs.

control—overlook the A20 road some eight km from Folkestone.

However, the invasions which most influenced Kent during Tudor times were peaceful ones. Immigrants from the continent, often fleeing from religious persecution, brought new crops and new industries to the county. The woollen industry established two hundred years previously by the deliberate installation of Flemish weavers was diversified by the manufacture of serge cloth at Sandwich and linen thread at Maidstone, both introduced by the refugee Flemings, while French Huguenots brought silk weaving to Canterbury. Papermaking, an important industry in Kent to the present day, was started at Dartford in 1588 by a German and flourished with the arrival of French refugees at the end of the seventeenth century. A Fleming set up the first English slitting mill at Dartford which cut iron bars into rods. The iron bars came from the flourishing Wealden iron industry. The smelting of iron needed charcoal, and to provide this as well as timber for houses and for shipbuilding there was large-scale clearance of the remaining Wealden woodland around this time.

Market gardening came to Kent with the Flemings, initially around Sandwich. Their memory lives on in farmhouses of Dutch style and Poulders as a name for the marshland they drained. They also encouraged rotations with root crops for which the credit is usually given to a Norfolk farmer, 'Turnip' Townshend, who advocated root crop rotations some 40 years later. Hops, the crop so typical of Kent, also had a Flemish origin, and became widespread in the county in the sixteenth and seventeenth centuries. Kent was early famed for fruit, probably because of the happy juxtaposition of favourable soils, suitable climate and proximity to the continent from where the trees for planting and expertise first came. The picture of Kentish agriculture painted in 1570 by William Lambarde in his *Perambulation of Kent,* the first history of any county ever written, is not unlike that of the present day. He says:

'The soile is for the most part bountiful, consisting indifferently of arable, pasture, meadow and woodland, howbeit of these, wood occupieth the greatest portion even till this day, except it bee towards the East, which coast is more champaigne [i.e. open] than the residue. [The same is true today.] As for orchards of aples and gardeins of cheries, and those of the most exquisite and delicious kindes that can be, no part of the Realme [that I know] hath them, either in such quantitie and number, or with such arte and industrie set and planted . . .'

Lambarde and other writers also stressed the generally prosperous nature of agriculture at the time, noting the new or improved farmhouses and the huge herds of cattle and flocks of sheep which came to Kent from other parts of the country for fattening. The productivity of Kent agriculture was providential, for the population was steadily rising, from 90,000 at the start of Elizabeth's reign to 150,000 a hundred years later. This population lived mainly in villages, although there was some migration to London. No Kentish town housed more than 10,000 people before the eighteenth century.

GEORGIAN KENT

A major factor discouraging the development of towns was poor communications. Before the 18th century roads were generally atrocious, so that goods from East and North Kent went to London by sea. Road conditions varied considerably with the geological substratum. Watling Street, according to a contemporary traveller was 'in general a very good and well beaten way, chiefly chalky and gravelly'. Another described the Ashford to Tenterden road across the Weald Clay in wet seasons as 'so miry that the traveller's horse frequently plunges through them up to the girths of the saddle; and the waggons sinking so deep in the ruts as to slide along on the nave of the wheels and the axle of them'. The 'roads' across areas of clay were usually very wide (up to 25 metres) so as to allow the traveller to pick his way round the holes and ruts and it was even permissible to detour through adjoining land. Wheeled traffic, the main cause of the deterioration, often became hopelessly stuck, and there is an account of a load of timber taking two years to travel from Tonbridge on the Weald Clay to the dockyard at Chatham.

Individual parishes through which these roads passed had the responsibility of their maintenance, but could not afford the complete reconstruction required. By a series of special Acts of Parliament between 1709 and 1825 Turnpike Trusts were set up empowered to raise the capital cost of new roads and to recover their expenditure by levying tolls. In a few places the cottages built for the toll-collectors still survive. So do the roads, for in large measure the Turnpike Trusts created the road system we have today (fig. 13). The first to be turnpiked (1710) was the road from Sevenoaks to Tunbridge Wells and Pembury, which crosses the Weald Clay. This was part of the main London to Hastings route, and it also carried much traffic to Tunbridge Wells which Charles II had made a fashionable spa. Much of the traffic from London to Kent and the continent came first by river to Gravesend, and it was not surprising that the next road to be turnpiked (in 1712) led onwards from Gravesend to Rochester and Chatham, a major centre of population. Then came turnpikes from Rochester to Maidstone (1720), Gravesend to Canterbury (1730) and Canterbury to the port of Whitstable (1736). The Gravesend to London and most, but not all, of the London to Hastings roads were turnpiked before 1750. The only part of this latter road missing was a four mile section across London Clay from Bromley to Farnborough, a surprising omission, but typical of the piece-meal development of the turnpike road system.

The period between 1750 and 1780 saw most of the major roads in West and Mid-Kent turnpiked with a few, for example the Ashford–Hythe'–Folkestone–Dover road, in East Kent. Most of the East Kent roads were turnpiked after 1780, including the Ashford to Wrotham road and routes from Canterbury to Thanet and Folkestone. Some, for example, the Canterbury to Sandwich road were not dealt with until the nineteenth century, by which time a number of Kent turnpike roads were regularly served by stage coach.

The initiative for turnpike roads usually came from local landowners, and such men were sometimes unwilling to take the

Fig. 13.
Georgian Kent
Towns and transportation around 1800.

Landscapes of the Past 17

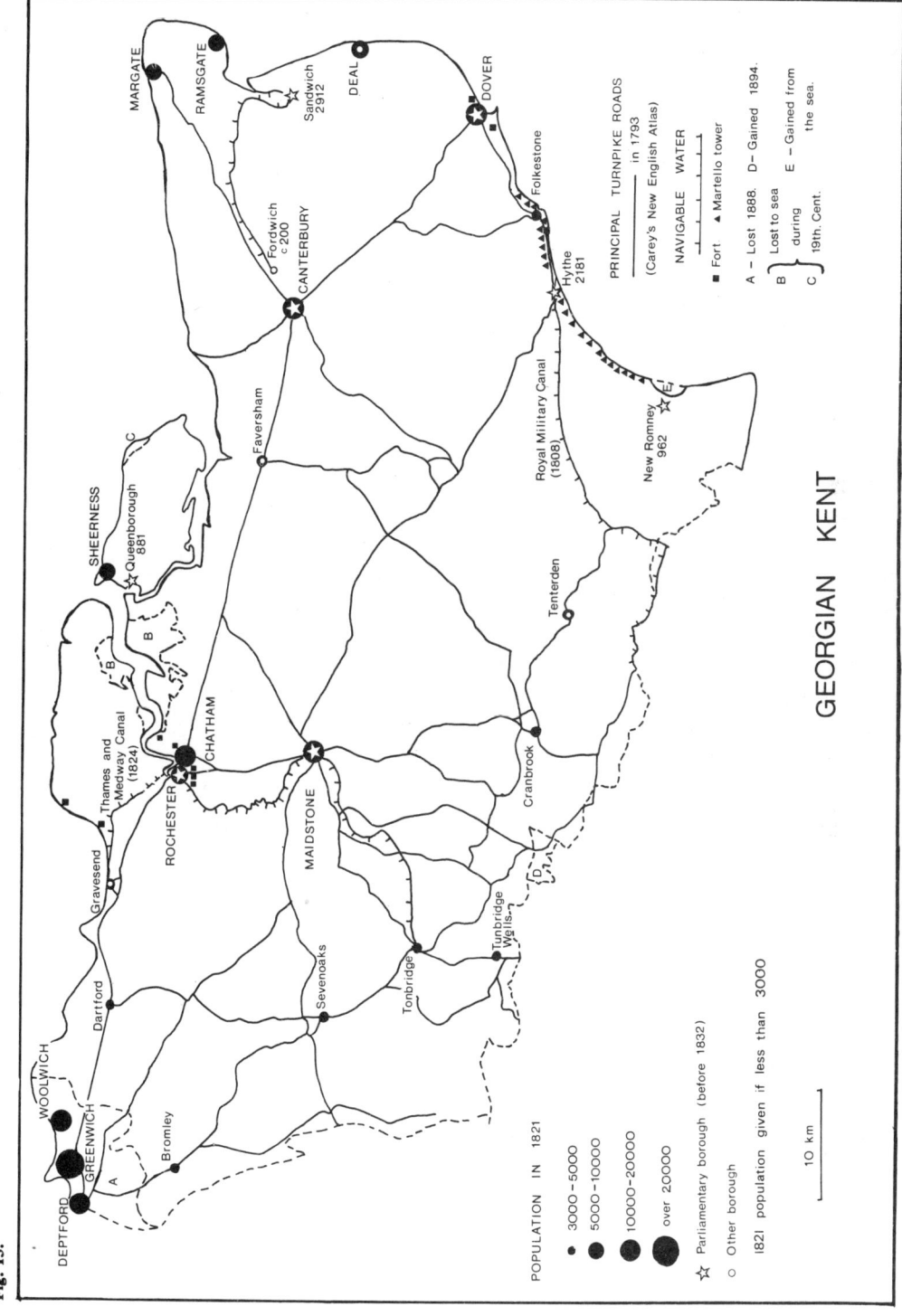

Fig. 13. GEORGIAN KENT

risks and responsibilities entailed. The farming community was often actively opposed to turnpikes, since improved communication would open the London markets to produce from further afield and threaten the favoured position of Kent suppliers. Most of the important bridges in the turnpike system were the responsibility of the county and were well maintained. These included several fine mediaeval bridges over the Medway, Teise and Beult, for example at East Farleigh (fig. 14).

The Medway was itself an important inland waterway, being navigable, after improvements made about 1740, as far upstream as Tonbridge (fig. 13). Fordwich, about five km down the Stour from Canterbury, could be reached from the coast at Sandwich, and small vessels could come up the Rother from Rye as far as Small Hythe. By far the busiest river was the Thames itself, and Gravesend was a major port with a fleet of ferries sailing to and from London. A canal involving a three km tunnel was built between 1805 and 1824 across the base of the Hoo Peninsula to link the mouth of the Medway with Gravesend. Other proposed canals to link Yalding on the Medway and the Rother with a branch to Ashford and Wye never materialized. Water transport, although slow, was comfortable and very suitable for bulky or fragile loads (e.g. fruit), and it was not until the development of the railways in the nineteenth century that this means of transport became unimportant.

For over 250 years after the time of the Spanish Armada, Kent figured only intermittently in matters of national importance. During the Civil Wars Kent was remote from most of the military activity, although there was a rising in Kent in 1648, more as a result of the unpopularity of the parliament and its edicts than because of royalist sympathies. This finally ended with a small running battle in the vicinity of Maidstone on 1 June 1648, followed in the next three months by the surrender of Walmer, Deal and Sandown Castles to parliamentary forces. With the Restoration Charles II arrived back in England at Dover to universal acclamation, but the end of the Stuarts, in which Kent also figured, was more ignominious. James

Fig. 14.
East Farleigh Bridge
Built in the 14th century of local ragstone. Its capture by Fairfax in 1648 led to the final defeat of the Kentish royalists.

II, fleeing from the forces of William of Orange, was picked up off Whitstable and was returned, with little ceremony, to London. William arrived in peace, although some 20 years earlier in 1667 the Dutch had attacked the mouth of the Medway and carried off Britain's largest warship from the dockyard at Chatham. In the eighteenth century struggles with France for overseas possessions, General Wolfe, born in Westerham, won a notable victory at Quebec.

With the Napoleonic Wars, Kent was once again, literally in the front line of the nation's defences. Wordsworth described the county in a sonnet addressed to the men of Kent at the height of the invasion fears as

'. . . a soil that doth advance
Her haughty brow against the coast
of France'.

Fig. 15.
Martello Tower, No. 3
At Copt Point, Folkestone, built 1806 with brick walls 1.5–2.5 m thick, as part of the defences against a possible invasion by Napoleon.

Fortifications against possible French invasion began as early as 1758 with the Chatham Lines, and further works were added around Chatham and along the Thames towards Gravesend following the renewal of war with the French in 1778 (fig. 13). The most likely stretch of the coast to be invaded by Napoleon lay between Folkestone and Rye. To defend this there was built a series of small circular forts shaped like a child's sand pie and known as Martello Towers because they were based on the plan of a defence work at Cape Martella in Corsica (fig. 15). Each was garrisoned by 20 to 30 men, who lived on the upper of two storeys below a vaulted roof, on which was mounted a traversing gun surrounded by a parapet. Twenty-five towers were built in Kent (fig. 13), from Copt Point, Folkestone to Littlestone. Tower number 24 at Dymchurch has been restored and is open to visitors. The Marsh was considered particularly vulnerable and a 'glorified ditch', the Royal Military Canal, was dug along its landward side. The line of the Canal is staggered at intervals, and at each bend an embrasure with a heavy gun was constructed. The idea was that the gun would fire along the line, and the length of each section, about 400 metres, represented the range attainable by the guns. Other preparations included troop encampments, a semaphore signalling system reminiscent of the Armada beacons and elaborate but impracticable schemes for transferring livestock and other foodstuffs from the east to the safer west of the county.

Napoleon of course, never invaded, and at Boulogne there is a tall monument, the 'Colonne de la Grande Armée', surmounted by a statue of the Emperor turning his back on the Kent coast and facing eastwards into Europe. Military defences, notably around Chatham, along the Thames estuary from Sheerness to Gravesend and at Dover, continued to be built during the nineteenth century, while naval installations became very extensive in Chatham and Gillingham, and Maidstone and Canterbury had large infantry barracks.

The late eighteenth and early nineteenth centuries were also a period of agricultural innovations, great enough to be called an Agricultural Revolution. Kent, already a county renowned for its agriculture, took to the new crops and techniques with enthusiasm. We have a clear picture of these changes from three contemporary accounts of Kent agriculture, by John Boys, of Betteshanger (1796, with a second edition in 1805), William Marshall, a visitor (1798), and John Bannister, of Horton Kirby (1799). These give a much more balanced account than those of travellers through Kent, who have always tended to exaggerate the amount of fruit and hops because the main routes tend to run through those parts of Kent where they are concentrated.

New crops included turnips, clover, sainfoin and lucerne grown in rotation with the traditional cereals, peas and beans. This led to new techniques of animal husbandry, sheep being folded on fields of turnips for example, so that the amount of permanent grassland could be much reduced. Large areas were turned over to arable cropping, particularly cereals, especially during the Napoleonic Wars when imports of corn virtually ceased. Areas traditionally thought of as permanent grassland, such as the Thameside Marshes and Romney Marsh, were tilled, and in an effort to bring as much land as possible into cultivation the hedges were cleared from the Isle of Thanet. They were never replanted, and to this day Thanet has a prairie-like appearance. Besides wheat, barley for brewing was also grown (except on the heavy Wealden soils), as was oats, much of which went to feed the rising horse population of London. The London market also encouraged large scale production of cabbages (previously only a market garden crop) and potatoes (formerly only a cattle and pig food) for human consumption. Fruit and hops continued to flourish, the former concentrated in the North and Mid Kent fruit belts, the latter still widely distributed through the county. Some traditional crops such as woad and madder for dyes disappeared.

Kent farmers were not highly thought of as livestock farmers, but were renowned for their skills in crop production. They were expert in the use of organic manures, including seaweed where available, and fully realized the necessity of adequate liming. The main problem was weeds, usually controlled by a fallow every three to seven years during which the land was cross ploughed with the traditional Kentish wrest-plough, a huge, heavy implement (fig. 16). The introduction of the seed drill in the later part of the eighteenth century, sowing the seeds in regular lines, allowed hoeing between rows either by hand or horse drawn implement to overcome the weed problem.

These changes ensured that agriculture in Georgian Kent remained a prosperous section of the community, although with a depression immediately after the Napoleonic wars for about two decades. Not until imports from America and Australasia began to appear in the 1850s did Kent (and indeed English) agriculture go into decline. The prosperity was never uniformly distributed, however, for three distinct strata had appeared in the Kent farming community. At the top of the tree were the builders and owners of the country houses (Chapter 6) which were appearing particularly in North-West Kent, East Kent and the High Weald. Profits from agriculture financed some of these, but the majority were built with money made in commerce, and other than landscaping their grounds they had little contact with the land. The social life centred on these country houses in Kent is vividly described by Jane Austen, who often visited Godmersham Park, believed to be the original of 'Mansfield Park'. A summer house in the form of a temple is still known as Jane Austen's Bower (fig. 17). The practising farmers, the successors to the yeomen of Kent, had profited from the high corn

Fig. 16.
Kentish Turn-Wrest Plough
An engraving from Boys Agriculture of Kent *(1796)*.

prices at the turn of the century, but at the lowest stratum of society, the farm labourer had fared badly. Wages fluctuated wildly, while prices did nothing but rise, and by the 1830s many farm labourers survived only because of payments out of the parish poor rate. Many emigrated, while for the remainder the spread of mechanized agriculture in the form of Boys' threshing machines meant the loss of the few extra shillings with which to make ends meet. Matters came to a head in August 1830 at Hardres near Canterbury with a revolt of farm labourers, which spread to other parts of East Kent and later to Maidstone and Sittingbourne. The modest demands of the Kentish farm workers for regular work and half a crown a day wages were met.

Fig. 17.
Jane Austen's Bower
One of two 18th century summer houses at Godmersham Park.

Georgian Kent was still predominantly rural, with about a fifth of the 300,000 population (at the first official census in 1801) living in towns. At the 1821 census, the population had risen to over 400,000, and there were 12 sizeable towns within the county, of which only two — Canterbury and Maidstone — were inland (fig. 13). Three—Deptford, Greenwich and Woolwich—were to be swallowed by London on the formation of the County of London in 1888. Dockyards were responsible for the large populations of Chatham and Sheerness. Ramsgate and particularly Margate had become fashionable seaside resorts, reached by boat from London. From both, packet boats plied to Boulogne and Ostend and the continent could also be reached from Dover. Deal was not a cross-channel port, but traded with ships sheltering at anchor offshore in The Downs. Prior to 1832 Kent sent 18 MPs to parliament, from boroughs essentially unchanged from the Middle Ages, and all east of the Medway (fig. 13). Some of the boroughs were fairly democratic, while others, notably Romney, were not. Romney had eight electors, all tenants who were obliged to vote for their landlord's choice. The Reform Act of 1832 brought the constituencies more nearly in line with the new pattern of population.

VICTORIAN KENT

The rise in importance of North-West Kent was to continue even faster in the Victorian age as a shift took place from a dominantly rural to dominantly urban population. The population in 1851 was double that of 1801 and, if the area lost to London is included, doubled again by 1901, by which time the vast majority lived in towns. Although conditions in the villages improved, with the appearance of free schools, for example, migration to urban centres was widespread especially from East Kent.

The major factors in determining the growth of towns in the latter half of the nineteenth century were the increasing industrialization of North-West Kent and the Medway Towns, and the coming of the railway (fig. 18). The first line in Kent opened in 1830 from Canterbury to Whitstable. It was a curious hybrid. Winding engines operated the two steepest inclines, one with a tunnel under the present site of the University of Kent at Canterbury, horses drew the carriages on the flat summit, while a locomotive, the Invicta operated the final short section at the Whitstable end. The Invicta has the distinction of being the first locomotive in the world to pull a regular passenger train, but proved so inadequate that it was replaced by horses in 1838. It stands today in the Dane John Gardens at Canterbury.

In 1836 the London and Greenwich Railway reached Deptford, then in Kent, and its terminus at London Bridge soon came to be shared with the London and Croydon, the London and Brighton, and the South Eastern Railway (SER). The South Eastern reached Ashford by way of Redhill in 1842, and by 1857 served most of the main urban centres in Kent, but often by very circuitous routes. To set off to Redhill was an unpromising start for a journey from London to Margate, totalling 163km. The routes, however, took full advantage of the flat land on the Weald Clay (from Redhill to Ashford) and the river gaps of the Medway and Stour. The Ashford to Hastings line (1851) also lay mainly on flat land, initially on Weald Clay, then the reclaimed marshes of Romney Marsh and Rother Levels. One of the aims of the SER was to capture the cross-channel traffic at Dover and the line had to claw its way along the coast from Folkestone to Dover. The unstable undercliff at the Warren was used for the southern end of this line, and was the scene of a spectacular rotational landslip in December 1915 (plate 5) which closed the line for nearly four years, and resulted in the construction of a massive concrete apron. North of this the work of William Cubitt, the engineer of the SER, has stood the test of time. Under the supervision of Lieut. Hutchinson, RE, the Round Down Cliff was blown up over a length of 90m with 8,400kg of gunpowder and Cubitt then constructed the Abbot's Cliff and Shakespeare Cliff tunnels.

The roundabout routes created by the South Eastern Railway left it very vulnerable to a competitor, and sure enough the East Kent Railway, an independent line from Strood to Faversham, was promoted as an independent route to Thanet, Canterbury and Dover, named the London, Chatham and Dover Railway, with termini at Victoria and Holborn Viaduct. The South Eastern Railway quickly matched these by extensions to Charing Cross and Cannon Street and by engineering a direct line to Tonbridge (1868) with long tunnels through the Chalk and Hythe Beds. Over the next 20 years both companies promoted further lines (fig. 18) specifically to compete for traffic, a process so unprofitable that the London, Chatham and Dover Railway only once paid a dividend and had very poor rolling stock, although the nickname 'London, Smash'em and Turnover' was hardly justified. The competition ended in 1899 with the creation of the South Eastern and Chatham, whose gentler nickname was 'Slow, Easy and Comfortable'. The legacy of duplicated stations (shown in fig. 18) was less easily removed, and still survives at Bromley, Canterbury and Maidstone and indeed the services in a modern timetable still follow a nineteenth century pattern.

The railways gave a huge impetus to the towns they served, and those missed by the main routes, such as Tenterden, hardly grew at all. In Kent, the most rapid growth was around London, and Beckenham, Bromley, Chislehurst, Sidcup, Bexley, Erith and Orpington mushroomed with the homes of those who could now

Fig. 18
Victorian Kent

Plate 5
Landslip at Folkestone Warren in 1915.

Landscapes of the Past 25

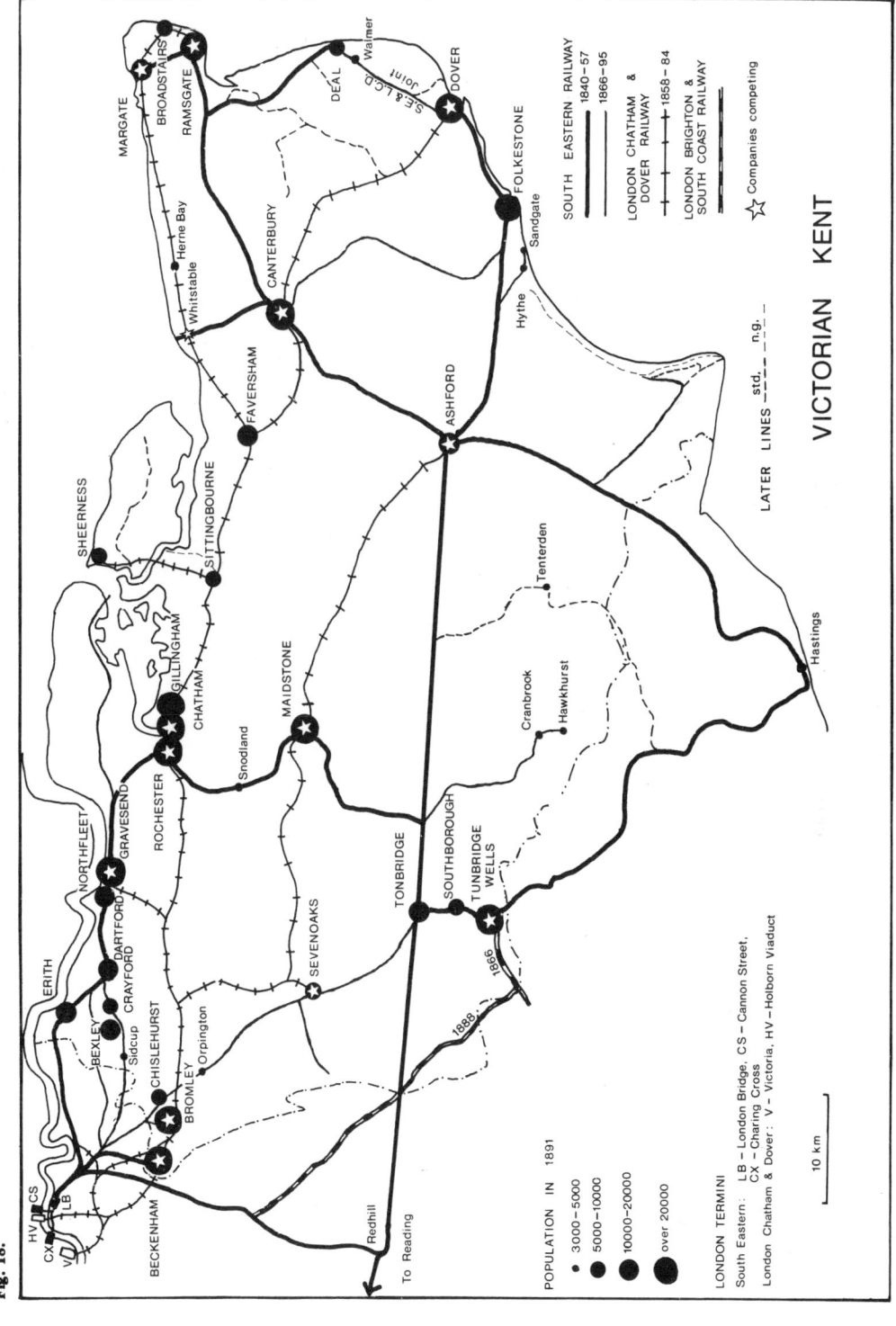

Fig. 18.

reach London easily by train. Further into Kent, Sevenoaks, Tonbridge, Tunbridge Wells, Snodland and Sittingbourne all doubled in size in the two decades following the arrival of the railway.

The effects were most marked in Ashford, which, from little more than a village in Georgian times, grew to be the hub of the South Eastern Railway in Victorian times, and Folkestone which was transformed from a sleepy fishing village to a cross-channel port.

Fig. 19.
The 'house on the cliff' (David Copperfield) at Broadstairs, open to visitors.

Railways also provided the opportunity for Londoners to reach the country or seaside. Each September, large numbers of East Enders came to work in the hop-harvest, and hoppers huts, hardly superior to pigsties, can still be seen. Railways also opened up the seaside resorts of the Isle of Thanet to the bulk of the population. Hitherto they had been the preserve of the gentry. Seaside holidays became a feature of Victorian life, and Margate, Broadstairs and Ramsgate thrived. One of the frequent visitors to Broadstairs was Charles Dickens and several houses in the town bear plaques showing where he stayed. His main residence, Fort House, is considered to be the original Bleak House, while the so-called Dickens House (fig. 19) was the 'house on the cliff' inhabited by Betsey Trotwood in 'David Copperfield'. However, Dickens was most at home in and around Rochester where a summer house which he used for much of his writing is now in the grounds of the Eastgate Museum. Gadshill, his favourite residence, still stands by the road from Strood to Gravesend.

TWENTIETH CENTURY KENT

Twice during the twentieth century Kent has been on the edge of a battlefield. In World War I Kent became host, as it had been 350 years earlier, to refugees from the Low Countries as German forces overran Belgium. Folkestone became a huge transit base for soldiers, while ammunition left from a secret base at Richborough. Dover was the home of the Dover Patrol (a destroyer flotilla) and attracted some attention from enemy aircraft and ships. Ramsgate, Margate and Folkestone were also attacked.

With the rise of Hitler's Reich, Kent once again welcomed foreign refugees, this time Jews who were accommodated at Richborough. World War II for Kent started with troop embarkations and naval patrols, but in May 1940 the full impact of war was felt. Hundreds of small ships set off from ports in Kent to evacuate the Army from Dunkirk while on shore, many civilians helped with the disembarkation at Dover, Folkestone and the Thanet ports.

Landscapes of the Past

Defences against invasion—barbed wire, pillboxes and hideouts—were prepared and some of the civilian population left the immediate potential invasion area. The Battle of Britain was fought over Kent with aircraft from the famous fighter stations at Manston, Biggin Hill and West Malling. During the War over 3,000 civilians in Kent were killed by bombs, flying bombs, rockets and even shelling from the French coast. Shells from Cap Gris Nez could land as far inland as Maidstone. Kent suffered badly from bombing, both from bombs jettisoned en route to or from London and from deliberate attacks. The worst attack was on Canterbury, when much of the city centre was gutted by incendiary bombs. In the later stages of the war flying bombs destined for London were deliberately brought down by aircraft over less populous parts of Kent, while rockets falling short of the capital also caused damage. Both the first and last V2 rockets to land on Britain fell on Kent. Kent had little chance to participate in retaliation, since only a dummy invasion fleet was marshalled along the coast. A large part of the Mulberry Harbour was, however, assembled off Richborough. Winston Churchill had his home at Chartwell, near Westerham, in a house now owned by the National Trust and open to the public.

Plate 6
Dover harbour, the Western Docks, with in the background (left to right) *the Castle Keep, Roman lighthouse and Saxon church, cliffs with former railway incline to harbour works and new road access to Eastern Docks (car ferry).*

Peaceful invaders of Kent have become increasingly numerous since the development of motor transport, aided by one of the greatest landscape innovations of the twentieth century: the tarred road. One of the first plants for coating crushed stone with asphalt for rural roads was erected by Chittenden and Simmons at Borough Green, between Maidstone and Sevenoaks, in 1913. From 1920 to 1970 the major cause of road congestion in Kent was weekend traffic to and from the coast. The 1920s saw a useful beginning to road construction aimed at relieving this congestion. Sidcup, Farnborough, Farningham and Dartford were bypassed, the Thanet Way was constructed between Faversham and Birchington and the disused section of Watling Street between Dartford and Strood was reinstated. In 1933 expenditure on roads was heavily cut and did not return in real terms to the level of the 20s until 1959. By this time motorways were being planned, the first stage of the A20(M), now the M20, was completed in 1961, and the M2 from west of Strood to Brenley Corner, near Faversham, in 1963.

Since 1970 traffic to and from the cross-channel ferries has become important. A total of 1,200,327 cars and 406,042 freight vehicles passed through Dover in 1977 (plate 5). Cars now predominate as a means of reaching employment in local centres if not in London, and weekend outings tend to be more diverse: National Trust properties being as popular as bathing beaches.

One of the most popular trips is in May and early June when the fruit trees are in blossom and Kent is indeed the Garden of England (plate 7).

Fig. 20.
Kingsferry Bridge
Built in 1960 to link Sheppey to the mainland. The giant concrete towers enable it to be lifted for ships to pass.

Geology and Landscape   2

Anyone interested in landscape will linger at a viewpoint on a clear day. He will orient himself by recognizing towns and villages, often from prominent buildings, such as church towers. The pattern of settlement is not random, it is channelled by valleys and focused by water supply. Roads and buildings are attracted to substrata offering firm, dry foundations and avoid dank clays and alluvial flood plains. The very material of older buildings, whether stone, brick or timber, is often derived directly or indirectly from the ground on which they stand.

Then the observer will note the vegetation with which the landscape is clothed. Nowhere is this 'natural' in the full sense, but nevertheless natural factors of soil and site have everywhere prompted the influence of man. Some geological formations show by the predominance of grass and a proliferation of overgrown hedges and woodland that the soils they bear are not highly valued for cultivation. On others, large fields with few stock-proof barriers are obviously rarely used for anything other than arable cropping.

Elsewhere orchards may clothe an entire slope, but disappear abruptly as the land becomes flat and liable to winter waterlogging and spring frosts. Nearby, rushes in the fields betoken waterlogged soils, travellers joy in the hedgerows chalky soils or heather acid ones. In turn, these soil properties enable one to pick out the clay, chalk or sandstone from whose very nature they spring, almost as certainly as the brickworks, the chalkpit or the quarry whose significance is also immediately apparent to those aware of local geology. Most striking of all to the initiated observer would be the comprehensive effect of geology on the layout of ridges and valleys, of escarpments and long even dipslopes which almost draw a geological cross section in the mind. Indeed this relationship of geology and relief is so close that separate chapters would be artificial and wasteful of words (figs. 21 and 22).

THE DEVELOPMENT OF THE WEALD

The rocks exposed at the surface in south-east England are sedimentary, laid down, sometimes by the sea sometimes by fresh water, in a period beginning about 135 and ending about 40 million years ago during the Cretaceous and Tertiary periods. Subsequent earth movements have gently folded these into two large basins or synclines, the London and Hampshire Basins and an intervening domed structure or anticline known as the Weald, bounded by the North and South Downs and in the west by the edge of the Salisbury Plain. The Cretaceous rocks of Kent represent most of the north-eastern quarter of the Weald while the Tertiary rocks along the North Kent coast form the south-western part of the London Basin.

Denudation of the area, mainly by the action of rivers, has exposed the core of the Wealden anticline, the Hastings Beds, in much of East Sussex and south-west Kent. Traced northwards across Kent the beds become progressively younger so that the very youngest are to be found in Sheppey. Each stratum, dipping to the north in Kent is matched more or less exactly by similar beds dipping to the south in Sussex. Between the outcrops the formerly continuous cover has been removed by erosion. This erosion has picked out the more resistant beds to form ridges or lines of hills with intervening low vales marking the outcrop of the soft and easily eroded clays (fig. 31).

Covering parts of the outcrop of these 'solid' geological formations are a variety of superficial 'drift' deposits, usually relatively thin (a matter of a few metres) and geologically quite young, hundreds or thousands of years old instead of the many million years of the solid formations. The drift deposits include materials laid down by rivers, such as alluvium along their present courses and spreads of sand and gravel marking former courses at a higher level.

No true glacial deposits occur in Kent, but the cold conditions associated with the Ice Ages produced an assortment of drift deposits. The end-product of the deposition of various sedimentary rocks, their folding by earth-movements, subsequent denudation and partial covering by the latter superficial drifts is a number of well defined natural regions. Each is associated with a particular geological formation, has its own distinctive landscape, soil pattern, natural vegetation and agricultural use (fig. 21).

Fig. 21.
Landscape Regions of Kent. *Compare with the geological map (Fig. 22).*

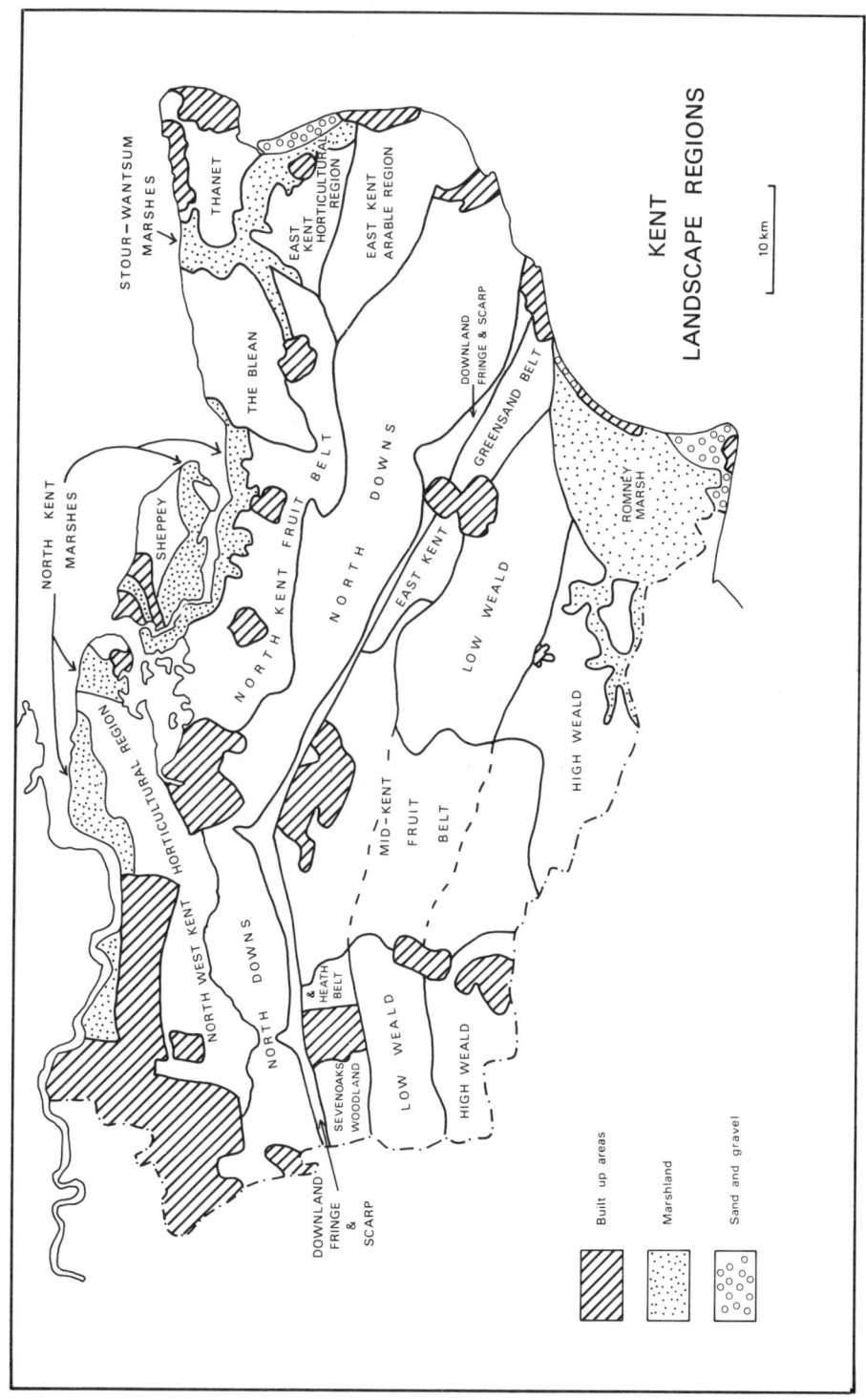

Fig. 21.

GEOLOGY AND NATURAL REGIONS

The Hastings Beds (The High Weald)

About 135 million years ago at the start of the Cretaceous period, hilly land ran along what is now the Thames Valley, eastwards to the Ardennes. From this several major rivers flowed southwards through deltas into a shallow freshwater lake, probably connected with the sea to the south, but kept nonsaline by the copious supply of fresh river water. The situation has been likened to the present-day Brahmaputra Delta. The material carried down by the rivers, mainly silt and clay, has formed the Hastings Beds which make up the High Weald of south-west Kent and East Sussex. At intervals, deposition of fine sandy material, the Ashdown Sands and Lower and Upper Tunbridge Wells Sands marked major periods of delta growth, although within each of the formations there is ample evidence of repeated short term fluctuations between lacustrine and deltaic conditions. Fossils are relatively rare, but include small lamellibranchs and ostracods (a distant relative of the shrimp). Occasionally the footprints or even actual remains of the land dinosaur *Iguanodon* have been found, and soil layers also occur in which the remains of the horsetail *Equisetites lyelli* can be discovered.

In Kent the main formation outcropping is the Tunbridge Wells Sand, with smaller areas of Wadhurst and Grinstead clay but relatively little Ashdown Sand. The landscape is hilly (reaching nearly 150 m near Tunbridge Wells), with round topped hills and steep-sided valleys or ghylls marking the courses of streams fed by numerous springs. The relationship of the actual beds to topography is complicated by a number of faults, but in general the Tunbridge Wells Sand is found mainly on the higher ground, with Wadhurst Clay on the sides of valleys, whose floors are underlain by Ashdown Sand often concealed by alluvium. Exposures of the rocks are rare, with the exception of crags, often used for mountaineering practice, e.g. Harrison's Rocks near Tunbridge Wells.

The Weald Clay (The Low Weald)

The broad flat featureless clay vale formed by the succeeding Weald Clay is in marked contrast to the hills of the High Weald. The Weald Clay is a thick deposit of fresh to brackish water shales and mudstones similar to the Wadhurst and Grinstead Clays, but containing bands of freshwater limestone crowded with the shells of the water snail *Viviparus* (formerly called Paludina). The limestones

Fig. 22.
Geology of Kent
Shows the main solid formations of Cretaceous and Tertiary Age and the more extensive relatively recent superficial drift deposits.

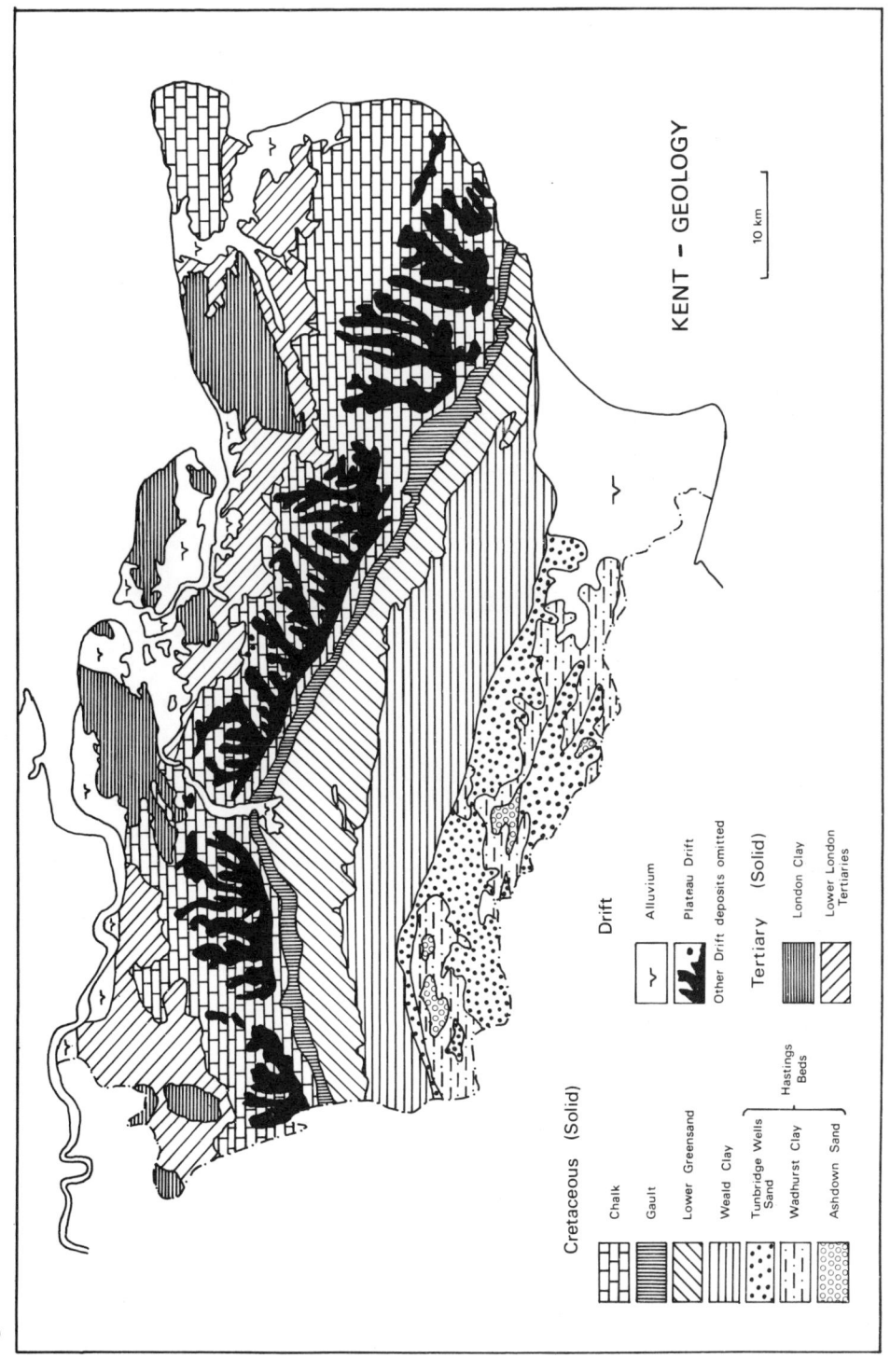

Fig. 22.

give rise to small ridges and were once worked as an ornamental stone called 'Bethersden Marble'.

Much of the Low Weald is below 30 m in altitude and, because of this and the impermeable nature of the underlying Weald Clay, the overall drainage of the region is poor. The central portion, however, in an area bounded by Marden, Yalding, Hadlow and Tonbridge is in marked contrast to the rest of the Low Weald. Here the Weald Clay is hidden by a cover of drift deposits associated with the Medway and Beult giving excellent soils greatly prized for hops and orchards.

The Lower Greensand (The Greensand Ridge)

About 120 million years ago the freshwater lake in which the Hastings Beds and Weald Clay were laid down gave way to marine conditions, and the shoreline withdrew to the north as most of southern England became sea for the succeeding 50 million years. The first series of sediments laid down by this sea are known collectively as the Lower Greensand, and in Kent consist of four members—the Atherfield Clay, Hythe Beds, Sandgate Beds and Folkestone Beds. These vary in character and thickness, not only from one to another from north to south across their outcrop but also along the outcrop from the coast at Folkestone and Hythe to the county boundary at Westerham. The name Greensand derives from a greenish coloured mineral called glauconite which appears as sand grains in the rocks of the type local in Dorset. In Kent, however, the Greensand is 'rarely green and seldom a sand' and the epithet is most true for the earliest member, the Atherfield Clay. This is virtually indistinguishable from the Weald Clay which preceded it, and is differentiated only by its content of true marine fossils including corals and ammonites. Its outcrop is, at most, only a few hundred metres wide, running along the bottom of the main scarp formed by the overlying Hythe Beds and usually hidden by landslipped material and hillwash from above.

The Hythe Beds can lay claim to being the most distinctive rock in Kent, the source of Kentish Ragstone from which many fine buildings have been constructed including parts of the Tower of London and many Victorian churches in the metropolis. Ragstone is a hard, bluish grey limestone occurring in bands about 15 to 60 cm thick with intervening layers of Hassock, a soft, creamy-white calcareous sand (plate 15). Quarrying, at present concentrated west of Maidstone, has produced some fine exposures of this rock, and individual layers of Ragstone have been given names by the quarrymen such as Dirty Dick, Little Diamonds and Square Rock.

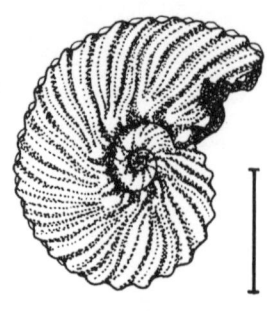

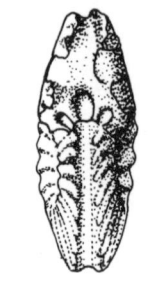

Fig. 23.
Fossil ammonite.
Hoplites dentatus, *from the Gault Clay. Scale 2 cm.*

Fossils are common, including several types of ammonites, brachiopods, gastropods, lamellibranchs, sea urchins and even an occasional dinosaur, such as the celebrated *Iguanodon,* discovered at Maidstone in 1834, and now in the Natural History Museum, London (fig. 24).

In general the Hythe Beds weather to give good soils, and the wide dipslope south of Maidstone is one of the major concentrations of fruit growing in Kent. Some of the fruit soils are on loamy drift overlying and partly derived from the Hythe Beds, but some drifts, notably the Angular Chert Drift on the higher ground near the crest of the ridge give less valuable land although attractively wooded. Woodland and heath characterize the outcrop of the Hythe Beds around Sevenoaks where the poor soils are due to a change in character of the underlying rocks.

Gone are the calcareous rag and hassock, replaced by acid sands and cherts which, because of their resistant nature, form a very marked ridge reaching over 245 m in Kent at Toys Hill, near

Fig. 24.
Iguanodon
A harmless vegetarian dinosaur about 10 m long, whose remains and footprints have been found in the Hastings Beds and the Lower Greensand.

Westerham and rising westwards into Surrey where Leith Hill, formed by Hythe Beds is one of the highest points in the South East.

By contrast with the marked ridge formed by the Hythe Beds the succeeding Sandgate Beds are unresistant silty and clayey sands, usually occupied by a flat and marshy tract often containing an east-west tributary of the Medway or Stour. The beds are often green and glauconitic, and might help to justify the name of greensand if they were not so rarely exposed. Occasional seams of fuller's earth, notably around Maidstone, are not so well developed as those now exploited near Redhill in Surrey.

In contrast, exposures of the succeeding Folkestone Beds abound in sandpits, large and small. The most obvious of these is at the present western end of the M20 near Wrotham, but this is only one of many along the general line of the A20 and A25 roads. The material being quarried is a yellow or sometimes whitish, loose, current-bedded sand with abundant bands and lumps cemented with iron oxides and a few seams of clay. Around Folkestone, e.g. in the classic if atypical exposure in the cliffs behind the promenade, the Beds consist of yellowish greensands and bands of calcareous and glauconitic sandstone. One is called Folkestone Stone. Another hard band within the formation, the Ightham Stone, is composed of chert.

The Folkestone Beds, especially in Mid Kent, form a line of low hills to the north of the main Hythe Beds ridge, with attractive, undulating farmland interspersed with woods and occasional heaths, e.g. Hothfield Common near Ashford. East of Ashford the whole Greensand outcrop is relatively subdued, while from around Sevenoaks westwards to the county boundary the Folkestone Beds give land similar to the neighbouring acid cherty Hythe Beds and superficially indistinguishable from it.

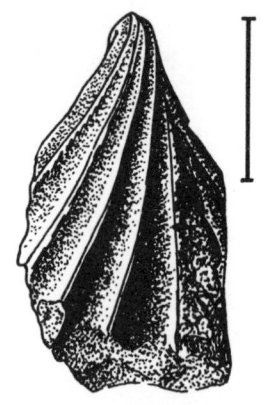

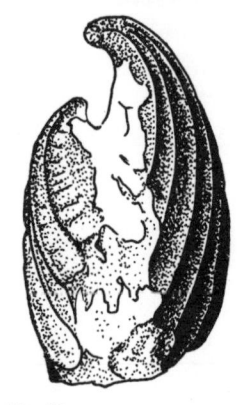

Fig. 25.
Fossil lamellibranch. Inoceramus sulcatus, *from the Gault Clay. Scale 2 cm.*

The Gault (The Vale of Homesdale)

The end of the Lower Greensand times, about 110 million years ago, was marked by an important advance of the sea, sweeping northwards and westwards over southern Britain, and depositing the Gault Clay in quieter offshore areas and the Upper Greensand in shallow nearshore areas. The latter deposit occurs in Kent only west of Sevenoaks, where about 9 m of a micaceous sandstone (the malmstone) containing some glauconite is found between the true Gault Clay and the overlying Chalk. Elsewhere there is only the Gault Clay, outcropping in a narrow vale, called Homesdale, between the Greensand Ridge and the North Downs.

The Gault is a dark bluish-grey clay, rich in clay minerals capable of considerable expansion and contraction on wetting and drying. Relatively few buildings and no villages are to be found built directly on the Gault because of the disruption of foundations. The instability of Gault Clay is responsible for the slumping still seen along parts of the M20 Maidstone by-pass. The spectacular landslips at Folkestone Warren can also be traced to the Gault Clay underlying the high chalk cliffs. In winter the water table in the chalk rises and the Gault can become saturated. Its failure causes a rotational slip, with the weight of the chalk squeezing the Gault seawards onto the foreshore. The railway line between Folkestone and Dover running across the Warren is thus at constant risk and has been closed several times this century because of land-slipping (plate 5). A concrete apron has been constructed on the foreshore to stabilize the toe of the slope and hence prevent further disruptive movement.

The Gault is highly fossiliferous, notably containing many ammonites by means of which the classic coastal locality at Copt Point, Folkestone has been divided into a number of paleontological zones which act as the frame of reference for studies elsewhere in southern England. The muddy conditions did not favour clear-water organisms such as brachiopods, sponges and coral, although examples of these can be found. Commoner are lamellibranchs, especially *Inoceramus,* and gastropods, but the variety is unusual and includes sea lilies, sea urchins, crabs, shrimps, lobsters, barnacles, fish, reptiles and plants. Probably the commonest fossils, especially in washed out debris, are the cylindrical pointed guards of belemnites, relatives of the present-day cuttle fish, and nobbly lumps of calcium phosphate called coprolites, believed to be the fossilized excrement of reptiles and fish (figs. 23, 25 and 26).

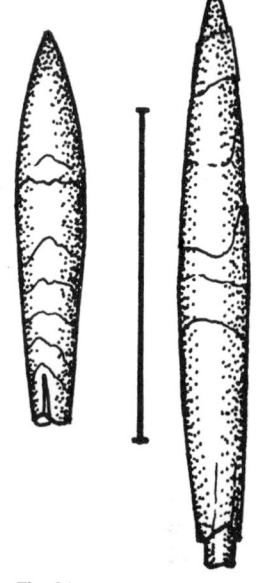

Fig. 26.
Fossil belemnite.
Neohibolites minimus, *from the Gault Clay. Scale 2 cm.*

The Chalk (The North Downs and Isle of Thanet)

The White Cliffs of Dover are one of the landmarks of Kent, and are continued westwards by the North Downs. Eastwards the chalk passes under the Straits to the cliffs of Cap Blanc Nez, visible from East Kent viewpoints on a clear day.

The Chalk was laid down between about 70 and 100 million years ago during the Upper Cretaceous period. At this time Kent occupied only a small part of the floor of a vast but shallow sea covering most of Central and Western Europe. In this sea vast numbers of minute planktonic algae flourished and the plates of their coccoliths together with foraminiferal tests and other shell debris produced a white calcareous mud which became the Chalk. The earliest beds making up the Lower Chalk also contain appreciable non-calcareous material, mainly clay, so that technically they are marls. The amount of non-calcareous material decreases towards the top of the formation being in excess of 50 per cent in the basal beds but less than 1 per cent in the Upper Chalk which is marked by the presence of flints, largely absent from the lower beds. Brown rusty nodules somewhat resembling small cannon balls or meteorites occur, especially in the lower beds. Broken up they reveal radiating needles of pyrite (fig. 27).

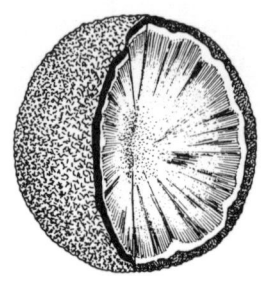

Fig. 27.
Pyrite nodule from the Chalk. Broken to show radiating crystals. Scale 3 cm.

The marly Lower Chalk occupies the footslope of the North Downs escarpment where it is often obscured by colluvium (hill-wash) and Coombe Deposits (chalky sludge) created during the tundra conditions which prevailed in Kent during the Ice Ages (fig. 36). Above a boundary coinciding almost exactly with the Pilgrim's Way, the Middle Chalk, purer, whiter and with a few flints near the top, makes up most of the scarp and crest of the Downs. The crest runs at about 190 m through most of Kent, but rises steadily west of the Medway to the highest point in Kent, Westerham Hill (251 m), where the Upper Chalk caps the crest. The scarp face is breached only by the river valleys of the Darent, Medway and Stour and by a dry 'wind-gap' near Lyminge. All of these yield important routes into the Weald proper from North Kent. The scarp face is often very steep, in excess of 20°, and in places is cut by coombes, the result of severe but localized erosion during late glacial times (plate 2).

The Upper Chalk is a remarkably pure, soft, white limestone with numerous bands of flint. It makes up most of the dipslope of the North Downs and underlies the Isle of Thanet. It would be highly misleading, however, to view this area as consisting entirely of chalk since it is extensively mantled with a variety of drift deposits and scattered outcrops of the succeeding Tertiary beds. Most widespread is a stiff, reddish flinty clay, usually called the Clay-with-Flints although this name is now being restricted to a particularly clayey variety. The name Plateau Drift now applies to other drift deposits on the upper part of the dipslope. These have a complex origin with components from a previous cover of Lower Tertiary rocks, Pliocene sands and gravels, insoluble residue from solution of the chalk and additions of wind blown dust (loess) during the Ice Ages.

The Chalk dipslope is also characterized by a well developed system of dry valleys, obviously a product of stream action, but now carrying no water. In some valleys intermittent streams called bournes used to appear in wet winters and former occurrences of these are shown by place names such as Sittingbourne. Water abstraction has so lowered the water table within the Chalk aquifer in recent years that bournes are now extremely rare. The dry valley system is too extensive to be due to erosion by these intermittent streams, and it is more likely that they were cut during Ice Age summers when meltwater ran over ground that was permanently frozen and impermeable below about half a metre. When this permafrost melted finally, rainwater once more soaked away into the permeable chalk. The dry valleys often have steeper west and south facing sides, with thin soils directly over solid chalk. The east and north facing slopes are gentler, usually with deeper soils in chalky drift which escaped erosion probably because summer thaws went less deep on slopes with a colder aspect. The floors of the valleys usually have deeper, less chalky drift while the interfluves between valleys and the undissected plateau near the crest of the Downs are covered with the clayey Plateau Drift, often wooded. Some sections of the North Downs dipslope, notably in North West Kent, Thanet and the triangle between Dover, Deal and Canterbury lack Plateau Drift entirely although they have dry valley systems and other chalky and silty drifts.

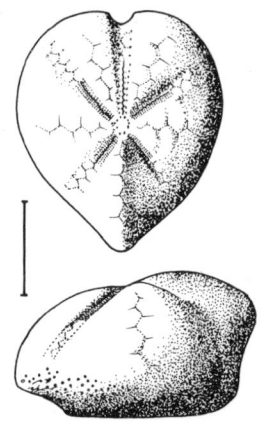

Fig. 28. Fossil sea urchin. *Echinoid* (Micraster coranguinum), *from the Chalk. Scale 2 cm.*

The Early Tertiary (North Kent)

The Alpine earth-movements, which were to culminate during the mid-Tertiary, probably began to form the Wealden anticline towards the end of the Cretaceous, for some of the recently deposited chalk was eroded away before the deposition of Tertiary sediments. It is thought that a large delta occupied central England, draining from land in the north-west into a shallow sea which stretched roughly from London into northern France and Belgium. In response to earth-movements the sea periodically advanced or retreated, especially during the deposition of the earliest beds, collectively known as the Lower London Tertiaries. These beds also vary in character between East Kent, mainly open sea, and areas further west and nearer the land mass. The succeeding London Clay was deposited in deeper water, after which the sea gradually retreated from the area.

The earliest Tertiary deposits are the Thanet Beds which derive their name from the Isle of Thanet whose southern edge they fringe and where, at Pegwell Bay, is their type locality. They consist of loamy sands, containing glauconite, with some seams of silty clay in East Kent where marine shells are abundant. In North West Kent the Thanet Beds are always fine sands and were probably deposited in shallow brackish water. At their base is a bed of unworn greenish-coated flints set in a dark greensand matrix called the Bullhead Bed which marks the unconformity with the Chalk. The beds occur as a discontinuous outcrop along the northern side of the Chalk dipslope from Sandwich to Woolwich. They are closely associated with later deposits of Brickearth and the two give rise to the excellent land of the North Kent Fruit Belt. It used to be thought that the Brickearth was simply redeposited Thanet Beds, but detailed studies have now shown the bulk to be wind blown dust (loess) carried from East Anglia by winds blowing off the continental ice sheets.

In East Kent the succeeding Woolwich Beds are a thin deposit of marine sands, becoming in West Kent shelly clays and finally passing laterally into the estuarine Reading Beds to the west of London. Their outcrop is small and fringes major areas of Tertiary deposits in the Blean north of Canterbury and in the Bromley-Bexley areas. The overlying Oldhaven Beds are again sandy in East Kent and are separated from the Woolwich Beds by a band of pebbles. This pebble band becomes much more important to the west at the expense of the marine sands and has merited the separate name of the Blackheath Beds. These have a large outcrop around south-east London marked, where not obliterated by urban development, by heaths and woodland, e.g. Hayes and Keston Commons.

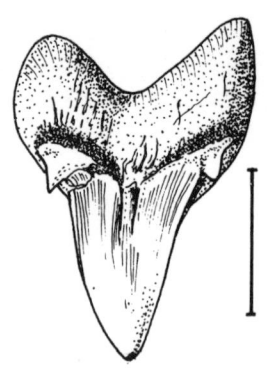

Fig. 29.
Fossil shark's teeth. Odontaspis *(a sand shark)*, *from the Tertiary Oldhaven Beds. Scale 2 cm.*

The thickest of the Tertiary deposits is the London Clay which outcrops as low plateaux and hills fringed by the earlier Lower London Tertiaries. It forms most of the Blean, north of Canterbury, much of Sheppey and the Hoo Peninsula and caps many of the small hills around Gravesend, Bromley and Beckenham. A blue marine clay, weathering brown, its fossil content is one of the most fascinating in south-east England. Fossils are best collected from the coastal exposures, such as on Sheppey and near Herne Bay, where coastal erosion is proceeding at an alarming rate (averaging 3 m per year in some places) although partly checked by sea defence works. The coarser material winnowed by waves from the clay has yielded fossil remains of star-fish, crabs, lobsters, snakes, fish, turtles and whales besides a multitude of molluscs and plant remains including palms, cinnamon and magnolia. It is often difficult to believe, standing on the foreshore at Sheppey searching for fossils in the teeth of a biting north-easterly wind, that these indicate a period of tropical conditions here in south-east England.

LATER STAGES OF LANDSCAPE DEVELOPMENT

The story of Kent from the tropical conditions of 40 million years ago to the present day has been pieced together by geomorphologists rather than true geologists, for, following the London Clay, no substantial geological deposits have accumulated. The situation has rather been of earth-movements, erosion, redistribution of material already present, and the development of the river systems.

The classic theory explaining the landscape development of south-east England is due to two eminent geomorphologists, S. W. Wooldridge and D. L. Linton, although it must be pointed out that some doubt is now being cast on it. One of the major problems was how to account for the Wealden rivers, almost all of which cut across the grain of the country, apparently picking the most difficult course to the sea. One of the headwaters of the Stour, for example, rises near Hythe only 3.5 km from the sea, but flows westwards and northwards a total of about 80 km through gaps cut in the Greensand Ridge and North Downs to reach the sea beyond Sandwich. Wooldridge and Linton believed that the drainage system of south-east England was initiated on the uplifted Wealden area produced by earth movements culminating in the Miocene period about 20 million years ago. These earth movements, associated with the building of the Alps and other southern European mountain chains left the Weald not as a smooth dome but as a series of east-west ridges and hollows looking rather like a gigantic crumpled tablecloth. The resulting drainage had a pronounced east-west trend, thought to be preserved to this day in the courses of most of the rivers of the High Weald.

It is thought that about two to three million years ago in the Pliocene or early Pleistocene period a sea invaded most of south-east England destroying the former east-west drainage system except on a postulated large island occupying most of southern Kent and Surrey and northern Sussex. As the sea retreated, perhaps because of continuing uplift of the land, the rivers flowed radially outwards (i.e. northwards in Kent) across the newly exposed sea floor. Small patches of sand, the Lenham Beds at about 180 m on the North Downs are relics of this former sea floor. In Kent, downward cutting of the rivers superimposed their northerly courses onto the underlying strata irrespective of the east-west trend of these. Once their courses were established, the rivers and associated erosion processes served to pick out the more resistant beds of the High Weald, Greensand and Chalk as ridges. The

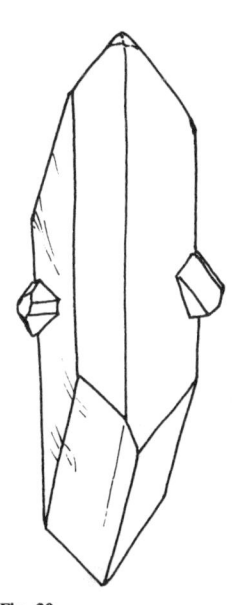

Fig. 30.
Gypsum crystal (selenite), from a clay seam in the Tertiary Oldhaven Beds. Scale 3 cm.

intervening less resistant clays became vales with tributary streams of the main rivers extending along them (fig. 31).

It is basically this differential erosion which has shaped the present day landscape of Kent, with some assistance from periglacial processes during the Ice Ages. Kent was never glaciated, the maximum limit of the ice sheets being southern Essex. In front of the ice sheets, however, tundra-like (periglacial) conditions prevailed. Permafrost was probably widespread, above which was an 'active layer' which underwent seasonal freezing and thawing. This caused disruption and churning of material and, where it occurred on slopes, downslope movement or solifluction. The products of solifluction widespread in Kent are known collectively as Head with the specific name Coombe Deposits for soliflucted Chalk. The dry valley systems of the North Downs and the Brickearths of North and East Kent have also resulted from these conditions, as has already been noted.

As the ice sheets waxed and waned, withdrawing and then releasing water, sea-level alternately fell and rose. The response of rivers to this has resulted in spreads of gravel at various heights

Fig. 31.
Geological Cross Section
From the county boundary near Tunbridge Wells to the Thames Estuary at Northfleet to show the relationship between geology and landscape.

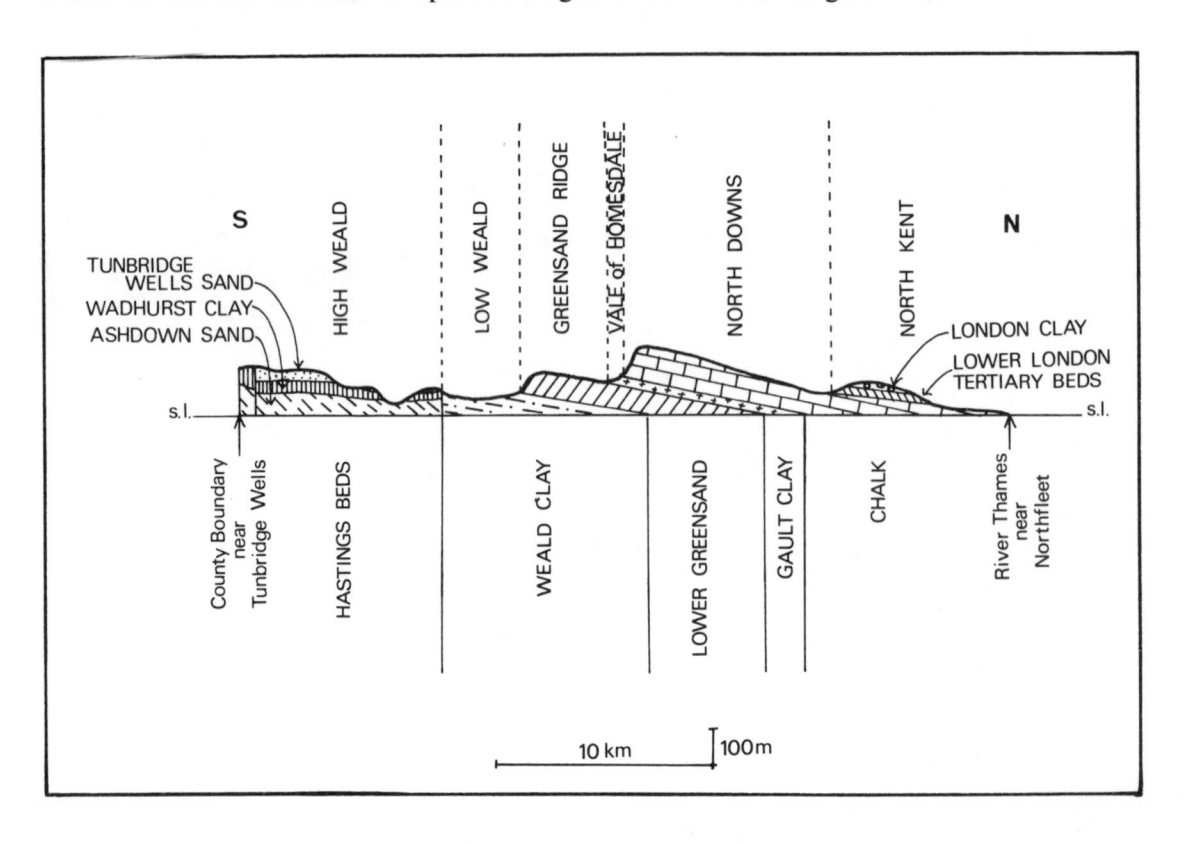

along their courses, notably along the Darent, Stour and Thames. The Thames was, in the early part of the Ice Ages, a tributary of the Rhine, both flowing northwards into an ancestral North Sea. At the period of maximum glaciation (Gippingian) ice from the north ponded the river waters in front of it and these eventually overspilled southwards along the valley of a neighbour of the river Stour and into the English Channel. As the glaciers retreated, northward drainage was re-established, but in the following interglacial period sea-level was probably sufficiently high to flood this overspill channel and temporarily sever Britain from the continent. The process was probably repeated in the following, final glaciation and with the post-glacial rise in sea-level, inundation of the Straits of Dover again took place. Contrary to popular opinion this was not the final breach with the Continent, since for some time a land bridge remained across the Dogger Bank which was not finally inundated till 8,600 years ago.

About a thousand years earlier the Straits of Dover were about half their present width with sea-level 40 m below present. Subsequent rise was rapid, in 300 years sea level had risen enough to inundate the now buried channels of the Thames-Medway and Stour-Swale systems. Eight thousand years ago the shoreline of Kent was more recognizably like today's, but with more land in north Kent particularly enlarging Sheppey and Thanet. Five thousand years ago sea level was about 10 m lower than at present, while in the Roman period it was about 2 m lower. Since Roman times there have been both gains and losses of land around the Kent coast (fig. 7). Erosion has eaten away at the North Kent coast and large areas of marshland near the Medway estuary have been lost since Elizabethan times. Conversely there has been reclamation from the Swale and Stour estuaries, notably on the Wantsum Marshes around Thanet, which, in Roman times, were an arm of the sea rendering Thanet truly an island.

The most significant, and relatively recent, change in the Kent coastline has been the formation of Romney Marsh. As sea level rose after the last glaciation a wide sandy bay existed between Hythe and Fairlight in East Sussex into which flowed the Rother (the river Leman of the Saxons) and other East Sussex rivers. The former coastal cliffs of this bay, now rather degraded, form the backdrop to the Marsh in an arc from Rye to Hythe. A succession of shingle spits fed by longshore drift from south-west then grew out into the bay from Fairlight Head and eventually formed a more or less complete bar across the bay. Alluvium, initially sands then mainly clays brought down by the Rother, started to build up behind the bar and even became forested. About 3,000 years ago the embryo Marsh was inundated back to the former cliff-line and a layer of peat with 'bog oaks' underlying much of the Marsh marks the former forest period. Thereafter the shingle ridge gradually swung round more or less to its present position at Dungeness (plate 18), locally breached at different places and times as the Rother found its way to the sea through the swamps. Reclamation of sections of marshland in the Roman and Saxon periods (fig. 32) gradually won the land from the sea, with frequent setbacks by sea-flooding notably a great storm in 1284 which changed the course of the Rother so that its mouth shifted from New Romney to Rye. By the seventeenth century reclamation was almost complete, and masonry sea defences added in the nineteenth and twentieth centuries secured the area against the sea.

This century the sea has had only one notable success, thankfully short-lived. The storm surge of 1953 breached the sea defences of North Kent, flooding all the north-facing marshland up to 5.5 m O.D., but not Romney Marsh. The Herne Bay to Birchington railway was undermined, but the Thanet road from Canterbury held firm. With this exception Thanet was again, for about three weeks, an island.

Fig. 32.
Romney Marsh
Some early features drawn on the present-day outline of the Marsh.

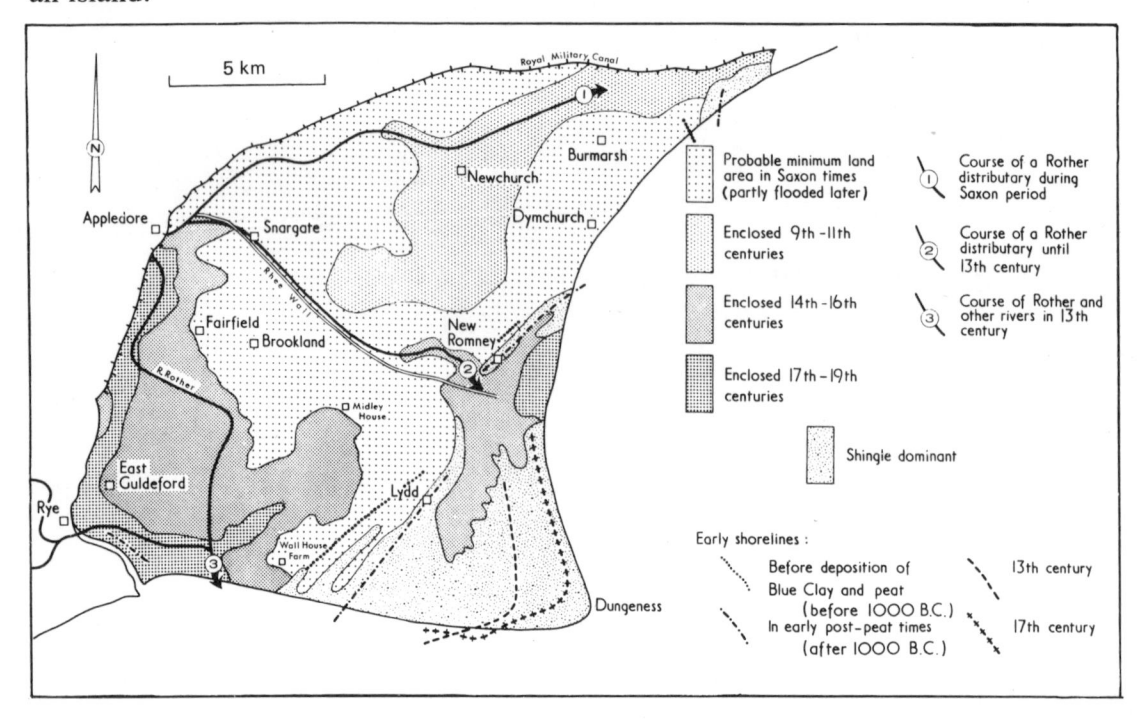

The Farmer's Landscape 3

Kent has every reason to claim the title of 'Garden of England'. Within the county are found almost half the orchards, half the hops and over one-fifth of soft fruit grown in England and Wales, with substantial areas of market garden vegetables and potatoes. Kent is not uniformly a garden, however, for these horticultural crops are located only in those parts of the county where the soils and climate are particularly favourable, although economic pressures also increasingly affect the location of the horticultural industry in Kent. Outside the mainly horticultural areas, Kent provides a wide diversity of crops and livestock, and virtually every British crop is represented.

LAND CAPABILITY

The character of land, whether it is considered as the natural habitat of plants or as a resource for human use, is largely determined by climate, relief and soil properties. Intelligent planning of land use implies knowledge of these factors, which is conveniently summed up by grading of the land using a capability classification. The two systems in common use both have numbered classes or grades, of which 1 to 4 are suitable for arable cropping, but with increasing limitations. The limitations may give lower yields, increased costs or difficulties of management, decreased choice of crops or a combination of these drawbacks. In the Ministry of Agriculture scheme Grade 5 comprises all land unsuitable for arable crops, but this land is divided in the British Soil Surveys Scheme used in this chapter into three classes. Class 5 is suitable for improved grassland, Class 6 can be used for forestry and/or rough grazing, and Class 7 is not agriculturally useful. Fig. 46 is a generalized land capability map of Kent.

CLIMATE

It is fortunate that Kent enjoys a climate which is warm and dry compared with most other parts of Britain. Fruit growing has benefited considerably from this warmth, and the only question that remains unanswered is whether Kent can compete with still more favoured regions overseas. Another great advantage of a favourable climate is the wider range of crops that can be grown. In Northern Scotland the arable farmer is restricted to oats, barley, turnips and potatoes. In Kent he can grow almost any crop grown elsewhere in Britain, while some crops associated with warmer latitudes are being tried, such as maize for grain, navy beans (the familiar 'baked beans') and even vineyards.

By British standards the climate of Kent is continental, warm in summer, cold in winter and relatively dry. This is because anticyclones centred over the European mainland often extend over south-east England and divert depressions arriving from the west towards Scandinavia. So it is not surprising that the highest shade temperature ever recorded in the British Isles occurred in Kent, 38.1°C at Tonbridge on 22 July 1868. Similarly, while the coast escapes great extremes of heat and cold, severe frosts are not

Fig. 33.
Rainfall of Kent (average of 1916-50).

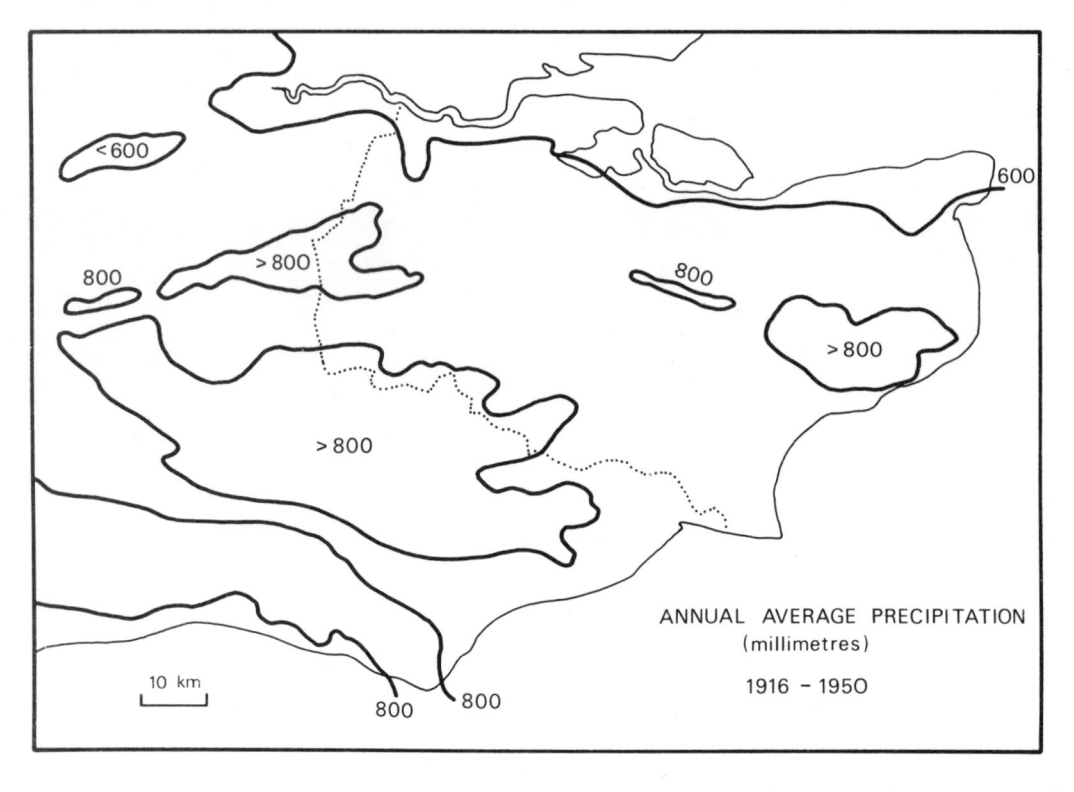

uncommon inland. Canterbury recorded an exceptionally low figure of −20°C in January 1940. Plants sensitive to winter frosts, such as the palms in Torquay gardens, rarely survive in Kent.

For many plants a good general index of climatic warmth is the length of the growing season. The actual growing season varies very much from year to year and even from one kind of plant to another in the same year. One definition, however, is the average duration of the period with a mean air temperature above 5.5°C. This decreases by an average of nine days for every 30 m increase in elevation. The Kent coast has a growing season of between 275 and 300 days. Hills above 150 m have a growing season of less than 240 days and bear very few orchards. In strawberries, however, the later fruiting at higher elevation may actually result in a bigger price for the crop.

Late spring frosts are the worst enemy of the fruit grower. The coast is relatively immune from them, but here exposure to wind and salt spray almost precludes commercial orchards. Inland, position in the landscape largely determines liability to frost. On clear nights cold air can flow down slopes like water, ponding in valleys and even behind hedges and windbreaks. It is generally possible to predict where frost pockets will occur, and to avoid them when planting orchards.

Information about climate is also relevant to the holiday-maker. Resorts on the Kent coast have warm, dry summer weather, particularly in the north-east, where Margate has a mean temperature in July and August of about 17.5°C. Most people have to take their holidays too late. For low rainfall and maximum sunshine May and June are, in general, the best months, when the sun shines along the Kent coast for an average of 7.3 to 7.5 hours a day. August is poor in comparison, with less sun and an average rainfall more than 50 per cent above the June figures in most places.

Overall, however, North Kent is one of the driest parts of Britain. In relation to its horticultural industry this has an advantage in early soil workability in spring, but to meet the needs of summer growth the waterholding capacity of its fortunately retentive soils is fully taxed. Indeed crops would benefit from irrigation almost every year. Regrettably, Thanet, where the need is greatest of all, suffers from a special shortage of water. In any case all private abstractions of water from rivers or boreholes now have to be licensed and a levy paid.

Conversely in winter more water reaches the soil as rain and snow than is lost by evaporation and transpiration and the surplus must be drained. This is small in North Kent, at Margate only 125 mm, but in the High Weald at Bedgebury, 330 mm in the average winter, and the difference greatly increases the need for artificial drainage of soils. Since sub-soils tend to be impermeable in the High Weald, it is not surprising that in that area sports fields are rarely in playable condition throughout the winter. Fruit growers too must give particular attention to drainage, for waterlogging for a few weeks can destroy the work of years.

Exposure to wind particularly affects tree crops. Little fruit is grown within 5 km of the open sea (fig. 39), and even woods are scarce. Orchards are rarely planted on hill crests, while hops are so sensitive that windbreaks of trees or netting are almost always provided.

RELIEF

Exposure to wind is intricately linked to relief, but there are several other ways in which relief affects the usefulness of land. Sloping land has an aspect: south facing slopes are warmer. An example is the south facing Hythe Beds escarpment between Yalding and Ulcombe, which has many orchards and a chain of villages, such as Sutton Valence. However, beyond about 7° slope affects mechanized farming operations, and slopes steeper than 15° are not normally in arable crops. Such slopes are common in the High Weald and also on escarpments and dry valley sides in Chalk country. In such areas, field boundaries often occur at changes in slope angle, so that parcels have odd shapes and may have difficulties of access.

Severe water erosion is not common in Kent, but slight sheet erosion of topsoils regularly occurs, even on fairly gentle slopes, if these are long, while rills form where cultivations leave wheel ruts straight up and down hill and an intense rainstorm follows. Over a period soil erosion can result in a 'step' of a metre or so where old hedgerows run along the contours of a cultivated slope. Parts of Lullingstone Villa were buried two metres deep in post-Roman hillwash. Conversely, shallow soils, depleted by erosion, occur on the upper parts of slopes, especially in chalk country. On very steep slopes (more than 25°) topsoil tends to slide down in a coherent sheet, and the resulting terracettes are often emphasized by paths trodden by animals, seen on the sides of coombes such as the Devil's Kneading Trough on Wye Downs (plate 2). Of course, special circumstances, due to geology or engineering works, may lead to more deep seated landslides such as those which have occurred in a number of places along the Hythe Beds escarpment.

Fig. 34.
Soils of Kent
The main soil associations of Kent, grouped into the four major categories of calcareous soils, brown earths, stagnogleys and alluvial soils.

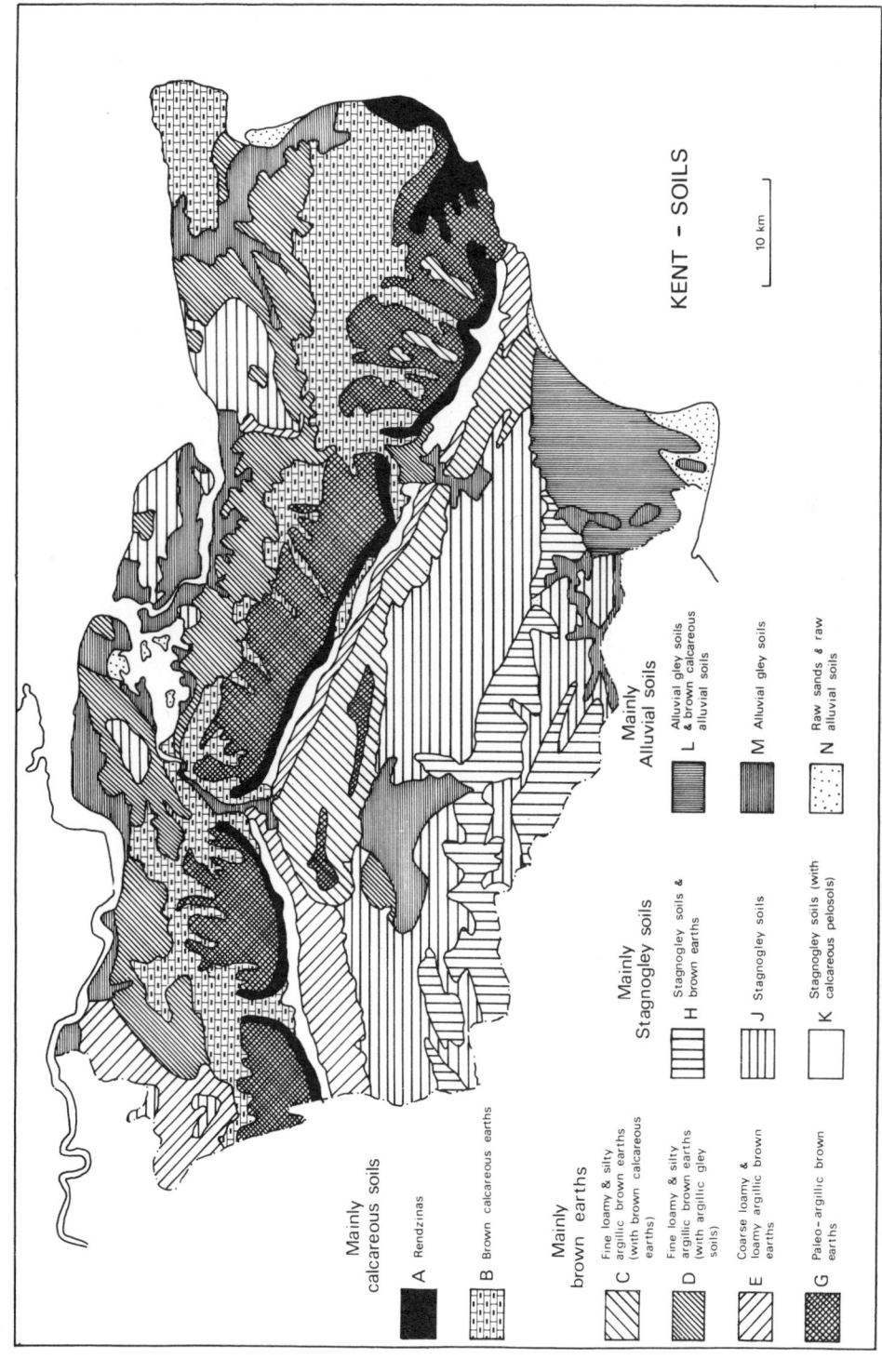

Fig. 34.

KENT – SOILS

10 km

Mainly calcareous soils
A Rendzinas
B Brown calcareous earths

Mainly brown earths
C Fine loamy & silty argillic brown earths (with brown calcareous earths)
D Fine loamy & silty argillic brown earths (with argillic gley soils)
E Coarse loamy & loamy argillic brown earths
G Paleo-argillic brown earths

Mainly Stagnogley soils
H Stagnogley soils & brown earths
J Stagnogley soils
K Stagnogley soils (with calcareous pelosols)

Mainly Alluvial soils
L Alluvial gley soils & brown calcareous alluvial soils
M Alluvial gley soils
N Raw sands & raw alluvial soils

SOILS

The study of the soil stands at a crossroad of many sciences. The soil is the surface skin of the physical landscape, the ultimate support of terrestrial life and for human activity both platform and storehouse. In history the location of fertile soils has generally determined the rise of civilizations; salt accumulation or erosion often led to their collapse, as soil pollution may well threaten our own. Even within Kent, boundaries between soil types have often marked changes in land use which have imposed a pattern on human activities, so that historians should vie with farmers in their interest in the soil.

For nearly 80 years Wye College has been a centre for the study of Kentish soils, beginning with the production of a bulletin by E. John Russell and A. Daniel Hall on the soils of Kent, Surrey and Sussex. Both co-authors moved from Wye to become successive Directors of Rothamsted Experimental Station, and both were knighted. No soil map accompanied their bulletin, for it was assumed that the geological map was a sufficient guide to the distribution of soils. Although this is more nearly true in Kent than in many other places, other factors have a profound effect, and it was the Rev. Dr. S. Graham Brade-Birks and Basil S. Furneaux, both of Wye College, who introduced the principle that soils should be classified and mapped as natural entities in their own right, beginning as early as 1929 to name and describe soil series following the same principles as those already used in the United States. Recently officers of the Soil Survey of England and Wales stationed at Wye have published a splendid detailed soil map of Romney Marsh, and have completed surveys of the Ashford, Deal and Rainham areas in terms of soil series. A complete coverage of Kent cannot be expected for some years but sufficient information exists to make a generalized map (fig. 34).

Classification of Soils

The early classification was geological (e.g. Gault Clay soils) and since the nature of soils does depend in part on the parent material from which they have been formed, this relationship has been used to complete the soil map (fig. 34) in areas for which little information was available. However the true parent material is often a thin surface deposit which may not be shown on a geological map. Modern soil classification into major groups is based on the presence of distinctive layers and other characteristics which reflect the process by which the soils have been formed. The sequence of layers from the surface to undisturbed geological material is called the soil profile. Major groups are subdivided into soil series according to parent material and examples are given in fig. 36.

The most important soil property is texture, which is determined by particle size. The coarsest particles are gravel and sand, the finest clay, while silt is of intermediate dimensions. A loamy soil is a mixture of sand, silt and clay, and is the most favourable for agriculture, while silty and fine sandy soils are also well favoured, despite a tendency to form compact surface cappings and subsoil pans. Soils high in coarse sand or gravel, though easy to till, are dry and chemically infertile. Clay soils on the other hand are difficult to cultivate, being wet and sticky in winter and hard in summer. In this section the soils of Kent are described in terms of texture and the major groups of the 1973 Soil Survey classification. Reference is also made to the soil associations shown on the map (fig. 34). These are areas dominated by the major groups shown in the legend, and indexed by letters. Typical land capability ratings are also mentioned, using seven numbered classes.

Fig. 35.
Cross-section from Greensand Ridge to North Downs. *Shows the relationship between geology, topography and pattern of soils.*

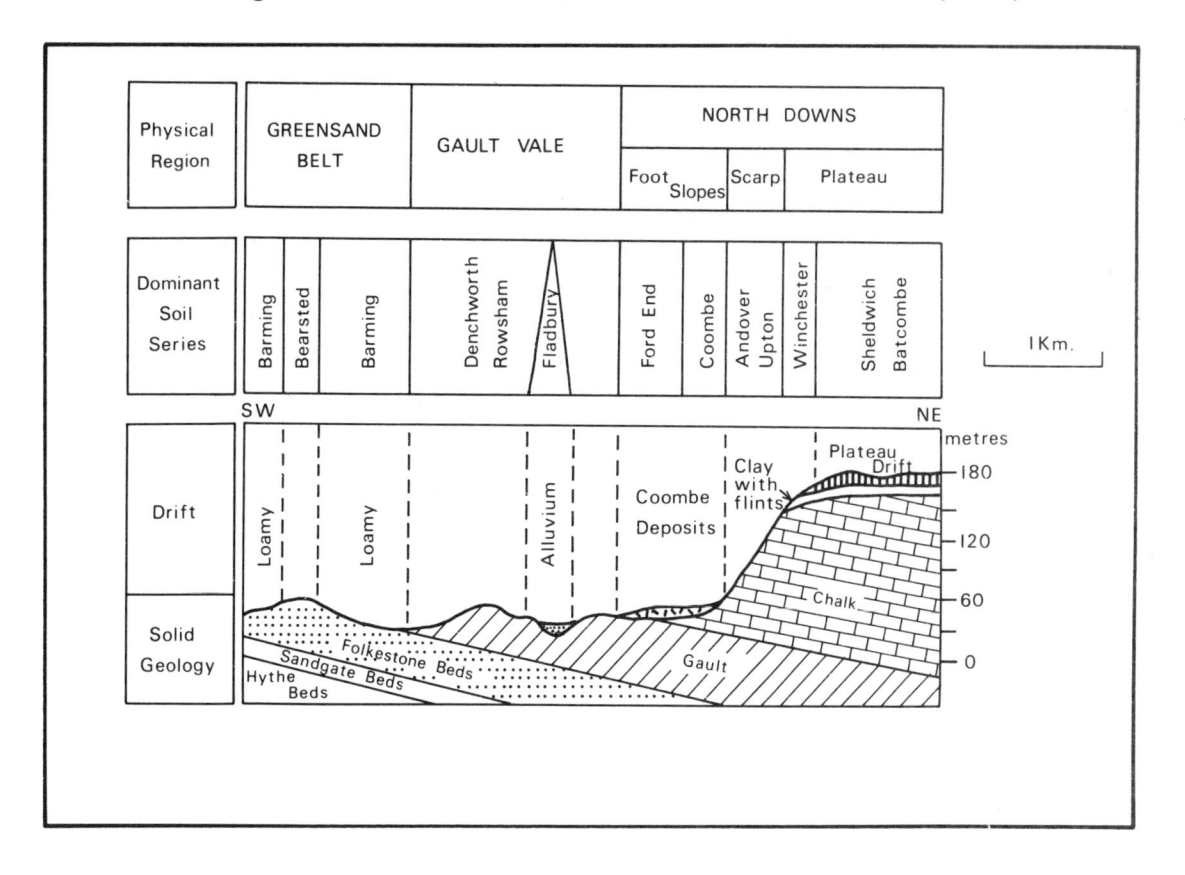

Calcareous (chalky) soils

In North Kent one is never far from the chalk, and chalk rubble and dust are often present in the soil. These soils have advantages for the farmer, for they never need lime and, being permeable, hardly ever require artificial drainage. Their medium texture (silty or loamy) makes them easy to cultivate and from Neolithic times they have been favoured in Kent for the production of cereals, particularly barley. Gardeners and fruit growers are less enthusiastic about chalky soils, for lime-hating plants such as azaleas die, while the leaves of others, e.g. pears, go yellow and may fall off before autumn, a condition called chlorosis which is frequently encountered in North Kent.

Very shallow soils on chalk or chalk rubble are called Rendzinas, and occur on the steep face of the Downs and the steep sides of dry valleys. When heavily grazed by sheep and rabbits, these give botanically rich downland pastures, but these are droughty and the yield of grass is low. Gentler slopes can be ploughed when chalk becomes mixed with the naturally dark topsoil, making it almost white. Good crops of barley can be grown, if adequately fertilized, but few other crops are suitable, and this is at best class 3 land.

Deeper chalky soils are brown calcareous earths, and will grow a much wider range of arable and horticultural crops, as in Thanet and along the northern fringe of the North Downs. Yields are high so that the land is in class 1 or 2, although they are not favoured for growing fruit or hops.

Fig. 36.
Rendzina and Brown Calcareous Earth
Two diagrammatic profiles of common calcareous (chalky) soils in Kent.

RENDZINA

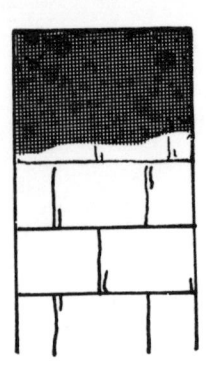

Dark calcareous topsoil, whitish when ploughed

BROWN CALCAREOUS EARTH

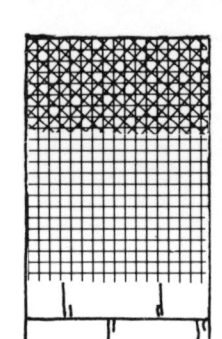

Brown, calcareous topsoil and subsoil

Brown Earths

These are the commonest well drained soils of Lowland Britain and in Kent, as elsewhere, form excellent arable land. Brown earths are non-calcareous (i.e. lack free calcium carbonate) and are acid if unlimed. The acidity is not strong enough to prevent earthworm activity, which mixes humus into the topsoil, but otherwise there is only indistinct layering in shades of brown which may have a yellowish or reddish hue (fig. 37). In many cases the subsoil contains more clay than the topsoil and feels distinctly more sticky when moist. These are argillic brown earths, or when the subsoil is also reddish in colour paleoargillic brown earths.

The texture of brown earths varies considerably, and this greatly affects their management by farmers and gardeners. The best soils, rating class 1, have a medium fine loamy or silty texture, and are greatly favoured by growers of fruit and hops. They occur overlying Thanet Beds and brickearth in a strip from Orpington to Sandwich which includes the North Kent fruit belt. In Mid-Kent they occur on brickearth and the ragstone of the Hythe Beds, especially south of Maidstone, and again are often occupied by hop gardens or orchards as seen in plate 7. The best soils on the Hastings Beds of the High Weald are similar and support fruit and hop growing southwards through Goudhurst and Horsmonden to the Sussex border near Lamberhurst.

Brown earths of lighter texture, which have a considerable proportion of coarse sand and are sometimes also stony, tend to be droughty and infertile. They rate only class 2 or 3 for agriculture but are well suited to woodland as is evident in the area concerned, mainly

Fig. 37.
Brown Earth and Humo-ferric Podzol
Diagrammatic profiles of a common agricultural soil (brown earth) and a soil characteristic of heathland (humo-ferric podzol).

BROWN EARTH

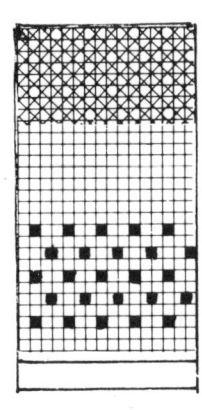

Brown, non-calcareous soil
Subsoil sometimes enriched in clay

HUMO-FERRIC PODZOL

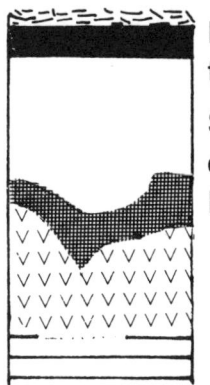

Bleached topsoil
Subsoil layers enriched in humus and iron

on the Lower Greensand outcrop in West Kent around Sevenoaks.

Small areas of heathy woodlands, with heather in open spots among birch or coniferous trees, carry podzols. This soil type is characteristic of Northern Russia and is rare in Kent where it is restricted to very sandy or gravelly parent materials, e.g. in Winterbourne Wood near Dunkirk, Pembury Walks, Hothfield Common, and near Ightham. Under the extremely acid conditions, the iron compounds (responsible for the brown colours in soils) are removed from a surface layer which takes on a bleached, ash-like appearance, hence the Russian name 'podzol' which means 'ash soil'. The iron, together with organic matter (humus), is carried down into the subsoil where it is deposited in black and rusty coloured layers (fig. 37). Without heavy manuring and liming, podzols are agriculturally sterile.

Brown earths with reddish clay subsoils are associated with Clay-With-Flints and Plateau Drift and occur along the relatively level top of the North Downs. Similar soils occur on the highest parts of the Greensand Ridge. The soil scientist calls these paleo-argillic brown earths, the prefix 'paleo' implying 'old'. Indeed, these are the oldest soils of Kent and their reddish colour is believed to have developed a million or so years ago in a sub-tropical climate before the Pleistocene Ice Ages. Difficulty of cultivation, slow drainage and abundant flints together with less favourable climate downgrade this land to class 2 or 3.

Stagnogley soils

Gley is another Russian word implying a soil which is waterlogged for at least several weeks in most years, favouring the activity of anaerobic bacteria. One result is the reduction of the iron in the soil from rusty brown ferric oxide to ferrous compounds of a faintly greenish or bluish colour. If the soil dries out in summer, as generally happens, a characteristic mottling in rusty and greyish colours results. This mottling is a permanent clue to the occurrence of winter waterlogging capable of killing roots in the soil, and thus detrimental to farm crops but calamitous to the fruit grower.

Three kinds of gley soil are found in Kent (fig. 38). Stagnogley soils are underlain by an impermeable clay subsoil, and suffer from surface waterlogging in winter. Alluvial gley soils are saturated at depth up to a limit (i.e. the water table), and are found in valley bottom or coastal situations. In a third type of soil, waterlogging is due to seepage from springs, which affects only small patches of land, but occurs frequently in the High Weald.

Stagnogley soils in the flat country overlying the Weald Clay are particularly difficult to farm, and are rated in Class 3 or even 4. Soils developed directly on the Wadhurst Clay and the London Clay resemble those on the Weald Clay. On the Weald and London Clays, however, loamy surface deposits blanketing the actual clay often give patches of more tractable soils. Stagnogley soils on the Gault Clay tend to be less acid than those on the Weald and London Clays and have more natural cracks, giving a better structure. They rate class 2 or 3 and can grow good crops of winter wheat.

The agricultural drawbacks of stagnogley soils can be reduced by artificial drainage. Pipe drains are of little use unless the subsoil is broken and made more permeable. Mole drainage, which involves drawing a steel plug through the subsoil to form a channel, is not very common in Kent although some of the stagnogleys are suitable. Normal subsoiling with a tine to loosen the subsoil is common, but is often ineffective. More effective is the Wye College 'double digger' which systematically loosens the subsoil with a specially mounted rotovator.

Alluvial soils

The alluvium underlying the flood plains of rivers and coastal and estuarine marshes is quite recent, particularly in its upper part. The 'Graveney Boat' found in 1971 buried by about 2 m of alluvium nearly a kilometre from the sea is probably of Saxon age. The land around the Thames and Medway estuaries has been gradually sinking so that around Grain alluvium deposited near high tide level

Fig. 38.
Stagnogley and Ground-Water Gley
Two poorly drained soils, the stagnogley common on impermeable clays, the ground water gley where the water table affects the lower part of the profile.

STAGNOGLEY SOIL

Mottled subsoil over compact clay

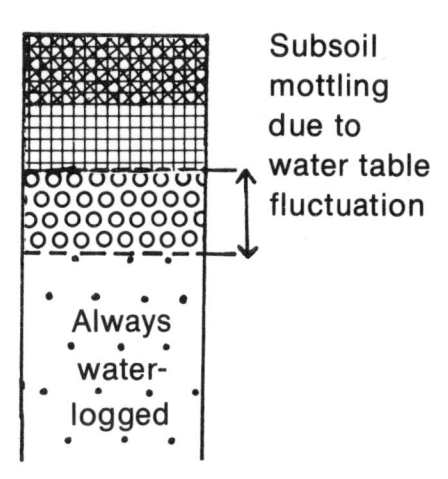

ALLUVIAL GLEY SOIL

Subsoil mottling due to water table fluctuation

Always water-logged

has accumulated to a depth of 45 metres in about 10,000 years.

The North Kent Marshes, associated with the estuaries of the Thames, Medway, Swale and Stour, have alluvial gley soils which are always of heavy clayey texture and very difficult to drain. Little unreclaimed saltmarsh remains, except in the Medway estuary where the effects of land subsidence have combined with those of mud digging for the cement and brick-making industries between 1850 and 1914. The reclaimed marshes were all flooded with seawater in 1953, but afterwards the embankments were raised and whereas all was grazing land some is now cropped, usually with winter wheat. In the Wantsum marshes there is some good arable land, but elsewhere the land ranges from Class 3 to Class 5, depending on drainage.

Romney Marsh is far better for agriculture than the North Kent Marshes. The soils, though very variable, are often more loamy and are considerably more permeable, so that drainage is more effective.

Many of the famous sheep-fattening pastures have been converted to productive arable land. However, as soil structure is damaged by cultivation when wet and the high earthworm and ant populations decline, soil permeability is often gradually impaired. Most of the land is graded class 1 or 2, except for a few low-lying patches, often produced by the shrinkage after drainage of a layer of peat in the subsoil.

The sand dunes around Sandwich Bay and the shingle of Dungeness and West Hythe are of no agricultural value, and little soil formation has taken place.

FRUIT GROWING IN KENT

The dominance of Kent in British fruit growing is partly a historical accident. While it is true that certain areas in the county have the prerequisites of suitable climate and good soils, probably the geographical position of Kent between the Continent and London most favoured the introduction of fruits. According to Pliny, the Romans introduced cherries to Kent, but no doubt only a few scattered orchards survived their final departure. Thereafter, until around the late fifteenth century, fruit growing was largely in the hands of the monasteries. By Tudor times Royalty and the nobility had acquired a great taste for fruit and one Richard Harrys, fruiterer to Henry VIII, 'did in the year 1533 obtain 103 acres of good ground in the parish of Teynham (in the North Kent fruit belt) which he divided into ten parcels and with great care, good choice and no small labour brought from beyond the seas the sweet cherry, the temperate pippin and the golden reinette'.

Some 30 places, all in Kent, benefited from plantings made by Harrys, and it is probable that the second major concentration of fruit—the Mid Kent fruit belt round Maidstone—had its beginnings at this time, although the southern extension into the Low Weald did not come until communications improved in the twentieth century. By the beginning of the nineteenth century fruit growing, particularly cherries, was well established in the North Kent and Mid Kent fruit belts, principally for local consumption and the growing market in London, although exports reached Scotland. The major period of expansion was in the latter half of the nineteenth century, especially top fruit in North Kent and strawberries near London. Early orchards were planted between hops, but problems such as canker and lack of expertise in pruning limited the production and life of many. It was common to underplant with soft fruit or to grass down and run flocks of sheep beneath the trees (plate 7). During the early twentieth century the situation improved and, encouraged by the practical advice coming from East Malling Research Station, founded in 1913, fruit growing became more precise and scientific. East Malling is now an

Plate 7
Old style apple orchard of standard trees undergrazed by sheep.

58   'Kent: The Garden of England'

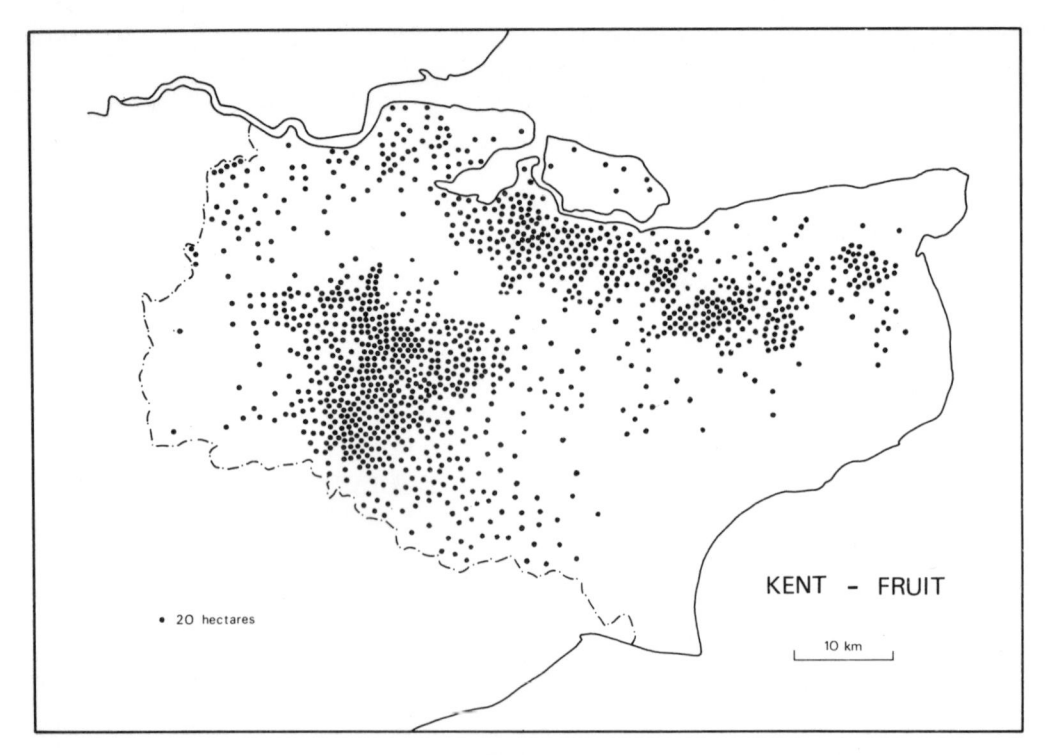

KENT – FRUIT
• 20 hectares
10 km

Fig. 39.

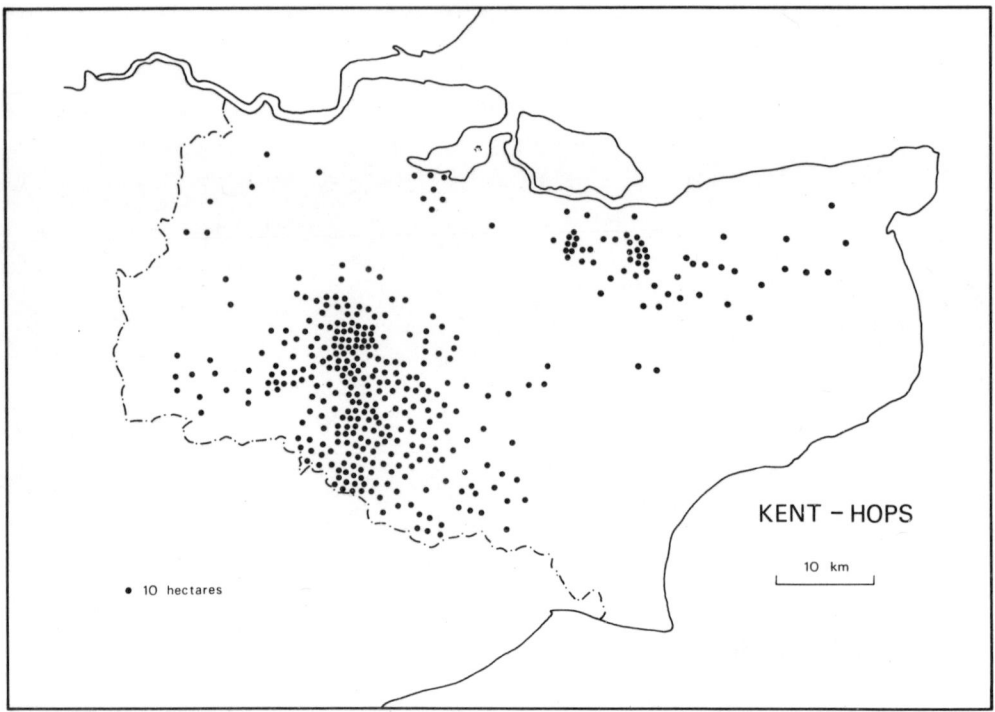

KENT – HOPS
• 10 hectares
10 km

Fig. 40.

internationally known research institute specializing in all aspects of the production and storage of fruit. Since 1945 the decline in the total area of orchards has been more than compensated by increased yields resulting from greater expertise, mechanization and more intensive planting (plate 8).

Orthodox dessert apple orchards have about 250-300 trees per hectare growing to about 4-5 m in height. Harvesting, pruning and other cultural operations are difficult, involving the use of ladders. Many modern orchards are being planted with trees on less vigorous rootstocks to produce mature trees only 2.5 to 3 m high but at rates of over 1,000 per hectare. The traditional Kent orchard may become a thing of the past since the trend is towards smaller trees with easier cultural and harvesting operations, perhaps in the future even including mechanical harvesting.

Modern top fruit growing is expensive, planting an orchard could cost £2,000 a hectare in 1976, and is a highly skilled business in which there is no simple formula for success. The grower has to choose the site, the varieties, rootstocks, pollinators (most modern varieties are not self-fertile) and the planting rate and pattern. Following this come skilled operations such as pruning, spraying and fertilizing. The grower is also very much at the mercy of the weather and it is not unknown for propane heaters or large candles to be lit in orchards, or water sprinkling devices to be erected, to prevent damage by late spring frosts. The Kent grower has proved highly successful at surmounting all these difficulties, making Kent the foremost county in England and Wales for fruit.

Fruit-growing in Kent is concentrated in two main areas (fig. 39), the North Kent fruit belt and the Mid Kent fruit belt, where over a third of the agricultural land is given over to fruit, compared with about a tenth in Kent as a whole. The North Kent fruit belt is the central part of a zone of deep, well-drained loamy soils mainly derived from Brickearth which extends through northern Kent from Sandwich to the outskirts of London. At either end of the fruit belt, fruit gives way to other horticultural crops, due probably in North-west Kent to the proximity of the London vegetable markets and in East Kent to the greater exposure to wind and the long tradition of vegetable growing. In general, the North Kent fruit belt has an ideal climate, with low annual rainfall, favourable summer temperatures, adequate sunshine and freedom from damaging frosts. It is therefore not surprising to find that the National Fruit Trials are situated here at Brogdale, near Faversham.

The North Kent fruit belt owes its existence not only to the

Fig. 39.
Fruit in Kent
Distribution of top and soft fruit in Kent.

Fig. 40.
Hops in Kent
Distribution of hops in Kent.

Plate 8

excellent soils and climate but also to their happy juxtaposition with the main line of communication through Kent, Watling Street (A2), from London to the continent. From Gillingham eastwards, orchards extend about 3 km on either side of the A2 to just beyond Faversham. Thereafter the A2 climbs over the Blean to Canterbury while the area of fruit growing keeps to the better soils around the south-western end of the Blean through Chilham, running south of Canterbury to end roughly at the valley of the Little Stour.

The main top fruits of North Kent are dessert apples, plums and cherries. The main apple variety is Cox's Orange Pippin with some Worcester Pearmain and a number of subsidiary varieties including Golden Delicious, the main competitor from continental orchards. The two main pear varieties are Conference and Doyenne du Comice while the main plum variety is Victoria. Cherries, a Kent speciality, have declined markedly in recent years but a few orchards are still to be found in North Kent. Black currants and gooseberries are the commonest soft fruit in North Kent, but are of little importance compared with top fruit.

The Mid Kent fruit belt originated on the excellent soils of the dipslope of the Hythe Beds division of the Lower Greensand around Maidstone. This area was also favoured by a convenient, if slow, way of transporting the fruit to the metropolis via the Medway and Thames. This water-borne transport prevented damage to the produce which the rough roads in the eighteenth and nineteenth centuries would have caused. George Buckland, writing in 1846 said 'The district known as Mid Kent in which is situated the county town of Maidstone, presents several interesting and remarkable features. Taking its agricultural resources altogether, the range and variety of its produce, there cannot be found any spot to compare with it in the United Kingdom. It has been truly designated 'The Garden of England'. The many visitors who come to this area in spring to see the orchards in flower, following specially signposted 'Blossom Routes' would surely agree.

The region has spread southwards on to the Low Weald, but only that central portion, between Tonbridge, Hadlow, Yalding and Paddock Wood, where the Weald Clay is covered by lighter Brickearth deposits associated with Medway, Teise and Beult. Sometimes these deposits are quite thin, and not shown on a geological map, but they are quite thick enough to produce the type of soil favoured by the fruit growers. Where the soils are formed directly in the Weald Clay, orchards stop, and they are similarly absent from the lowest poorly drained clayey soils on the alluvium

Plate 8
Picking apples on Wye College Farm.

bordering the rivers. Expansion of the Mid Kent fruit belt has also taken place onto the most favourable of the very variable soils of the High Weald, probably by transfer of expertise from the more favoured regions to the north.

In general, Mid Kent is not such a suitable area for fruit as North Kent. The land under fruit is mainly Class 2 (Class 1 in North Kent) because of the shallower or stonier soils (in the Hythe Beds zone) impeded drainage and danger from flooding (in the Low Weald) and soils which restrict rooting (in the High Weald). Climatically, Mid Kent is not ideal for fruit. The north facing Hythe Beds dipslope is 'late' but free from frost while the Low Weald pays for its 'early' climate by being very subject to spring frosts.

The main fruit crop of Mid Kent is apples, with culinary varieties, mainly Bramley's Seedlings, more important than in North Kent. Pears and plums are grown, but cherries, a sensitive and demanding crop, are even scarcer than in North Kent. The one speciality of Mid Kent is a crop unique to the county and once the most distinctive of Kent. This is the Kentish Cob, a large hazelnut, of which a few orchards still remain around Maidstone. Soft fruit is also grown, especially in the Hythe Beds zone, where it is much more important than in North Kent, and in the High Weald zone. Strawberries, blackcurrants, raspberries and blackberries are the main crops. In North Kent, fruit growing is accompanied by potatoes and market garden crops, but in Mid Kent, hops are the main companions.

Fig. 41.
Hops
A leaf and cluster of 'cones' of the cultivated hop (Humulus lupulus).

HOPS

The cultivated hop *(Humulus lupulus)* (fig. 41) is a herbaceous perennial plant, a relative of Cannabis. It dies down each winter to a fleshy rootstock just below the soil surface and in spring sends up new climbing shoots or bines which are trained up coir strings attached to a system of overhead wirework. The speed of growth is prodigious, as much as 15-20 cm per day, so that before long the bines reach the rop of the wirework. In the days of handpicking wirework 4 m high was common, but with machines 5.5 m is now more usual and even 7–8 m in some gardens. The vast majority of the hop plants in a garden are female (hops are unisexual, i.e. there are individual male and female plants). The female inflorescence appears in July. It can scarcely be called a flower, since there are no visible petals, the cone like appearance being due to enlarged bracts, modified leaves which in typical flowers act as a sort of cup into which the petals are set. The bracts of the female hop carry glandular hairs which secrete a yellow resinous substance, lupulin, which gives the characteristic bitter taste to beer. Brewers are the sole customer for the crop, which is harvested by cutting down the whole bine and stripping off the cones. These are then dried in special buildings called oast houses which are an attractive part of the rural scene (plates 22 and 23). A few bines will be saved, for there is a belief that a house containing a hop-bine will never lack money. Another belief is that a hop pillow (a small muslin bag filled with dried hops) is a cure for insomnia.

The hop-growing year starts during late autumn and winter as the hop gardens (called hop-yards in the West Midlands) are cultivated and manured. Hops are pampered by their growers, traditionally receiving large, often excessive amounts of fertilizers and organic manures, incorporated by hand digging by which means weeds were also controlled. In recent years rational use of inorganic fertilizers coupled with herbicides such as simazine and paraquat have reduced the need for cultivations by hand or by machine. This system of 'minimal' cultivation is now preferred by most growers and can be advantageous as it does not disturb the root systems of the hop plants, which can extend from the surface to a depth of as much as 4 m.

Hops were traditionally grown on small mounds, called hills, about two and a half metres apart and in February and March dressing (Weald) or cutting (E. Kent) takes place. This is a form of pruning to remove the remnants of the previous year's bines and the underground lateral shoots or runners. Diseased or dead hills are grubbed out and replanted. Minimal cultivation techniques are reducing the need for these earthing and dressing procedures.

In March and early April stringing is carried out. This consists of tying a number of coir strings, usually four, from a wire peg in the ground at each hill up to the overhead wirework. Sometimes a stilt-walker is employed to attach the upper ends of the strings with an assistant on the ground. There are several systems of overhead wirework and methods of arranging and tying strings (plates 9 and 10) and while some have particular advantages, for example in machine harvesting, local tradition is still important. The maintenance of normal tensioned wirework, which has to bear a great weight by the end of the season, and difficulties with stringing have led some growers to experiment with new systems, including a cheaper 'low pole density' wirework with widely spaced poles and more sagging wires.

In early to mid April the growth of the bines begins. Some of the shoots may be infected with downy mildew, one of the many diseases which afflict hops, and these are pulled out by hand in a

Plate 9

Plate 10

process called 'spiking', prior to dusting or spraying with fungicide. Some of the earliest bines (rank bines or pipers) are sometimes also pulled out because they were over-vigorous, but with new varieties, machine picking and stronger, higher wirework these are now less of a problem. The bines are trained clockwise round appropriate strings in late April and May, two or three to each string, after which surplus bines are removed. This training is normally done by women on piecework and it is one of the problems of hop growing to obtain sufficient skilled labour at this time as well as on other occasions during the year when a large labour force is required for a relatively short period.

During the summer the bines grow rapidly, but need constant attention. The lowermost leaves up to about 1.5 m are removed, formerly by hand stripping but now with chemical defoliants. This was to reduce the dangers of plant disease but because it also reduced yield a compromise of stripping to about a metre above ground level is now practised. Bines which have been blown off their strings have to be retrained. In mid-June the hills are earthed up, formerly by hand, now by tractor-mounted plough or disc. While these activities are proceeding, applications of fertilizers are made, and routine measures against pests and diseases are carried out.

By the end of June the bines will have normally reached the top of the wirework and subsequently and unpleasantly for the workers growth thickens with lateral shoots, often uncomfortably prickly, extending to form a barrier across the alleys, which may have to be pruned if very dense. The weight on the wire is now considerable, with much of the growth high above ground and the quality of the wirework is severely tested, especially during high winds. Wind is one of the hop growers' chief menaces and hop-gardens are usually situated in sheltered spots, and surrounded by high hedges or windbreaks of netting (lewing).

In July short branches carrying round buds develop from the leaf axils in the lateral branches. These buds throw out short stalks carrying the female flower or 'burr' about 0.6 cm long which has protruding stigmas giving a brush-like appearance. These catch the pollen from the few male plants scattered throughout the garden so that the final crop carries seeds. Continental brewers insist on seedless hops and for continental beers such as lager British brewers have had to import seedless hops. A few British growers are now growing seedless hops on a trial basis, but this requires great vigilance in eradicating male plants in the gardens or wild relatives in the hedgerows.

Plate 9
Richard Huckstep stringing hop wirework at Spring Grove, Wye. Method using stilts.

Plate 10
Method using stringing pole.

Plate 11

During the summer regular spraying to control pests and diseases is carried out, for hops are subject to a wide variety of disorders which can be very damaging to the crop. The main aerial pest is the Damson-hop aphid, which regularly invades hop-gardens each summer, sometimes carrying a virus disease, hop mosaic. As its name implies, the aphid is also connected with damsons or other members of the plum (Prunus) family, especially sloe or blackthorn. These carry the overwintering eggs which hatch in spring. The first few generations, produced in a matter of weeks, feed on the Prunus host, then a winged version appears which fly or are wind-borne into the hop-gardens from June onwards to behave similarly to the common greenfly on roses. In September the aphids return to the host Prunus where the eggs are laid to complete the cycle. Infections in hop-gardens are difficult to control and there is increasing evidence of a build-up of resistance by the aphids to commonly-used insecticides.

The two most serious diseases to which the hop is subject are Downy Mildew and Verticillium Wilt. The former is a fungal disease and can reach epidemic proportions if not controlled by fungicides and the removal and burning of infected parts. New varieties being bred at Wye College such as Wye Challenger have a markedly better resistance to downy mildew than traditional varieties. A more recent but equally dangerous mildew, powdery mildew is now being fairly effectively controlled by new fungicides. More difficult to control is Verticillium Wilt, a strain of which causes progressive wilt which is lethal to the hop. This disease was first noted at Paddock Wood in 1930 and has since spread steadily. The apparent ease with which it can be spread is one of the chief dangers and sensible hop growers rightly object to casual visitors to a hop-garden who may easily be carrying the disease in the soil on their footwear. Disinfectant baths and washing footwear, wheels and implements may all help to check the arrival of wilt on a previously wilt-free garden, but the grower has to be on guard against all imported material to his farm, especially if it has come from another hop-garden. If the disease appears the only control is complete grubbing and burning of the infected and neighbouring plants, and it is a statutory duty of growers under the Progressive Wilt Disease of Hops Order 1965 to comply with these and other preventative measures. As for the mildews, wilt-resistant varieties are now being bred.

Assuming no disasters have befallen his crop, by hail, wind, pest or disease, the grower can look forward to the busiest time of the

Plate 11
Cutting hop bines at Spring Grove, Wye.

year, harvesting. In Kent this traditionally begins on 1 September. Picking used to be by hand and a large labour force was required. In the eighteenth and early nineteenth centuries local labour, the families of farm workers, was supplemented by gypsies drawn to Kent for the hop and apple harvests, and perhaps staying on to help in potato picking. With the relative decline of rural population and the expansion of the cities in the nineteenth century a new work force appeared, easily brought to Kent by the new railways. These were the 'hoppers', working class families mainly from the East End of London (plate 12). Entire families came, looking on it as a sort of holiday, but living under appalling conditions and treated with contempt by local people. They were employed on piecework, the number of bushels of hops picked being recorded on a tally stick or by means of coin-like hop tokens (figs. 42-44). These were usually made locally, often bearing only the grower's initials and the number of bushels. Others are charming examples of rustic art bearing sprays of hops, elaborate monograms or other appropriate emblems such as the Kentish horse or in one case a pair of oast houses.

Nowadays machine picking is universal. The bines, string and all, are cut down (plate 11) and brought to a stationary machine where they pass through rotating drum to which wire-loop fingers are attached. The cones and leaves which these pluck from the bines are then passed through mechanical cleaning devices which are now as effective at separating cones from extraneous matter as previous hand sorting.

The hops then pass for drying to the 'stowage' section of the oast house from where they are loaded into the kiln, the changes in the actual design of which are described in Chapter 6. The hops are spread on horse-hair cloths over an open-slatted wooden floor through which warm air is passed. Originally the air current was a natural draught and the hops were relatively thinly spread (about 50 cm deep), but with the modern forced draughts layers double this depth and more can be successfully dried. During the first half hour or so of the drying sulphur is burned below the hops mainly to change their colour to the yellowish green which is esteemed on the market. The drying is a highly skilled process and although attempts have been made to control and quantify it with recording instruments, the human element is still indispensable. In a well managed kiln the hops have dried (from an original moisture content of about 80 per cent) to about six per cent in ten hours. They are then brittle and have to be carefully unloaded onto the cooling floor where they also pick up a little atmospheric moisture to end up with

Fig. 42.
18th Century Hop Pickers' Token.
John Toke, Godinton, near Ashford. Brass, diestruck, 1767. Scale 2 cm.

Fig. 43.
Early 19th Century Hop Pickers' Token.
Aaron Pinyon, Boxhurst Farm, Sandhurst. Lead alloy, cast.

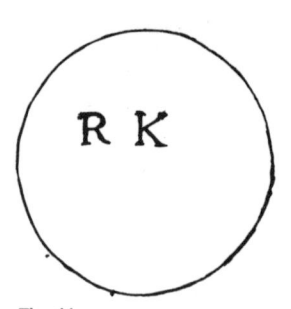

Fig. 44.
Late 19th Century Hop Pickers' Token.
Robert Kennett, Harville Farm, Wye. Zinc punched.

a uniform ten per cent moisture content. They are then packed into stout jute sacks, called 'pockets' each containing about 75-90 kg (1½ to 1¾cwt), standing about 2 m high when filled and worth about £120 (1977). A typical yield is around 1200 kg hops per hectare (11 cwt per acre), although good growers would expect about 1800 kg per hectare. Seedless hops give 20 per cent lower yields.

The marketing of hops is a complicated matter. They are sold on a quota system operated by the Hops Marketing Board which since its inception in 1932 has served to bring stability to a situation previously beset by gross price fluctuations and overproduction. Quota may be bought and sold and may have cost the grower as much as, if not more than, the value of the land on which the hops are grown. Most growers engage the services of a factor who submits samples to the valuation committee of the Board. Formerly every pocket was sampled, but now only one in three is actually judged. The committee set a mandatory price based on the quality of the hops and the hop merchants who buy on behalf of the brewers must abide by this price. An element of competition is introduced by the 'call option' whereby the purchaser in any year has the first option to buy hops the following year from the same producer. Thus a merchant may buy hops of slightly inferior quality in order to obtain the option to buy the following year from a producer normally having a high quality hop. Recent trends have been towards more efficient utilization of hops in brewing and a preference for less bitter beers, so that the area under hops has decreased from about 8,000 ha to 7,000 ha over the past few years. The resurgence of interest in 'real ale' with a more bitter taste has meant that traditional varieties of hop such as Fuggle may make a come-back against the newer 'high alpha acid' varieties. English hops are traditionally grown with seeds, whereas in most countries brewers prefer seedless hops. This militates against any export of English hops, and indeed the English hop industry faces competition from the continental imports. A fairly recent development is the processing of hops (seeded or seedless) to powders or extracts which have advantages in brewing and can also be exported.

Brewing used to be carried out in small-scale establishments scattered throughout the country and hops used to be widely grown too. At the height of production in 1878, coinciding with a rapid growth in population and beer consumption, a total of 29,000 ha (72,000 acres) was under hops, in every county of England and Wales and even as far north as Aberdeenshire in Scotland. Since then there has been a steady decline in acreage and a concentration into a few localities. At the present time over half the hops grown in Britain are in Kent the rest being found in a continuation of the Kent area in East Sussex, between Farnham (Surrey) and Selbourne (Hants) and in the West Midlands. Even within Kent, hop growing, once widespread as still testified by the distribution of oast houses, is now localised in the Mid Kent and North Kent fruit belts (fig. 40). In the former, hops take up eight per cent of the agricultural land, but only three per cent in the latter. The association with fruit in both cases is obvious since hops and fruit both require a pool of highly skilled and specialized labour which has grown up over the centuries. The deep, moisture retentive, yet well drained soils which have proved so suitable for fruit are also admirable for hops, although hops prefer slightly heavier soils, which partly explains the relative concentration of hops in Mid Kent. Environmental, historical and economic factors have combined to make Kent pre-eminent in hop growing. The crop was introduced to England via Kent by Flemings in the sixteenth century and since then a favourable environment has been coupled with the proximity to London which provided a ready market and an ample supply of cheap, temporary labour for picking.

Plate 12
Hop pickers, near Boughton Aluph in September 1936.
(Rev. R. W. H. Ackworth)

Plate 13
Tallyman in hop garden, at Stuppington, near Canterbury in September 1936. The tallyman used to measure the hops and record the number of bushels either by notching a wooden 'tally stick' or by giving tokens (also sometimes called 'tallies', see figs 42-44).
(Rev. R. W. H. Ackworth)

Many hop varieties have Kentish names. For many years the predominant variety was Fuggle, introduced by a grower of that quintessentially Kentish name from Brenchley, and another common variety, Golding, was similarly named after a grower from East Malling. From the early 1920s onwards many new varieties were raised, named and introduced by Professor Salmon at Wye College, notably Bullion and Northern Brewer which became well established. Wye College has continued this tradition, and specializes in creating new varieties combining increased disease resistance with the required brewing quality. One of these new varieties, Wye Target, has been keenly sought by growers in recent years.

VEGETABLES

There are four major areas of vegetable growing (including potatoes) in Kent, making the county one of the major producers in England and Wales (fig. 45). Two of the areas, in the hinterland of Sandwich and in North West Kent have a long history of vegetable growing, but Thanet and Romney Marsh have only relatively recently become noted for vegetables.

Vegetable growing was introduced to the Sandwich area by refugees from the Low Countries in the late sixteenth and early seventeenth centuries. The excellent soils (mainly loamy well drained soils on brickearth and Thanet sands) and favourable climate encouraged the unique type of farming and the region prospered. In recent years the growth of road transport bringing the London markets within easy reach has further encouraged vegetable growing in this area. The proportion of agricultural land devoted to vegetables (about 14 per cent) and potatoes (nine per cent) is exceeded in Kent only in the adjacent Isle of Thanet. The main concentrations are around Ash and Sandwich with radishes, spring onions, marrows and early runner beans, proximity to the sea giving a relatively early season. The amount of glass has increased markedly over the last few years, growing tomatoes, cucumbers and lettuce.

Formerly the major area for glasshouses in Kent was round Swanley in the north-west Kent Horticulture region, but this has declined drastically, although flower-growing is still a local speciality. Horticulture in north-west Kent began around Deptford, then on the outer limits of London. It was favoured by the proximity to the Thames which afforded easy transport of produce to the London markets and the return of horse manure. The growth of

London and of industry and towns along the banks of the Thames has moved the zone of vegetable growing southeastwards so that it now runs in an arc from around Swanley up into the Hoo Peninsula. In many respects this area resembles the other main vegetable areas around Sandwich and in Thanet in terms of light easily worked yet moisture retentive soils derived from Thanet Beds, brickearth and chalky drift and a warm, dry and generally early climate. The specialities of the area are early potatoes, collards (unhearted spring cabbage) and peas but a wide variety of crops is grown, including some fruit and, in recent years, increasing acreages of cereals.

The Isle of Thanet was traditionally a cereal-growing area, renowned, then as now, for high quality malting barley produced on the light chalky soils. An influx of farmers from Scotland, however, at the beginning of the twentieth century transformed this into the major vegetable growing area in Kent. Vegetables, especially spring cabbage, cauliflower and broccoli take up almost a quarter of the agricultural land, and potatoes a further fifth or so. The emphasis is on early potatoes, and the equable climate favours first earlies which have a ready market in London, now easily reached by improved roads. The climate is particularly favourable to vegetables, with an early spring free of late frosts and high sunshine. The low rainfall is somewhat of a problem, however, and irrigation water is rather difficult to obtain due to lack of streams. Nevertheless many farmers are prepared to purchase mains water for irrigation. Rotations are variable, and growers often manage to produce two crops in one year (potatoes followed by broccoli or spring cabbage) or else three crops in two years (potatoes, broccoli and autumn cauliflower), with interspersed barley or grass seeds. Herbage seeds, which make better use of the well-fertilized soils following potatoes and vegetables than does barley, have increased, and onions and carrots have also recently been introduced. The climate of Thanet is not favourable to fruit, due largely to exposure to wind. For the same reason, and because of tainting caused by the salty atmosphere, hops are almost completely absent.

Thanet is, itself, too dry for good pasture, and traditionally livestock has been restricted to the marshes around Thanet, with crops in the drier uplands; two different enterprises often in different hands. The general absence of livestock in Thanet, with the exception of a few dairy herds, has meant that the hedges, grubbed during the Napoleonic Wars, were never replaced. In recent years, much of the marshland around Thanet has been drained and converted to arable, particularly wheat and potatoes.

Fig. 45.
Vegetables in Kent
Distribution of vegetable crops for human consumption in Kent, including potatoes.

Fig. 46.
Land Use Capability of Kent
Shows the overall quality of land for agriculture.

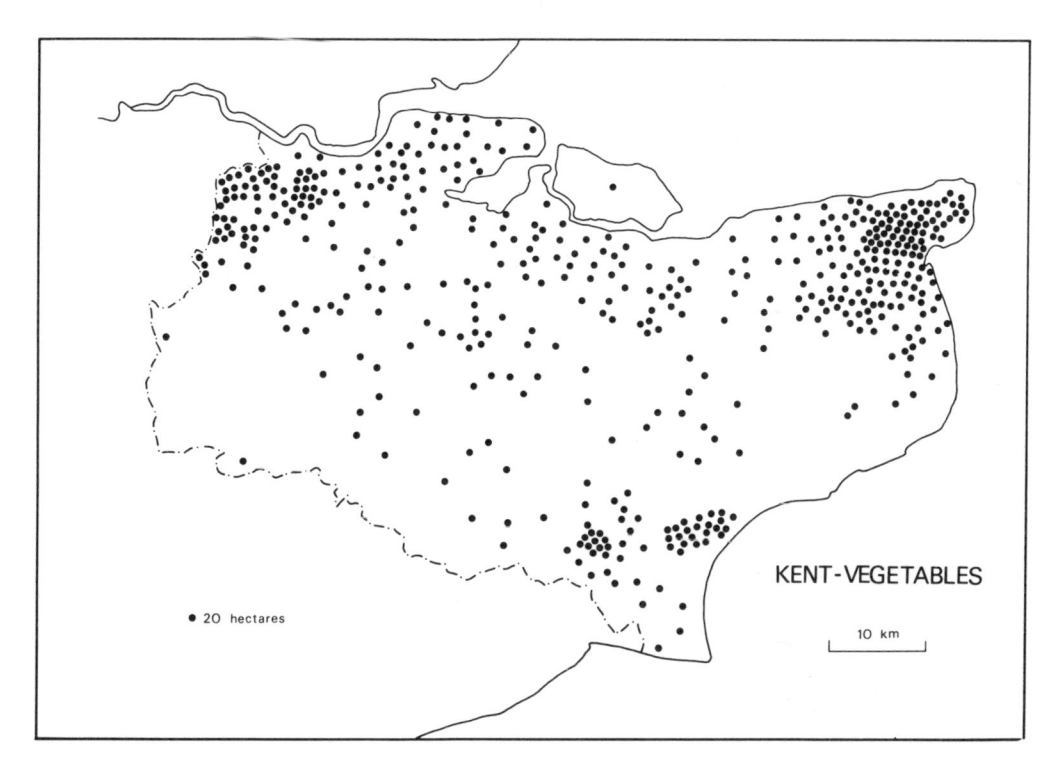

Fig. 45.

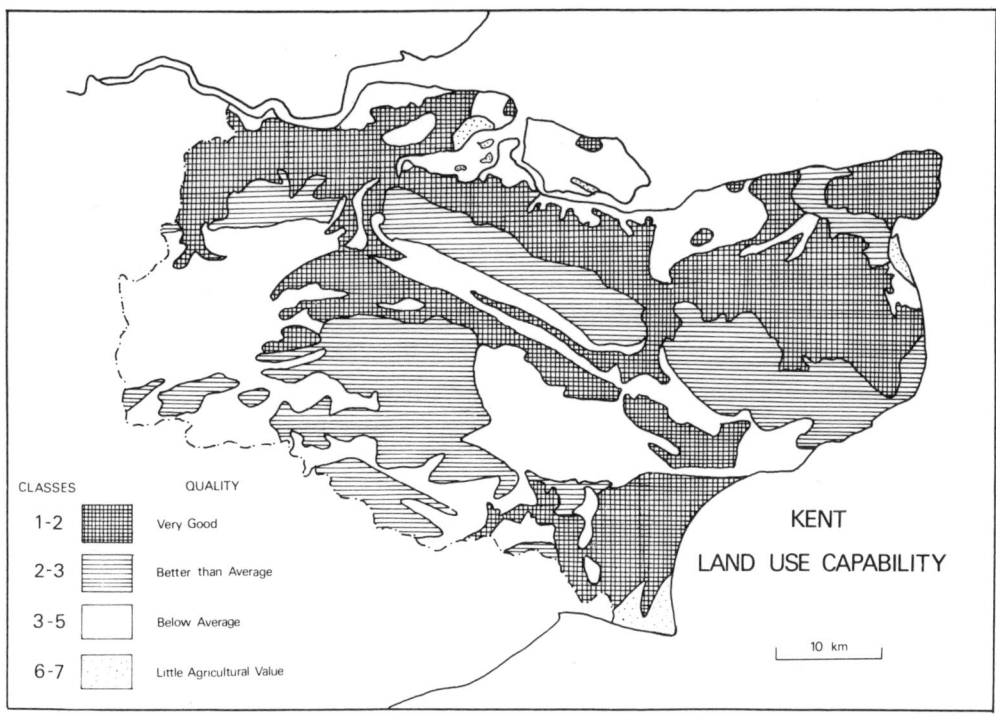

KENT-VEGETABLES
● 20 hectares
10 km

Fig. 46.

CLASSES | QUALITY
1-2 Very Good
2-3 Better than Average
3-5 Below Average
6-7 Little Agricultural Value

KENT
LAND USE CAPABILITY
10 km

Romney Marsh was once virtually synonymous with high quality fattening pastures and sheep. After the second World War, however, the general trend has been towards arable crops and this coincided with the arrival of several large-scale arable farmers from Lincolnshire who had left their native Fens following problems due to potato cyst eel-worm. The introduction of potatoes on a major scale was followed by other vegetable crops, notably field peas and beans. More recently bulb-growing has transformed some of the Marsh to scenes reminiscent of Holland. A further specialist crop for which the Marsh is renowned is herbage seed, which is also grown in north-east Kent. Both areas are favoured by a mild, relatively frost free climate and geographical remoteness limiting cross-pollination of the crop (fig. 47).

OTHER ARABLE CROPS

Apart from its fruit, hops and vegetables, the farming of Kent has followed national trends remarkably closely with the amounts of arable land increasing and decreasing as the fortunes of farming fluctuated. Thus in the mid 1930s, arable land was only about 25 per cent of the total agricultural land compared with 40 per cent in the late 1870s and about 60 per cent today.

The main arable crop in Kent is cereals, mainly barley, but as with horticultural crops, arable farming tends to predominate in a few favoured areas. The main cereal growing area is in the triangle between Dover, Deal and Canterbury which rivals the recognised arable counties of East Anglia in terms of the percentage (over 60 per cent) of agricultural land given over to cereals, and in the high yields attained. In this East Kent arable region, the silty, calcareous soils are ideal for barley, which alone occupies over 40 per cent of the land. Wheat tends to be grown on heavier soils than barley. In Romney Marsh 45 per cent of the land is in arable crops, and half is wheat.

Cereals are also common in other parts of Kent, although often mixed with other enterprises. Barley is the main crop of the thin band of chalky soils running along the foot of the Downs and in places, enterprising (or foolish) farmers have extended their arable land right up the scarp face. The East Kent Greensand Belt provides a more varied farming pattern, still dominated by cereals but with local concentrations of horticultural crops especially on the more sandy soils, for example around Charing Heath and Lenham Heath, where strawberries, raspberries and beans are grown, often with the aid of irrigation from the nearby Len and Stour. Nevertheless, this

Fig. 47.
Wild White or Kentish Clover (Trifolium repens). *Kentish seed of this hardy pasture legume has contributed to the improvement of grassland throughout Britain.*

belt has a relatively large proportion (over 50 per cent) of grassland, showing the extent of rather poor soils.

The southern fringe of the North Kent fruit belt gives way to a zone of mainly arable crops as the altitude increases and the soils decrease in quality up the North Downs dipslope. Arable crops, chiefly barley, then became restricted to the dry valleys or patches of lighter textured Plateau Drift or Brickearth. Indeed, some of these patches, for example near Biggin Hill and West Kingsdown, are used for market gardening. Elsewhere the heavy, stony soils on the Plateau Drift are left under grass or even woodland. Other heavy soils traditionally under grass but now increasingly used for cereals include the northern part of the Isle of Sheppey and parts of the Blean. Perhaps the greatest change has been in the alluvial marshes, both in Romney Marsh and North Kent, particularly the Wantsum Marshes round the Isle of Thanet. Drainage schemes, attracting considerable Government aid, and economic factors have encouraged this swing to arable cropping, especially wheat, a trend which will probably continue.

GRASSLAND

Today grassland is mainly confined to the areas of poorer soils (fig. 46). Thus it is not surprising to find the heavy and ill drained soils of much of the High and Low Weald as the main grassland areas in Kent. The High Weald has been described as 'a sportsman's paradise but a farmer's hell'. Many factors combine to make farming difficult, hilly land deeply dissected with many steep slopes, springs and wet patches requiring drainage, and a highly complex soil pattern. Over 60 per cent of the agricultural land is grass, much of it permanent pasture, and only the Low Weald and Sheppey have a greater proportion of grassland. This grassland has been traditionally utilized by sheep and beef cattle and the Sussex breed of beef cattle is indigenous to the area, but now dairying is the mainstay.

The highest proportion of grassland in Kent (over 70 per cent) is in the Low Weald both east and west of the central fruit-growing area, where the soils are heavy poorly drained stagnogleys, described as 'like cement in summer and soup in winter'. Regional drainage is also a problem, as the land is low-lying and the rivers have little fall. Formerly river flooding was a severe hazard, especially along the Medway, but this is now less common. The overall wetness of the area makes the soil slow to warm up in spring and the length of growing season is thus reduced.

With these limitations it is hardly surprising that most of the area is permanent pasture (almost 60 per cent of agricultural land) usually in small fields with thick hedgerows. In spite of a general reduction in grassland in the county there seems little downward trend in permanent grassland here, although cereals could increase if drainage improvements and field amalgamations were effected. The mainstay of agriculture is dairying and, with effective grassland management, large and expanding dairy herds are found, often at reasonably high stocking densities. The disposal of farm effluents is a major problem for dairy farmers in the area. Beef cattle are also kept at a density greater than the county average. Substantial numbers of sheep are kept, particularly in the east, where doubtless proximity to Romney Marsh has affected farming policy. This eastern section is the lowest and most poorly drained part of the Low Weald of Kent and the most wooded. It was traditionally an area of small graziers with sheep, Sussex cattle and some cereals, but, as elsewhere on the Weald Clay, these have largely given way to dairying.

Two areas of Kent have long been renowned for their sheep—the Isle of Sheppey (Isle of Sheep) and Romney Marsh. In Sheppey, the numbers of sheep have declined in recent years, but the density is still one of the highest in the county. Beef cattle have increased markedly and there are now more per hectare in Sheppey than anywhere else in Kent. Romney Marsh is now a marsh in name only, but remains distinctive, as expressed in the phrase 'the fifth quarter of the world'. It is criss-crossed by a system of dykes which act as field boundaries and which connect with larger drainage ditches whose outfall to the sea is controlled by sluices. The Royal Military Canal now serves as an important drainage channel for the parts of the Marsh nearest the former shoreline, which are often underlain by peat whose shrinkage has caused subsidence so that some parts are now well below high water levels at spring tides. For example the Dowels near Appledore lie at only 0.6 m (2 ft) OD, and drainage into the Royal Military Canal must be by pump.

The agricultural use of the Marsh has fluctuated over the centuries. Arable phases occurred in the Middle Ages, during the Napoleonic Wars and in the decade following 1850. By 1866, much had reverted to permanent pasture and in that year only 15 per cent of the marsh was tilled. This tillage area fluctuated between 15 and 20 per cent until the end of the first World War and declined to less than 10 per cent in the inter-war years. During the second World War, the area under tillage rose four-fold to 37 per cent in 1944, while the number of sheep decreased from 178,176 in 1939 to 99,990 in 1944, although cattle remained constant at around 3,500. This trend to greater arable use of the Marsh continued in the post-war years due to economic factors favouring arable farming and the influx of fenland farmers from Lincolnshire.

Today, only about 30 per cent of the Marsh carries permanent grass, although there has been a slight increase in temporary leys which has gone some way to maintaining the total area of grass. The traditional breed of sheep is the Romney Marsh (fig. 48), the most numerous breed internationally but confined in Britain to Kent and East Sussex. This breed has evolved to tolerate the winds and wet, bleak winter of the Marsh but still yield a good clip of wool with a large carcass. It also grazes individually, not as a flock, and tolerates high worm populations. Traditionally the graziers tended to live in the towns such as Rye, New Romney and Lydd, and because of this and the pastoral system which required few buildings villages are small and farm buildings few.

Fig. 48.
Romney Marsh Sheep

WOODLAND

Although the dense forests of the Weald, such a barrier to early human endeavour in Kent, are now gone, Kent is still one of the most heavily wooded counties in England and Wales with about 12 per cent of the total area under woodland. The distribution is not uniform but closely related to soils and their capability for agriculture so that in general only low quality land is left in woodland (fig. 46). Thus woodland is commonest in the High Weald, Low Weald (especially the eastern section), the Sevenoaks Heath Woodland Belt (stony, acid soils) the Blean (on London Clay) and on the poorest soils of the North Downs and Hythe Beds Ridge. Although the land they cloak may be of poor quality the woods, still predominantly deciduous, give a pleasing effect to the landscape and complement the hops, fruit, vegetables and other crops of the Garden of England.

Plate 14
Chestnut coppice with oak standards near Hawkhurst showing on-site production of palings.

Wildlife in the Landscape   4

Even in a small garden many unintended plants are tolerated willing or not, and wild birds and animals come and go. In a county such as Kent a number of widely varying habitats exist, all subject to some degree of management or disturbance by man, but providing homes for a characteristic range of wildlife. Some, like heaths, bogs and salt marsh, have become relatively rare and nature reserves have been established to preserve these and other habitats.

WOODLANDS

Moist Oakwood

A prehistoric traveller would have found the Weald covered by dense moist oakwood. The subsidiary trees varied with soil conditions; ash favouring less acid soils, birch more acid and alder the most poorly drained sites. Crab apple and wild cherry trees were common, looking forward to the orchards of today. In places, hornbeam and elsewhere holly, were abundant. Hazel, sloe and hawthorn were the main shrubs, with twining brambles, ivy and honeysuckle joining wild roses to make passage difficult. Bracken sprang up each year where the soils were relatively sandy and well drained. A great variety of wild flowers and other herbs grew near the ground, varying with the degree of shade and soil conditions.

Coppice

One eighth of Kent is still occupied by woodland, but man has intervened to manage the woods when this was profitable, and at other times to neglect them except as game preserves and as reserves of timber to meet the emergency needs of the owner or the nation. Before cheap transport enabled the use of coal, winter warmth and supplies of bricks, pottery, lime and iron depended on firewood. For this large trees were not essential, and requirements were too pressing to await their development. So nearly all Kentish woods were coppiced, and as late as 1924 three quarters of the wooded area was still coppice. Every eight to 25 years the growth was cut, and then allowed to shoot again from the stumps. In the nineteenth century the value of the coppice cut from one hectare was about £100, very comparable with contemporary returns from agriculture. In the long term, however, coppicing is inefficient, yielding only about 60 per cent of the timber grown by 'high forest'.

Sweet chestnut (introduced in Roman times), hornbeam and hazel were the commonest coppice trees, while ash and sessile oak were also coppiced. Pedunculate oak was often grown on the same land, forming large widely spaced 'standard' trees, which offered both large baulks and naturally crooked timber for the shipbuilders of Deptford and Chatham. Many of the outlets for coppice timber—charcoal, hurdles, hop poles, etc.—have contracted or disappeared. Sweet chestnut, used for fencing (plate 14), still repays cutting. Other species go to Sittingbourne for pulp, but barely pay for management. Small areas of hornbeam and hazel coppice are maintained at Ham Street National Nature Reserve.

Fig. 49. Nightingale *(Luscinia megarhynchos) A bird especially common in Kent.*

Typical cutting rotations were every eight to ten years for hazel, 15 years for sweet chestnut, and 25 years for hornbeam and mixed coppice. The ground flora of coppice woodland is much influenced by the cycle of cutting. On moderately acid, retentive soils the early stages of regrowth encourage spectacular displays of wood anemones, primroses and bluebells in the spring, followed in early summer by bugle, red campion and yellow archangel. In older areas the heavy canopy in summer tends to shade out ground plants. If part of an area of woodland is cut each year a range of habitats is maintained which encourages a great variety of plants and of insects, such as butterflies and beetles. The coppiced section of Ham Street Woods shows this variety, which extends also to birds. A winter population mostly of woodpeckers, jays, jackdaws, titmice, blackbirds, thrushes and robins is diversified in spring and summer by breeding populations of blackcap, garden warbler, whitethroat, willow warbler, chiffchaff and nightingale (fig. 49). Visitors are rewarded by a rich variety of bird song. Woodland animals are less evident, but include weasels, foxes, badgers and stoats. Moist oakwood, and the 'coppice with standards' which has often replaced it, is associated with moderately acid loamy and clayey soils, usually gleyed brown earths or stagnogley soils on such formations as Wadhurst Clay, Weald Clay, Plateau Drift and

London Clay. The woodlands on dry, sandy soils and on calcareous soils overlying chalk need separate description.

Dry Oakwood

On dry very acid soils (brown earths and podzol intergrades), the climax vegetation is still oakwood, but the range of associated trees and other plants is different. Birch is abundant, both as a pioneer and also accompanying oak, while rowan, holly and aspen are frequent. Although beech and Scots pine grow well and regenerate, they are not generally considered to be native to these soils. Ash and hazel are scarce or absent and so are the shrubs found in moist oakwood or chalk scrub except hawthorn and sloe. The ground flora, similarly, is much poorer in species than moist oakwood, and sometimes bracken suppresses almost everything else. In bluebell woods, however, on Folkestone Sands and elsewhere, brambles, wood anemone and a limited range of other herbs and grasses are present. Locally heather is found in open places.

Chalk Scrub

The characteristic vegetation of the rendzinas and shallow brown calcareous earths of the North Downs escarpment and the steepest dry valley sides is known as chalk scrub.

This has greatly extended at the expense of chalk grassland during the last few years as the pressure of grazing by sheep and rabbits has relaxed. The most abundant constituents of chalk scrub are hawthorn, blackthorn and several species of wild rose, which combine to tatter the clothes of intrepid ramblers climbing the North Downs.

Also abundant are ash, hazel, spindle tree, privet, whitebeam, elder, dogwood, wayfaring tree and field maple. Juniper, common buckthorn and spurge laurel are other characteristic chalkland scrubs which are more local in their occurrence. Box is now very rare, despite the name Boxley. Traveller's joy, giving the characteristic greyish, shaggy 'old man's beard' in autumn, is a ubiquitous climber, accompanied frequently by ivy and honeysuckle, and sometimes by white bryony or brambles. Dog's mercury frequently dominates the ground flora and among other plants that occur are both deadly and woody nightshade and the otherwise rare stinking hellebore and columbine. The most distinctive flowering plants are orchids, including rarities like the lady orchid (fig. 50), which is almost exclusive to Kent. The Wye and Crundale Downs Nature Reserve includes areas of chalk scrub, as well as chalk grassland and serves to protect some rare orchids in both formations.

Beechwoods

Beechwoods are less extensive on the chalklands of Kent than in West Sussex or Hampshire or on the Chilterns, although it is probably the climax vegetation that would ultimately replace chalk scrub. The beechwoods that occur have few subsidiary species. Yew is almost the only smaller tree that can stand the dense shade, while the leaf litter is often almost uncolonized. Where the canopy is relatively thin, dog's mercury usually covers the ground and helleborine orchids are sometimes found.

Planting in Kentish Woodlands

For centuries woodlands were cut, and then allowed to grow again naturally or otherwise replanted with deciduous species or completely grubbed. One effect of piecemeal clearance was the creation of an immense length of woodland edge. This makes fencing and management expensive, and also provides refuges for wildlife, such as rabbits, pigeons, owls and foxes, which go out to forage in nearby fields.

In the eighteenth century landowners began to plant exotic trees, including conifers, for visual effect, and about 1850 close planting of conifers, particularly Douglas fir, was introduced to Kent by Edward Faunce, of Sharstead, south of Sittingbourne. The Forestry Commission now has over 2,100 ha of conifer plantations in Kent and nearly 1,300 ha of mixed deciduous and coniferous trees. The extent of conifers is partly concealed by edgings of hardwoods, and in any case will decrease as conifers are removed from mixtures, leaving beech and oak. However, some private owners have planted conifers since 1945, encouraged by tax concessions. Species planted have been few, notably Douglas fir on deeper, better drained brown soils and Corsican pine on shallower brown soils or on ill-drained gley soils. A much wider range of species could be grown, as every visitor to Bedgebury Pinetum can judge by examining the Forest Plots. These were begun in 1929 to compare, under normal forest conditions, the growth of relatively uncommon species, both coniferous and broadleaved. Each species or variety is planted pure in a small block of about one tenth of a hectare. In 1969 there were

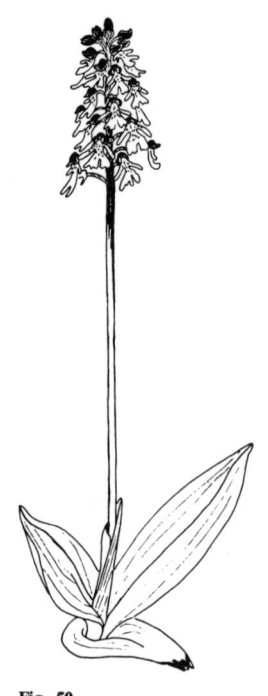

Fig. 50
Lady Orchid *(Orchis purpurea)*
Also called Maid of Kent and virtually confined to chalk woodland in Kent.

130 plots, representing 107 species, giving glimpses of a fascinating range of forest types. Particularly successful are the plots of Wellingtonia, coastal redwood, bishop pine and Chilean beech.

Many Forestry Commission properties have been provided with Forest Walks to encourage, but control, public access (fig. 61). Several parcels of woodland, particularly in West Kent, are owned by the National Trust. Many private woodlands are valued most as game preserves and public access is understandably discouraged.

AGRICULTURAL LAND

It might be supposed that the ecology of agricultural land was sufficiently covered by the chapter on agriculture and horticulture. But, in reality, many unsown plant species are found in pastures and hedgerows, and as weeds in arable land.

Permanent Pasture

Before 1939 just two thirds of Kent was occupied by grassland, very little of which had been artificially sown. In 1970 only 28.5 per cent was permanent pasture and 2.8 per cent rough grazing, but this residue is still of considerable ecological interest.

The sheep fattening pastures of Romney Marsh are, at their best, dominated by perennial ryegrass. A botanical analysis of one yielded 74 per cent perennial ryegrass, 9 per cent wild white clover, 8 per cent bent, 4 per cent rough stalked meadow grass, 4 per cent Yorkshire fog. The pastures of the North Kent marshes have a very varied flora, including some ryegrass mixed with a considerable proportion of bent. The permanent pastures on non-alluvial soils are less good, being dominated by bent, although there is a little ryegrass in North Kent. Wild white clover is still an important associate, but other grasses such as crested dogstail, sheep's fescue, meadow barley and golden oat grass are also frequently of significance. Although around Bethersden and High Halden some better-drained pastures yield seed crops of indigenous perennial ryegrass and Kent Wild White Clover, the general standard of permanent pastures on the Weald Clay outcrop is particularly low, bent being accompanied by much Yorkshire fog and meadow barley, and in the wettest fields by rushes and tufted hair grass.

Where permanent pasture is not acid and is reasonably well drained, an active soil fauna is present. This ensures good structure and hence good rooting in the topsoil, while deep exploration of the subsoil by earthworms and ants has been shown to increase the permeability of silty and clayey soils to an enormous extent. This was a notable factor in the productivity of fattening pastures on Romney Marsh, but has been largely lost where they have been converted to arable.

Chalk Grassland

Chalk hills are commonly called Downs, and were associated with short, springy thyme-scented turf, very attractive to walkers and picnickers and containing an enormous variety of plants. Now less than 0.5 per cent of the Chalk outcrop in Kent and Surrey is occupied by semi-natural grassland, although there is more in Sussex. One of the largest areas remaining, about 50 ha, forms part of the National Nature Reserve on Wye and Crundale Downs.

The dominant grass of chalk grassland in Kent is sheep's fescue, sometimes with red fescue. There are several herbs of the thyme family, not only wild thyme but marjoram, self-heal and wood-sage. Many, although not all, of the plants are definite lime-lovers (basicoles), for example rock rose, hairy violet, salad burnet and Carline thistle. Apart from lime the soils are not very fertile, so nitrogen-fixing legumes are prominent, such as red clover, kidney and horseshoe vetches and birdsfoot trefoil. Blue flowered milkworts are abundant, including locally a great rarity, Kentish milkwort, now confined to Kent. The most distinctive group, however, is the orchids, among which are many rarities. The scented common, the spotted, the pyramidal, the fragrant and the bee orchids are often abundant in chalk grassland. Among the rarities are the spider, the man, the lady and the monkey orchid. The names are evocative of their shapes, the lady orchid for example is supposed to resemble a Victorian lady with a crinoline and bonnet. The late spider orchid is confined to East Kent. In all the Wye and Crundale Downs Nature Reserve contains 17 species of orchid (figs. 50-52).

Chalk grassland has a varied insect population with many species of moths, butterflies, beetles and bugs, some of which are special. The black-veined moth is only found on Wye Downs and the pretty chalk blue and the chalk carpet moth are virtually confined to chalk grasslands. In the rendzina soils a leading role in breaking down roots and other plant debris is taken by chafer grubs, for summer dryness discourages earthworms. Apart from larks and meadow pipits, birds prefer adjacent scrub for nesting.

Chalk grassland is a plagioclimax conditioned by heavy grazing,

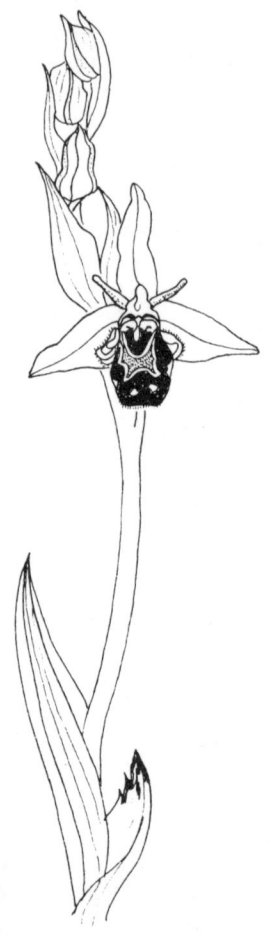

Fig. 51.
Bee orchid (*Ophrys apifera*) Fairly common on the North Downs.

particularly of sheep and rabbits. Today the sheep population of the chalklands is actually lower than elsewhere in Kent, and since myxomatosis rabbits, too, are few. In past times sheep were often pastured on the Downs by day and folded on the low ground during the night. This led to the slow but steady depletion of the downland soils in the nutrients contained in the wool, mutton and night time dung of the sheep. Even rabbits tended to concentrate nutrients near their burrows and thus depleted outlying areas. Continual grazing and nutrient depletion are believed to prevent tall-growing plant species from competing strongly with dwarf ones, and so maintain species diversity. Cutting can only serve the same purposes if frequent and if the cut material is removed. Where grazing is light or absent, therefore, the short turf is quickly replaced by tall grasses, such as upright brome, tor grass and cocksfoot. Tor grass, especially, is unpalatable to animals and shelters seedlings of hawthorn and blackthorn which initiate a third stage in the succession, chalk scrub.

Hedgerows

Hedges and hedgerow trees are perhaps the most characteristic and attractive features of the agricultural landscape in Kent as in most parts of England. Except in Romney Marsh and in the arable north east, Kent has a pattern of small irregular fields, mostly hedged, characteristic of early, piecemeal enclosure. A feature of the hop growing areas is the specially high hedge sheltering the hop gardens. In the Weald narrow strips of woodland (shaws) sometimes replace hedges as field boundaries. Hedges in general and especially high hedges and shaws are excellent windbreaks.

A group of ecologists working at Monks Wood Experimental Station has established that the variety of trees and shrubs in a hedge increased steadily with age. Taking the mean of several 27 m sample lengths, the rate of increase is about one species per century.

Around Wye, for example, hedges seem to fall into two groups: those that are almost pure hawthorn, and therefore presumably no more than a century or so old, and those which are very mixed, with five to ten species. These must be very much older, probably mediaeval. In the latter hawthorn, blackthorn, hazel and field maple are almost always present with larger trees of ash, pedunculate oak and English elm at longer intervals. A number of other shrubs and creepers are sometimes present including traveller's joy, dogwood, holly, honeysuckle, wild rose, bramble and wayfaring tree. This list,

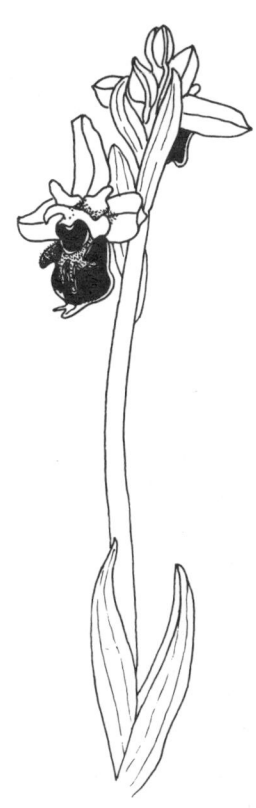

Fig. 52.
Late Spider Orchid (*Ophrys fuciflora*)
A real rarity, its only British occurrences are a few localities in East Kent.

especially traveller's joy, dogwood and wayfaring tree, reflects the wide occurrence of chalky soils in the area.

Another factor besides age encouraging species diversity is proximity to woodlands, and this operates strongly in the Weald, reflected in the abundance of hazel in hedges. Dog's mercury, primroses, bluebell and wood anemone are other characteristic plants of hedgerows near woodland.

Until recently, English elms were the most prominent large hedgerow trees, although oaks are also common especially in the Weald. All three species of elm occur in Kent; the English elm much predominates in North Kent, but the smooth leaved is important in East Kent, and the Wych elm in the Weald. All three are liable to Dutch Elm Disease, which is caused by a fungus and spread by a bark beetle which feeds on dead and dying trees. The disease reached England in 1927, but had stabilized at a low level. By 1971 a new outbreak had reached epidemic proportions and North Kent was badly affected. The disease has continued to spread, and in Sheppey, for example, has killed almost all hedgerow trees, as no other kind is common on the island. Even elsewhere the importance of trees in the landscape is declining, for Dutch Elm Disease has reinforced a steady loss of trees from other causes. Hedges contain many species of the family of Rosaceae which also provides our main tree fruits. Thus hedges can harbour orchard pests and diseases, of which the most serious recent example has been fireblight, a disease mainly affecting pears. Growers of seedless hops also need to cast a suspicious eye over local hedgerows, in this case to remove cross fertilizing plants of wild hop.

The 'laying' of hedges in which selected stems are nicked and bent nearly horizontal has almost died out in Kent and mechanical trimming is the main management operation. In conjunction with their mixed composition this means Kent hedges are much less stockproof than for example in the West Midlands where laying is still practised. In recent years stubble burning has led to many damaging fires in hedgerows. Weed killers too may drift from adjacent fields. For these reasons, gaps bridged with barbed wire are all too common in Kentish hedges.

More disquieting still is the wholesale grubbing of hedges, sometimes to enable larger and more conveniently shaped fields to be formed, occasionally to facilitate drainage schemes, often simply to avoid the costs of regular maintenance.

The narrow world of the hedgerow often acts as a complete ecosystem. Hundreds of invertebrate species can be found in a few metres length of hedge. Over a hundred species of moth caterpillars feed on hawthorn and nearly as many on blackthorn, the small ermine moth being the commonest. Hawthorn and blackthorn also attract bees and other flower visiting insects, particularly beetles. In turn the cuckoo combs the hedgerows for caterpillars, while fieldfares, thrushes and blackbirds could hardly survive the winter without berries from hawthorn hedges. On the other hand owls, rooks, crows and wood pigeons nest in hedgerow trees and sally forth to feed elsewhere. Voles, field mice and shrews co-exist in the complicated system of small mammal runs and burrows that exists under every hedge. This makes hedges attractive to their predators, such as weasels, vipers and owls.

In summary the farmer finds the hedgerow a mixed blessing. It is an attractive and still fairly cheap barrier between fields, but undoubtedly it harbours some pests and diseases. To the observer, however, further drastic removal of hedges would lead to a serious loss of diversity in the life of the countryside.

Fig. 53.
Hoary Cress (*Cardaria draba*)
Introduced to Britain through Kent.

Arable Weeds

The weed population of Kent has been much depleted by the use of selective chemical weedkillers, but it remains difficult to control grass weeds in cereals and broad-leaved weeds in established dicotyledonous crops. There is less continuous cereal growing in Kent than in most eastern and southern counties, and so wild oats are correspondingly less important and blackgrass not a serious problem. Couch grass, however, is a serious pest in places. Populations of more easily controlled weeds, such as poppies, survive on headlands and waste land.

Particular ecological interest attaches to weeds which have invaded Britain from the Continent through Kent. Hoary cress, an untidy plant with a cluster of small white flowers, was first firmly established in Thanet and acquired the name 'Thanet weed' (fig. 53). It is said to have been introduced through the bedding straw brought back with sick and wounded soldiers from the ill-fated Walcheren expedition of 1812. It is still spreading west and north into Ireland and Scotland. Similar in name and origin is hoary mustard, now well established on waste ground in a few places. This is said to have been introduced through Richborough when the port there was a supply base for the campaigns of 1914-18. Longleaf, a perennial weed resembling garden gypsophila, has no such peg in history. It is common on chalky soils in parts of France, was first found in Kent near Wingham in 1858 and is still confined to southern and eastern England. Wool waste used in some hop gardens is also a source of unusual alien weeds. Twenty-two species of 'wool alien' have been found in fields manured with wool shoddy around Swanley, and New Zealand burweed is well established around Mereworth.

HEATHS AND BOGS

Heaths

Unlike Surrey, Kent never had much heathland and with the decline of the rabbit and the disappearance of the gipsy's horse and the commoner's goat these few small areas have been colonized by birch and are developing into dry oakwoods. At Hothfield Common, near Ashford, which is a public open space and a local Nature Reserve, the heath community is losing ground, but has not disappeared entirely. Of about 60 ha within the Reserve only about 6 ha is dominated by heather, which is associated with cross-leaved heath and Molinia, and ill drained peaty gley soils (fig. 54). Before 1950 heather associated with wavy hair grass occupied dry slopes with podzols also, where it has now been replaced by bracken. The small area of heather is the most easterly in Kent, and has a rich insect fauna including 23 species linked by feeding habits to heather.

Bogs

Hothfield Common includes four small hollows where seepage from

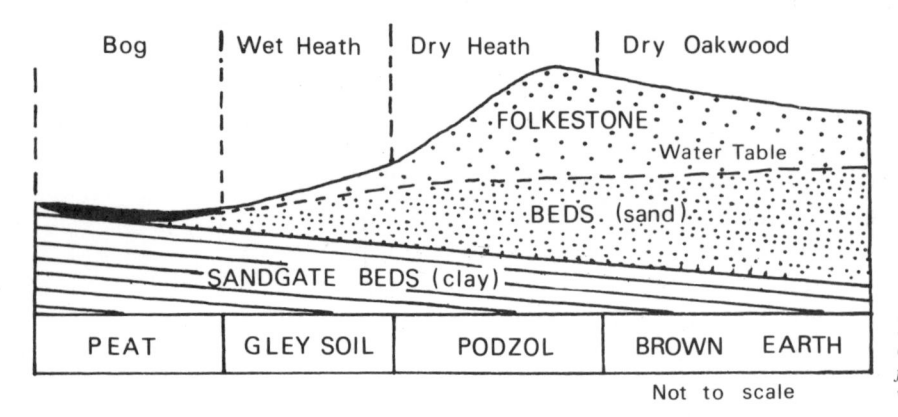

Fig. 54.
Hothfield Common
Cross section to show the different soils and associated vegetation.

the water table in the Folkestone Sands has encouraged the formation of acid peat (fig. 54). Twelve species of the characteristic moss *Sphagnum* occur here, and for two it is the only Kentish locality. Common cotton grass (really a sedge) is prominent, developing a cluster of 'cotton wool' covered fruiting heads in summer, and is accompanied by true sedge and rushes. The tiny insectiverous common sundew is frequent in the main bog, and so is the bog asphodel with yellow flowers in July and August. Small areas of acid peat also occur at Bedgebury and at Hawkenbury Bog, near Tunbridge Wells. Near neutral peat is formed in occasional spots saturated by springs arising from the chalk, and gives fen carr, a wet woodland with willows and alders. A small area of sedge fen, reminiscent of the Norfolk Broads is found within a nature reserve at Ham Fen, north of Deal. Most of the former wetlands, however, have been drained for agriculture, including Naccolt Bog, near Wye, probably the largest area of peat in the county.

Fig. 55.
Wall Pennywort (*Umbilicus rupestris*)
Found occasionally in Kent.

DISTURBED GROUND

Human disturbance, even of an unwelcome kind such as rubbish dumping or wartime bombing, can create unusual ecological habitats, or, as when a piece of salt marsh is walled off (as happened at Egypt Bay, High Halstow), interesting vegetational successions are initiated. The following paragraphs indicate a few of these inherently variable habitats that exist in Kent.

Walls

Kent is not a mountainous county nor rich in hard rocks, but the activities of man have provided frequent opportunities of studying the colonization of bare rock by plants. Every churchyard is stocked with dated specimens of various rock types showing the pioneering activities of lichens which greatly speed the processes of chemical weathering and are succeeded by mosses. Passing then to walls, small ferns soon grow in crevices, such as polypody, spleenwort and wallrue. Flowering plants often occur on old walls, such as wall pellitory and the more showy yellow stonecrop and ivy-leaved and purple toadflaxes. Wall pennywort (fig. 55), an unusual plant in Kent with disc shaped leaves has been found on several churches. Could it be an escape from the collection plate? Another specialist is clove pink, a real rarity, growing on ruined buildings. It has been recorded on three Kentish castles and on Boxley Abbey.

Railways and Roads

Transport is another human activity with interesting ecological by-products. There are characteristic plants of railway cuttings which have spread from specialized habitats such as cliffs or gardens or from abroad. Examples are red valerian, snapdragon and pyrenean cranesbill. It has been suggested that stinking groundsel, a plant once mostly associated with seaside shingle, as at Dungeness, was moved to various parts of Kent with railway ballast. Rayless mayweed is an example of a plant that has spread along roadsides. It originated in Oregon and has been distributed in mud on tyres and boots.

Chalkpits

The commonest quarries in Kent are chalk pits, many of which are now abandoned and are becoming vegetated. The Great Culand quarries near Burham, for example, are being managed as a reserve by the Kent Trust for Nature Conservation. Here the initial colonization of bare chalk can be seen, in which small flowering plants generally precede grasses to give an intricately varied carpet, with about 12 species to the square metre, reminiscent of an alpine pasture. Blue scabious, purple felwort (a gentian) and marjoram mingle with yellow wort and birdsfoot trefoil. Red fescue comes in rather slowly to give chalk grassland, but this is soon colonized by scrub as the rabbit population remains rather low. The range of environments in chalk pits is extreme, from the very dry exposed faces to the sheltered, unusually moist pit bottom, so some relatively unusual plants occur in various pits. Examples are blue fleabane, several orchids and mulleins, including the rare large flowered and moth mulleins. The insect population is also rich in variety. Oddly enough, at Great Culand, certain rare spiders colonize derelict cars, obnoxious though these are in every other way.

Sandpits

Sandpits occur commonly in the Folkestone Beds, together with a few on the sandy type of Woolwich and Oldhaven Beds. The bare sand faces provide nesting sites for certain sand wasps and also for sand martin colonies. Foxes are said to prey on the sand martins, climbing vertical faces to drag out the contents of the nest holes. On the floor of pits conditions are varied, in places moist from a water table, elsewhere heaps of loose sand offer very dry sites. In a single pit at Charing Heath 69 species of plants were found. Willows were prominent in the moist areas, while the flora of the loose sands, not yet strongly acid, included pioneering legumes such as birdsfoot trefoil and white clover. Insects, for example the common blue butterfly, were abundant and attracted many birds, such as willow warblers, whitethroats, tits, goldcrests, wrens, grasshopper warblers and chiffchaffs.

Ragstone quarries

Many of these have been filled in or used as sites for development, but Dryhill Quarry, west of Sevenoaks, has been converted into a 'country park' by the County Council. Nearly a thousand people planted birch and beech trees there in 1969 through a scheme sponsored by the Automobile Association. When the site was landscaped and a picnic area developed points of geological interest were preserved.

Fig. 56. Thorn Apple (*Datura stramonium*) An invader from the United States which flourishes very locally in Kent during warm summers.

Spoil and Rubbish Heaps

Two colliery spoil heaps in East Kent are partly vegetated. Betteshanger is only 2 km from the sea, and some coastal species are present. Chislet, further inland and abandoned for some time, shows a distinct succession from bare shale debris on eroded slopes to scrub in which even pedunculate oak saplings are represented.

Rubbish heaps often harbour unusual casual and exotic species, for example the highly poisonous thorn apple (fig. 56), together with common nitrophiles such as elderberry and nettle and solanaceous plants (tomato, potato and black nightshade).

FRESH WATER HABITATS

Rivers

Because man has always regarded streams and rivers as convenient drains for human, agricultural and industrial effluents, and because the added materials usually move freely, fresh water is especially liable to pollution. Fortunately a survey in 1970 classified 92 per cent of the length of Kent rivers as unpolluted. The exceptions were the tidal section of the Medway, Milton Creek and a small part of the Swale, which are heavily industrialized, together with a short stretch of the Great Stour downstream of Canterbury and a few short lengths of small streams which were polluted by sewage works. The effect of Ashford and Canterbury sewage works is well seen in fig. 57. Organic matter and phosphate (from detergent) in the effluents encourage an excessive growth of filamentous algae downstream. Respiration of these algae and of micro-organisms degrading the organic matter depletes oxygen at night to a level detrimental to trout, so that the reaches below the sewage works are populated mainly by coarse (non-edible) fish. Fortunately for the trout in the middle reaches turbulent flow over the weir at Wye mill reoxygenates the water.

If a river is to remain healthy, a reasonable flow is required in dry weather. Direct abstraction of river water and the depletion of springs by pumping from boreholes both tend to reduce dry weather flow and have caused great concern to those interested in both the Great and Little Stour. Conversely the sealing of surfaces by roofs, roads and pavements as towns grow and rapid transfer of storm water to rivers by urban and agricultural drainage systems increases the risk of floods. Flooding is a particular problem in the Eden and Medway Valley and feasibility studies have been made for a major flood prevention scheme. Floods themselves and the artificial structures checking them may adversely affect the life of the river.

Many riverbank and aquatic plants still continue to thrive. Typical bank species are reeds, purple loosestrife, yellow flag, great water dock, comfrey and hemp agrimony. Somewhat more unusual is the handsome flowering rush, with pink flowers and hence not really a rush, which occurs along ditches and streams in the Stour and Medway basins. Crack and white willows are common trees by Kent rivers and streams, but they have often been planted. The aquatic flora of the Great Stour is dominated by river crowfoot, which belongs to the buttercup family, but has a white flower an inch

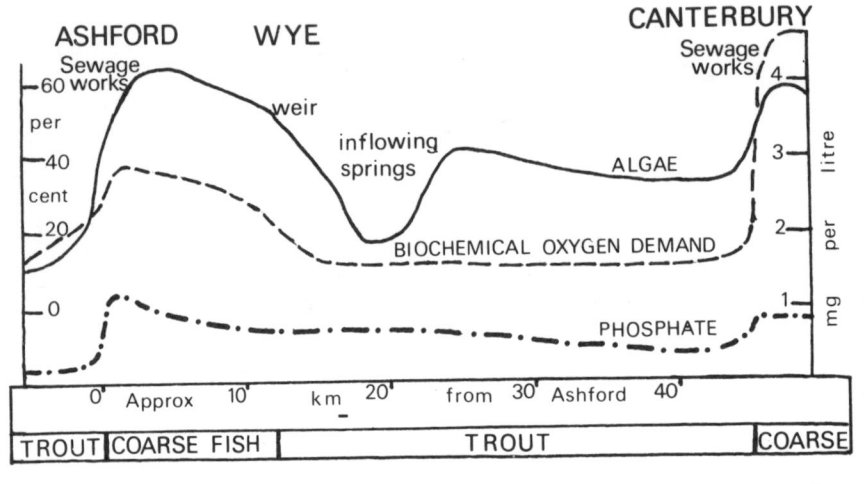

Fig. 57.
Pollution in the River Stour
Indications of pollution in the River Stour between Ashford and Canterbury and their effect on the fish. Algae as per cent of total plant dry material, phosphate and biological oxidation demand in milligrams per litre.

across, together with filamentous algae (most Cladophora). Pondweeds are abundant in the upper reaches: fennel pondweed especially, but also the Canadian, horned and curly pondweeds. The last is also called frog's lettuce. The Lower Stour has abundant river water dropwort, a floating umbellifer, rare in Britain as a whole, together with water starwort and spiked milfoil. Bur reeds become dominant in slow-flowing streams, including the Stour around Fordwich. The yellow water lily is found on the East Stour and between Wye and Chilham, and edible watercress in various tributary streams.

There are some fish in most parts of the larger Kent rivers. The Great Stour is well known for trout: the common river trout is numerous in places, the migratory sea trout visits the river. Perch, trout and carp are found in the non-tidal parts of the Medway. Among coarse (non-edible) fish, bream, roach, pike and tench occur in slow moving waters, while chub and dace are to be found in the faster, clearer reaches of the Medway and Stour. Nature's fisherman, the heron, may sometimes be seen, but the otter is probably extinct in Kent rivers, its 'ecological niche' taken over by the mink, an American invader. Another foreigner is the noisy marsh frog, introduced to the ditches of Romney Marsh in 1935, and still confined to that area.

Lakes and flooded gravel pits

In Kent lakes are an artificial feature of the landscape. Millponds were once very common and some survive, for example the water lilied 'hammer pond' at Cowden (plate 25).

No 'gentleman's seat' of the eighteenth and nineteenth centuries was complete without its lake to which would be brought not only waterlilies but exotic birds, such as the Australian black swans of Leeds Castle and Hall Place, Leigh. Lakes in nature are temporary and many are being gradually filled up. First colonizers are floating plants like pondweed and duckweed (which ducks do relish) followed by reed swamp, in which common reed may be joined by bulrush and the greater and lesser reedmace. Reed swamp also quickly chokes uncleared ditches in Romney Marsh and the North Kent marshes. Mineral workings have formed many modern lakes, especially where gravel has been extracted below the water table, and common reed and greater reedmace may be seen invading them. Some birds have benefited greatly from the appearance of flooded pits, and also from reservoirs, such as that at Bough Beech. The great crested grebe (fig. 58) and the little ringed plover, in particular, have shown great increases in numbers. The Stour valley lakes, which include Stodmarsh National Nature Reserve, flooded by mining subsidence, and gravel pits, have breeding populations of some relatively rare birds such as Savi's warbler, the bearded tit and the bittern. Unusual visitors to Britain seen there include the purple heron, the night heron and the great reed warbler. The flooded pits at Dungeness also act as a staging post for a great variety of fresh water birds. Those near Sevenoaks draw greylags and Canada geese, and nearby an osprey was recently observed.

Fig. 58.
Great Crested Grebe *(Podiceps cristatus)*
This species has increased markedly in Kent over recent years.

COASTAL HABITATS

Kent has about 170 km of coastline and well over 200 km of foreshore on estuaries of substantial width, quite apart from very narrow rivers and creeks and the periphery of small islands. Thus the habitats affected by tidal overflow or salt spray are very extensive, even if greatly reduced by the building of sea walls, especially since the great storm surge of 1953. In the account that follows only terrestrial and estuarine environments are considered, and not the fully marine life of beaches and the open sea.

Estuarine mudflats

With the exception of Pegwell Bay this ecosystem is only of significant extent in the lower reaches of the Thames, Medway and Swale, where it is largely protected from the full effect of North Sea waves by the Hoo peninsula and the Isle of Sheppey. Sedimentation of the finest particles (fine silt and clay) is predominant in the very sheltered conditions of the Medway estuary, and here the extent of mudflats has been much increased over the last three centuries through the removal of marshland by natural erosion and excavation for the brick and cement industries. Coarser sediment (sand and coarse silt) predominates in Pegwell Bay and at the more exposed end of the Swale near Whitstable, where the zone between low and high tide levels is almost two kilometres wide.

The mudflat ecosystem provides an elegant example of a food chain. It is well supplied with nutrients from land drainage and from the action of bacteria on organic detritus, resulting in a very dense growth of plants (seaweed and phytoplankton), which provide the food for many small animals ranging from tiny, floating zooplankton, to various shellfish and marine worms. In turn, a very large bird population is supported, especially in winter. Some birds feed directly on seaweeds, such as *Entermorpha,* and eel grass is a favoured food plant of Brent geese and wigeon. This is one of the very few flowering plants which flourishes on estuarine mudflats, and is particularly abundant at the east end of the Swale and in parts of the Medway Estuary, notably north of Lower Rainham, although it is not common in other British estuaries. Cord grass *(Spartina)* is much less desirable, as it multiplies explosively and may completely alter the foreshore habitat. In Kent *Spartina* is established near Seasalter and in Pegwell Bay. The East Swale is a Nature Reserve, and its intertidal fauna is the richest known in south east England with over 350 invertebrate species. All the exposed mudflats are important winter feeding and roosting areas for geese (especially Brent geese), ducks (mallard, wigeon, teal, shoveler, pintail and shelduck), waders (especially knot and dunlin) and common and black-headed gulls. Shelducks, for example, eat marine snails.

The foreshore is sometimes disturbed by bait digging and by pleasure boats, but there is more subtle threat from pollution. The proximity of the oil refinery at Grain is one obvious danger.

Salt Marsh

As plants like *Spartina* or glasswort trap sediment, the level is gradually raised, leading to colonization by a succession of other plants, until ultimately the surface is covered only by the highest tides. Areas affected by these processes are called saltings or salt marshes, and are normally broken up by a complex, branching pattern of creeks. In the Medway estuary, where erosion rather than accumulation is generally predominant, the boundary from saltings to tidal mudflats normally takes the form of a miniature cliff. Along the Swale, however, the saltings are generally growing seawards, and no erosion cliff occurs. This enables a fuller succession of

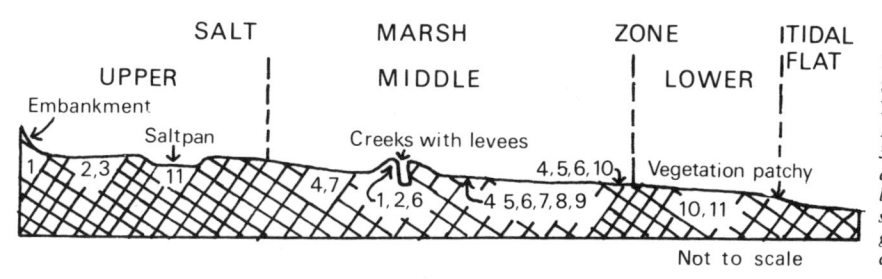

Fig. 59.
Salt Marsh Vegetation, Shell Ness, Sheppey
1, red fescue. 2, sea purslane. 3, golden samphire. 4, sea aster. 5, herbaceous seablite. 6, sea meadow grass. 7, sea lavender. 8, sea arrow grass. 9, sea plantain. 10, cord grass. 11, glass wort.

vegetation to be observed (fig. 59). Extensive salt marshes only survive in the Medway estuary. Reclamation for agriculture or industrial use has left only small remnants elsewhere. The flora of salt marshes is restricted to plants which can tolerate a salt content that would kill most species, and is therefore most distinctive. In many places the middle levels of the saltings are turned a deep lilac colour in August by the sea lavender and the sea aster which resembles a Michaelmas daisy. Even more common, but much less attractive, is the grey, untidy sea purslane which occurs along the creek edges and in other relatively well drained areas. The commonest salt marsh grass is sea meadow grass. Another attractive flower is the daisy-like golden samphire, which is not found much further north. Certain insects favour salt marshes, such as the rare moth, the ground lackey. Salt marsh has a rich bird population. Teal eat fleshy plants, such as glasswort and seablite; wigeon and Brent geese can feed on sea meadow grass. Curlews favour the creeks, while flocks of twite sustain themselves through the winter on the seeds of salt marsh plants.

Fig. 60.
Sea Holly *(Eryungium maritimum)*
Found around Sandwich Bay and at Dungeness.

Coastal sand and shingle

Shingle banks are extensive at Dungeness, and near West Hythe. The only substantial area of sand dunes is at Sandwich Bay, where the greyish sand couchgrass is the initial colonizer of mobile dunes, followed by marram grass. Further inland the dunes are older, and vegetation cover and the diversity of plants increase greatly. One very attractive species here and at Dungeness is sea holly (fig. 60). Its leaves resemble holly closely in shape, but are bluish green with whitish edges. Pinkish storksbills are also characteristic plants of coastal sands. At Sandwich Bay a large area of dunes has been modified to form golf courses, yet the Royal St. George's Golf Links shelters the rare Lizard orchid, whose flower looks like a lizard, but smells like a goat. On Dungeness the sea rocket and the yellow horned poppy are early colonizers of the shingle. Inland the series of dry ridges (fulls) and wet linear hollows (slacks) is only partly vegetated (plate 18). Some older ridges have gorse, bramble, blackthorn and burnet rose, and there is even a small wood situated rather inaccessibly within Lydd Ranges. The Dungeness slacks have a distinctive vegetation including the saw sedge that can be nearly two metres high. The damp slacks between the dunes at Sandwich Bay are also interesting, with an orchid, marsh helleborine.

At a few places within the North Kent Marshes there are beaches of shell sand which also have an interesting flora. One at Shell Ness, at the eastern end of Sheppey, is now a National Nature Reserve (fig. 61). The small North Kent beaches are a breeding ground for various waders, particularly the ringed plover. In the winter large wader flocks of oyster-catchers, knots, dunlins, bar-tailed godwits, turnstones and plovers roost on these beaches.

On the coast there are bird observatories at both Dungeness and Sandwich Bay, strategically situated to record many spring and autumn migrants to and from the Continent, as well as numerous seabirds, waders and ducks. The curlew is one summer visitor to Dungeness, and oyster-catchers nest there.

Cliffs

The most extensive cliffs in Kent are composed of chalk, on which stonecrops and plantains are common. Near Dover sea cabbage and sea kale are found. More attractive are thrift (or sea pink), red valerian and the white flowered sea campion. A rare relative of the latter, the Nottingham catchfly, is also present; it has sticky hairs, but is not really insectivorous. The rock samphire occurs on the cliffs between Folkestone and Dover, its only connection with the marsh samphire (glasswort) being that both are edible, and can be pickled. Cliffs are resting places for some sea birds, but several of those characteristic of the northern and western coasts of Britain, such as fulmar, gannet and shag, do not nest in Kent. The ubiquitous herring gull is by far the commonest bird of the Kent cliffs. However, several land birds, such as kestrels and jackdaws frequent them, and house martins have nested on chalk cliffs at Folkestone Warren.

NATURE CONSERVATION IN KENT

The Nature Conservancy Council, with its South-eastern Regional office situated at Wye, exists to establish and manage nature reserves, and also to advise the government and others on the conservation of flora, fauna and other features of the natural environment. The Nature Conservancy Council manages several National Nature Reserves in Kent, areas controlled by ownership, tenancy or special agreement (fig. 61). Two are woodlands: Ham Street Woods, moist oakwood and coppice on Weald Clay, and Blean Woods, oakwood ranging from dry to wet on London Clay and the overlying gravel. Two of the remaining reserves relate mainly to bird life, High Halstow Heronry and the marshes and

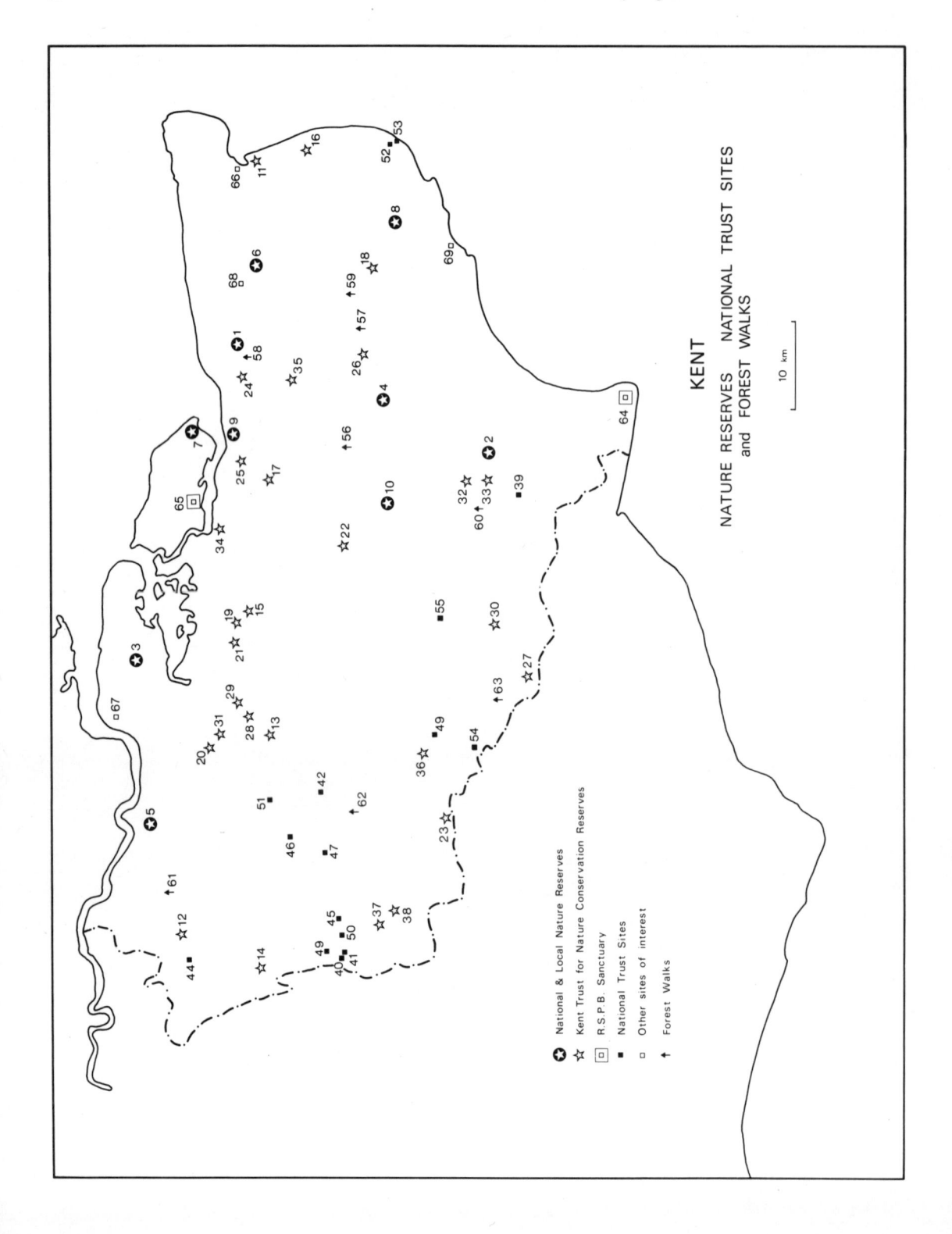

KENT

NATURE RESERVES NATIONAL TRUST SITES
and FOREST WALKS

10 km

● National & Local Nature Reserves
☆ Kent Trust for Nature Conservation Reserves
□ R.S.P.B. Sanctuary
■ National Trust Sites
□ Other sites of interest
↑ Forest Walks

Fig. 61. Kent—Nature Reserves, National Trust Sites and Forest Walks

National Nature Reserves

1. Blean Wood
2. Ham Street Woods
3. High Halstow
4. Wye and Crundale Downs
5. Swanscombe Skull Site
6. Stodmarsh
7. The Swale

Local Nature Reserves

8. Temple Ewell Down
9. South Swale
10. Hothfield Common

Kent Trust for Nature Conservation Reserves

11. Sandwich Bay
12. Ruxley Gravel Pits
13. Leybourne Lakes
14. Downe Bank
15. Stockbury Hill Wood
16. Ham Fen
17. Ospringe Down
18. Denton Banks
19. Queendown Warren
20. Red Wood, Luddesdown
21. Purple Hill, Bredhurst
22. Kiln Wood, Lenham
23. Hawkenbury Bog
24. Ellenden Wood, Whitstable
25. Oare Pond and Meadow
26. Yockletts Bank
27. Collingwood, Hawkhurst
28. Burham Marsh
29. Burham Down
30. Parsonage Wood, Benenden
31. Cuxton Warren
32. Orlestone Forest
33. Smallman's Wood, Ham Street
34. Murston
35. Hunstead Wood, Chartham Hatch
36. Brenchley Wood
37. Bough Beech
38. Chiddingstone

National Trust Open Space Sites

39. Royal Military Canal, Appledore
40. Chartwell
41. Crockham Grange Farms and Mariners Hill, Westerham
42. Gover Hill, Mereworth Woods
43. Golden Hill, Harbledown
44. Hawkwood and Petts Wood, Chislehurst
45. Ide Hill, Brasted
46. Styants Wood, Oldbury Hill, Wrotham
47. One Tree Hill, Sevenoaks
48. Parson's Marsh, Scord's Wood, Brasted
49. Sprivers, Lamberhurst
50. Toys Hill, Brasted
51. Wrotham Water
52. Bockhill Farm, St. Margaret's Bay
53. St. Margaret's Bay; The Leas
54. Scotney Castle, Lamberhurst
55. Sissinghurst Castle

Forest Walks

56. Kings Wood, Challock
57. Lyminge
58. Clowes Wood, Whitstable
59. Covert Wood, Barham
60. Faggs Wood, Orlestone
61. Joydens, near Bexley
62. Dene Park near Tonbridge
63. Bedgebury

Royal Society for the Protection of Birds Reserves

64. Dungeness
65. Elmley Marshes, Sheppey

Other Sites of Interest

66. Pegwell Bay
67. Cliffe Pools
68. Hersden Marsh
69. Folkestone Warren

pools at Stodmarsh. The Wye and Crundale Downs Reserve represents the flora and fauna of the chalk and includes both woodland and grassland, as well as several coombes, steep sided dry valleys of geomorphological interest, in the escarpment (plate 2). From the upper part of this Reserve, where there is a kiosk, splendid views can be obtained. Educational visits to this and other reserves can sometimes be arranged with the office in Wye. In addition to the Reserves there are over 70 Sites of Special Scientific Interest in Kent, each with some valuable biological or geological feature, on which the Nature Conservancy Council staff keep a watchful eye.

The most important private body is the Kent Trust for Nature Conservation, which has some degree of responsibility for about 30 reserves. Among these are represented nearly all the habitats discussed in this chapter. Comprised among them are about ten woods, several areas of downland and old pasture, Hothfield Common and several wetlands including Hawkenbury Bog and Ham Fen. There are lakes at Ruxley, Leybourne and Murston and part of the periphery of Bough Beech reservoir, where birds are the principal interest, as is also the case on the coastal reserves at Shell Ness and Sandwich Bay. The Royal Society for the Protection of Birds has a major observatory at Dungeness. The National Trust has a number of parcels of dry oak and birchwood on the Lower Greensand outcrop between Ightham and Westerham. They also control an attractive stretch of the Royal Military Canal, which has a considerable population of fish.

Fig. 62.
Greenshank (Tringa nebularia).
A regular passage migrant seen at all Kent coastal nature reserves.

The Industrial Scene   5

Industry would seem to be out of place in the Garden of England, yet Kent has its share of industry both past and present. In Tudor times the heart of industrial England was in the Weald of Kent and Sussex where the iron ore of the Wadhurst clay was smelted with charcoal from the Wealden woodlands. The products included cannon, and with oak for ships' timbers the Weald was a major supplier of the dockyards at Deptford and Chatham. Geological raw materials, in this case fuller's earth, also encouraged the woollen industry which thrived in Kent in late mediaeval times. Other textiles were also produced, for example linen at Maidstone, silk at Canterbury and serge cloth at Sandwich. Today all these industries are gone, but some of the replacements also exploit local geological or agricultural raw materials. The main concentration of industry in Kent is along Thamesside in the north-west of the county and here a major advantage is accessibility to water for industrial processes and navigation.

THE EXTRACTIVE INDUSTRIES

The earth offers to Man not only a platform for his activities and soils for growing food and timber but also a storehouse of useful materials. Kent is not particularly rich in minerals of high specific value, but more utilitarian materials such as sand, gravel, clay and chalk have been widely extracted. In his desire to wrest these materials from the earth Man has often paid too little attention to the effect he is having on the landscape and, particularly in respect of chalk workings in North-west Kent, he has sometimes been responsible for wholesale devastation. Luckily, however, Kent has been spared most of the adverse effects of large scale quarrying and mining which have despoiled many of the more industrial areas of Britain.

Sand and Gravel

Sand and gravel are in increasing demand by the building and construction industry. The softer fine sands are used mainly in plastering and mortar work but, increasingly, also in the manufacture of lime-sand bricks. Sharp sand and gravel are used for reinforced concrete and, when of poorer quality, for road construction and general filling purposes. The deposits are often worked 'dry' using scrapers and excavators but 'wet' excavation using hydraulic or bucket dredgers is practised along the Darent, Medway and Stour valleys and on the coastal shingle along the eastern coast of Romney Marsh and near Sandwich. These wet pits are often excellent habitats for a variety of interesting birds as well as providing recreational facilities such as yachting and angling when abandoned. In addition increasing amounts of gravel are now being dredged from the Thames estuary and landed on the North Kent coast.

The main 'solid' geological formation exploited for sand is the Folkestone Beds, whose outcrop roughly follows the A25 and A20 roads. Important workings are around Westerham, west of Maidstone and near Harrietsham, Charing and Sellindge, but the precise location of pits is constantly changing and the outcrop is studded with worked out pits. Sand from Tertiary deposits is dug mainly in the vicinity of Canterbury.

Silica sand, used in glass-making and foundry work, is extracted from the Folkestone Beds in certain localities around Maidstone. The siting of Woolwich Arsenal, formerly within Kent, was partly due to the ready supplies of moulding sand in the nearby Thanet Beds.

Building Stone and Road Metal

An examination of old buildings in Kent shows that a wide variety of building stones have been used (see Chapter 6). Only ragstone (see Chapter 2) was of sufficient importance to be sent outwith the county and was especially popular for Victorian churches in London. Its main and virtually exclusive use today is for road metal, although it is also used on a small scale for ornamental purposes. As a road metal ragstone has some desirable properties, such as good roughness, resistance to polish and a good affinity for bitumen (plate 15). The main workings are to the west of Maidstone, and some of the quarries are enormous. Production of road metal involves the installation of crushing and grading equipment which is often of sufficient size to impinge on the landscape. Many of the old quarries

Plate 15
Interbedded ragstone and hassock of the Hythe Beds at Coombe Quarry, Hayle Place, Maidstone, overlain by a deep brown earth carrying orchards.

are now infilled with domestic rubbish, but in the former large workings at Boughton, near Maidstone a housing development now occupies the quarry floor.

Bricks and Tiles

Kent has long been renowned for the variety and excellence of its bricks and tiles and these have more than adequately compensated for the general lack of building stone in the county. The main brick-making area in Britain is now in the East Midlands, with the resulting demise of many of the brickpits in Kent and elsewhere, and, as with sandpits and quarries, traces of abandoned workings are far more numerous than those still in operation. In the past brickworks were based on clay or brickearth, but in recent years the manufacture of sand-lime bricks has expanded.

Formerly the clays of the High Weald, and the Weald and Gault Clays were actively worked for bricks, but today only a handful of brickworks remain. There is still considerable activity, however, on the brickearth deposits of North Kent. Most of the workings were relatively small-scale shallow enterprises, easily restored to agriculture or horticulture when abandoned, and often detectable only by the use of an old map showing their location. The capital investment in the kilns has served to keep many of the larger brickworks open even when the brickearth in the immediate vicinity is exhausted, and several of the brickworks in North Kent use brickearth extracted from sites at considerable distances from the kilns. Large brickworks occur at Faversham, and near Teynham, Lower Halstow and Rainham.

Chalk Products

The Chalk, apart from making the most important landscape feature in the county, is probably also the most valuable economically. In the past it was widely worked for lime and whiting, but production is now more concentrated, a plant at Swanscombe producing over 20 per cent of the total British output of whiting. Chalk from the remaining small pits is now used largely for agricultural purposes, but the largest use is in the production of cement. The industry began in North-west Kent in 1846, exploiting the natural geographical advantages of the juxtaposition of Upper Chalk and alluvial clay, with proximity to the river allowing easy transport of the coal fuel and export of the finished product. Coal is now brought in by rail and much of the cement is distributed by rail and road, but riverside sites are still occupied and some cement and cement clinker sent out by barge and ship. The extraction of chalk has migrated southwards from the original pits and clay is now brought from considerable distances. Although the concentration of the industry near the Thames and Medway is less marked than was the case 50 or 100 years ago, there has been continued growth and 20 per cent of the British output is from the four remaining works. The largest, indeed the largest in Europe, with a capacity of 4,000,000 tons a year, is at Northfleet (plate 16), and belongs to the Associated Portland Cement Manufacturers Ltd. The same company has a smaller works nearby at Swanscombe and another at Holborough in the Lower Medway Valley, where Rugby Portland Cement Co. Ltd., also have a works at Halling.

The manufacture of cement requires one part of clay to three parts of pure chalk. Where pure Upper Chalk is used, clay, often of

Plate 16
Northfleet Cement Works (A.P.C.M.) with six coal-fired kilns, slurry tanks (upper left) and ship loading for export.

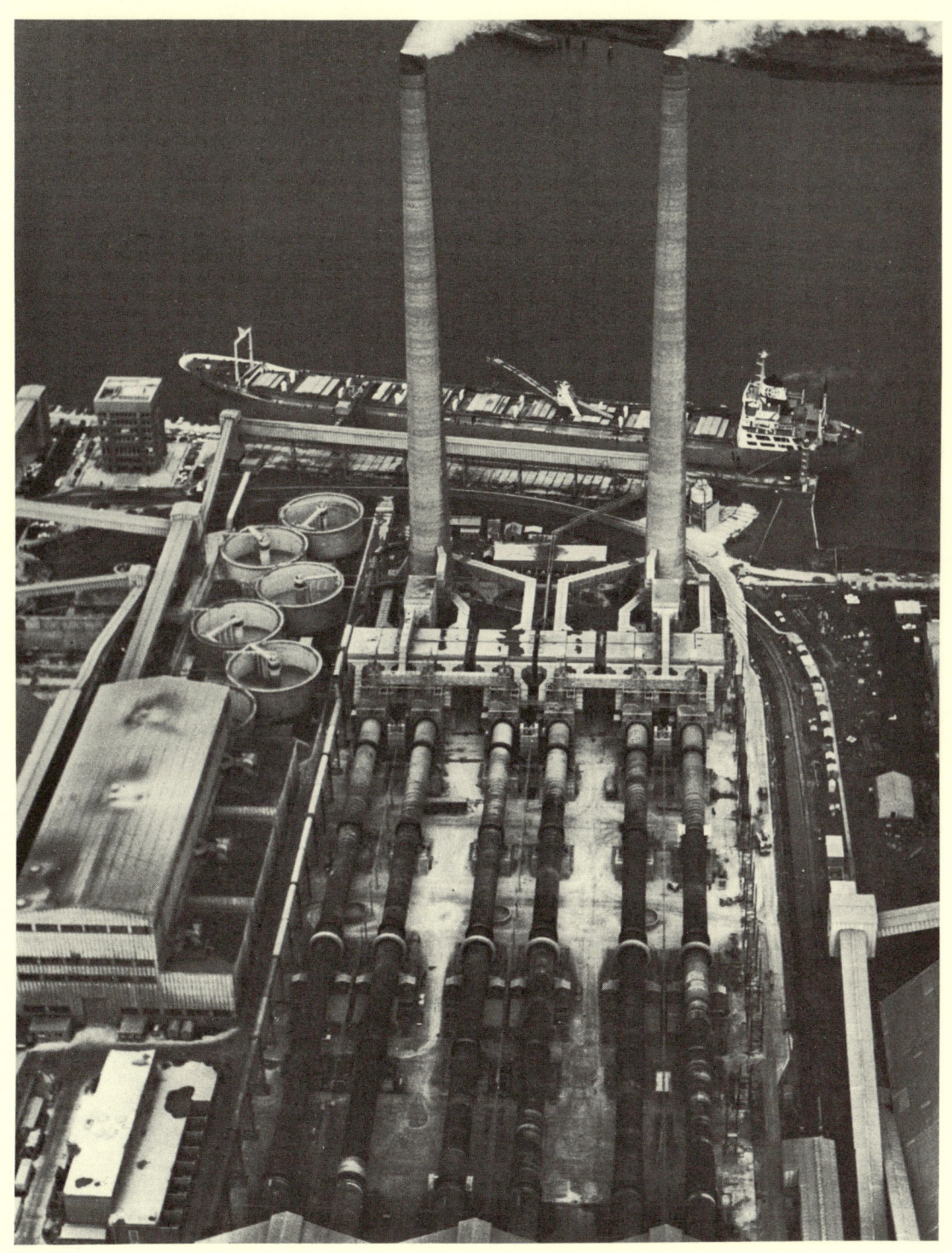

Plate 16

alluvial origin, has to be added to the mix. The very large system of flooded pits near Cliffe is a legacy of cement manufacture, together with the almost equally extensive abandoned chalk workings nearby. The clay pits give the appearance on maps of wholesale devastation, but the actual visual effect is much reduced by the low-lying nature of the ground. Shortage of local clay has been a problem for many of the cement works in North-west Kent, and clay is now brought to Northfleet from South Ockenden in Essex, piped across the Thames as a slurry. The works at Swanscombe sometimes uses Cornish china clay for the manufacture of special types of cement. The cement works in the Lower Medway valley require less clay because they utilize the more argillaceous lower horizons of the Chalk, and where the Lower Chalk itself is used no clay whatsoever has to be added. When clay is required it may be obtained by deepening the pit to reach the underlying Gault Clay or may be brought from clay pits on the Gault outcrop between Snodland and Wrotham.

The main legacy of cement manufacture, apart from the existing cement factories, is the abandoned chalk workings. These are often very deep, and isolate the roads and settlements which are perched on narrow causeways between the pits. Add to this the dust and smoke from the cement works and the tall chimneys of both the cement works and the paper works which now occupy some of the worked out chalk pits and the result is one of the least attractive parts of Kent. The main difficulty to be overcome in attempts to remove some of the worst scars of this industry is the two-tier topography which the chalk workings have produced, with deep pits separating habited areas perched high above them and preventing their expansion as villages. Both alternatives of infilling the pits to their former levels or abandoning townships such as Swanscombe to allow the removal of intervening spurs and give a uniform floor to the area seem equally unfeasible and the problem of how to cope with the pits remains.

Coal

The occurrence of Coal Measures beneath South-east England was predicted as early as 1856 but was not confirmed until 1890 when a borehole at the foot of the Shakespeare Cliff near Dover encountered Coal Measures at a depth of 353 m (1,158 ft) and a colliery was established. Thereafter four more collieries were opened at Tilmanstone, Betteshanger, Snowdown and Chislet, but today only the Tilmanstone, Betteshanger and Snowdown collieries still operate.

Fourteen coal seams have been encountered, but not all have been worked. The coal is excellent for coking and, in spite of difficulties in mining due to the parting and coalescing of seams, the remaining pits are economically viable.

Surface evidence of mining activities take the form of tip heaps, that at Betteshanger being the largest. The tip at the abandoned Chislet Colliery is now largely covered with natural volunteer vegetation, rendering it less unsightly, and encouraging optimism about the other tip heaps in the area. Coal tippings can be used as infilling and foundation material, for example, at the Hoverport and approach road at Pegwell Bay.

MANUFACTURING INDUSTRIES

As benefits a predominantly agricultural county Kent has industries servicing the needs of agriculture and also benefiting from the produce. There used to be many local manufacturers of farm implements but only a few today, an example being Stanhay's of Ashford, now of international repute for seed drills and harrows. The farmers' need for pesticides is met by the products from Plant Protection Ltd., of Yalding, while at the Shell Research Laboratories at Sittingbourne new weapons to overcome agricultural pests and diseases are being developed.

Processing and packing plants for the wide range of horticultural produce are widespread in Kent, with a major centre at Paddock Wood. If the Channel Tunnel had been built this was destined to become the major distribution centre for fruit and vegetables from Europe. Canning and food processing plants are found at Faversham, Maidstone and Ashford. At Ashford the odours from the dehydrated food factory on the eastern edge of the town mingle with the sweet scents of Proprietary Perfumes Ltd., who make a wide range of perfumes to be added, for example, to soaps and detergents. The characteristic smell of Maidstone, that of the Whitbread and Fremlin breweries, is now gone, for only a bottling plant remains, but brewing using local barley and hops still continues at Wateringbury and Faversham.

The two main industries in Kent are paper-making and engineering. There has been a long tradition of paper making in the county, favoured initially by a supply of clean water which also provided water-power. The linen rags formerly used were replaced first by imported esparto grass and later by Scandinavian and North American woodpulp. Thus the major paper mills grew up on navigable rivers. The main products are newsprint and board but a number of

Plate 17
William Balston (1759-1842), an associate of James Whatman, who founded, at Springfield Mill, Maidstone, W. &. R. Balston Ltd., manufacturers of high grade scientific and technical papers under the Whatman trademark.

(Whatman Ltd.)

mills produce more specialized material. Of world-wide renown are the 'Whatman' drawing, filter and chromatographic papers made by W. R. Balston at Maidstone (plate 17).

Engineering is now the major employer in Kent and the industry is found mainly in the large centres of population of North-west Kent and along the Thames Estuary to Gravesend and the Medway Towns. Most of the other large towns in Kent also have their own engineering companies. Ashford, for example, has British Rail Workshops making rolling stock, Stanhay's making agricultural machinery, and Houchin's producing aircraft ground handling equipment. Folkestone has the Martin Walter Dormobile Works, Sandwich generators and welding equipment, and at Maidstone, drying machines by Drake and Fletcher. In light engineering Kent has produced literally everything from A (adding machines by Facit at Rochester) to Z (zip fasteners by Optilon at Sevenoaks).

Heavy engineering is represented by the munitions factory of Vickers at Dartford and the AEI cable factory at Gravesend. The other end of the electrical spectrum is provided by a number of electronic companies at Dartford, Rochester and Maidstone and manufacturers of precision electrical measuring equipment at Dartford, Dover and Margate. Companies specializing in plastic and rubber products include Portex at Hythe (medical equipment), Haffenden Richborough at Sandwich, and Marley, founded at a hamlet of that name near Lenham and now making a wide variety of constructional materials, including the famous Marley tiles, there and at Riverhead near Sevenoaks. The real giant of the petrochemicals industry is, however, the BP Refinery at Grain on the end of the Hoo Peninsula, from an aesthetic viewpoint thankfully well away from

Plate 18
Dungeness. The pattern of shingle ridges (fulls) with intervening slacks forming the spit is clearly seen, together with Dungeness A Nuclear Power Station, then under construction.
(Aerofilms Ltd.)

the rest of Kent although its flames are easily visible from the M2 Motorway. The manufacture of chemicals and pharmaceuticals is concentrated mainly in North-west Kent, for example the Burroughs Wellcome Works at Dartford, but at the opposite end of the county Pfizer at Sandwich are also major pharmaceutical manufacturers.

All this industry needs power, and Kent has a number of large power stations including four conventional stations on the coast at Littlebrook (near the Dartford Tunnel), Northfleet, Kingsnorth (on the Hoo Peninsula) and Richborough with a further one under construction at Grain to use waste gases from the refinery. Pride of place, however, must go to the atomic reactor at Dungeness, to be joined at some indefinite time in the future by a second AGR station, still under construction. Thus one of the loneliest parts of Kent, has been taken over by the most advanced twentieth century technology (plate 18).

Buildings in the Landscape 6

'Wherever one goes in Kent,' writes John Newman, 'a view free from buildings can hardly be had.' Thus it would be quite unrealistic to describe the landscape of Kent without writing a substantial chapter on its buildings, a task made much easier by the inventories taken by Newman for the 'Buildings of England' volumes. Kent has indeed more buildings listed by the Department of the Environment as of special architectural or historic interest than any other county. The particular emphasis of this book leads to giving more space than usual to parks and gardens and to buildings connected with agriculture, such as windmills, watermills, barns and oasts.

BUILDING MATERIALS

Well mannered buildings can seem a natural outgrowth from the ground on which they stand. Until the railway era this was no mere figure of speech, for the heavy materials used in buildings were only carried long distances in exceptional circumstances. Indeed sometimes they were obtained literally on the site, as was the stone for Edward Hussey's house at Scotney Castle and the tiles for roofing Boxley Abbey. Many a timber-framed house in the Weald must have been built from oaks that grew nearby. Thus we find a happy adjustment to local conditions in older buildings.

Building stones are particularly distinctive. The fine sandstone of the Hastings Beds, often seen in and around Tunbridge Wells, can be squared and has often proved durable, as in the gatehouse of Tonbridge Castle. The Paludina limestones, locally called Bethersden Marble, are less durable but could be polished for interior work. Kentish ragstone from the Hythe Beds, on the other hand, can hardly be squared, but if softer selvages are rejected it is very hard. It is normally used in rubble work with dressings of brick or imported freestone. The foundations of the Roman villa at Little Chart were built of the ragstone on which it stood, and so were many

Fig. 63.
Shoreham church porch. *Much of the fine oak timber dates from the 15th century.*

of the more substantial Kentish buildings from before Tudor times. Situated on the outcrop, Maidstone and its environs were dominated by ragstone walls until recently, but the material travelled more widely as a favourite medium for Victorian churches. Chalk is not durable; Bicknor Church was almost ruined during nineteenth century restoration by the action of frost on walls of chalk blocks. Springs issuing from the chalk sometimes deposit tufa, a soft limestone but better than chalk as several Norman remnants show. The commonest durable stone of chalk country is flint, seen as unsplit nodules in some early churches such as Godmersham and Doddington and in the city walls at Canterbury. From the early fourteenth century the flints may be neatly split and laid in a banded pattern alternating with stone, as at Cliffe Church (plate 19), or brick, as at Dent de Lion near Margate. Such split flints are specially characteristic of Thanet.

While Kent is sparingly provided with building stone the reserves of brick and tile clays are inexhaustible. The colour of the product depends partly on the nature of the clay and partly on manufacturing technique. The North Kent brickearths may give the yellow London stock brick as well as red colours. Gault clay produces pale yellow

Plate 19
Decorated period (early fourteenth century) chancel of Cliffe church, built of alternate bands of knapped flints and ragstone blocks, right hand window has 'Kentish' tracery.

or pink bricks, while the Weald Clay gives a rich, glowing red. The Romans produced tiles in Kent, and by the fourteenth century the Old Naccolt tileyard near Wye was being operated by the Benedictines of Battle Abbey. Brickwork at Allington Castle may be late thirteenth century, and consequently among the earliest mediaeval bricks in Britain. The undercroft and chapel of Horne's Place, Appledore, was rebuilt incorporating some small yellow bricks after Wat Tyler had damaged it in 1381. By 1500 brick was the commonest material for walls, as tiles were already for roofs. Brick was used for the internal walls of the Bell Harry Tower (1496) of Canterbury Cathedral. During the seventeenth century brickwork became highly sophisticated, especially in East Kent.

Fig. 64.
Cast iron Fireback—The Old Hall, Wye College
The date is probably that when brick chimneys were added to the College buildings, hitherto of stone and wood. Similar firebacks occur widely in the Weald of Kent.

Kentish tiles have been so good for so long that thatched roofs are rarely seen, and even Victorian slate is less prevalent than elsewhere. Tile hanging on walls has always been a Kentish speciality, sometimes as a later clothing to the upper stories of timber framed houses (plate 28). Such tiles are usually slightly curved and overlap, giving a rippled texture to the wall, but others called 'mathematical tiles' were mortared together as a substitute for bricks when these were taxed (1784-1850).

The Kentish chalk affords plenty of lime for plasterwork, both inside and outside. External plaster decoration, called pargetting, was popular in the seventeenth century, especially in Maidstone (plate 27).

In the late mediaeval period windows became larger because of the greater availability of glass. Glass was made at Knole, for example, from 1585 for purposes including glazing the mansion (fig. 71).

The Wealden iron industry provided accessories such as railings for buildings and firebacks (fig. 64) from an early period. Indeed, the elaborately decorated door hinges of Staplehurst Church are believed to be twelfth century. The large scale structural use of iron dates from the nineteenth century, but came early to Kent in the case iron battlements and spire of Waterloo Tower (1819) in Quex Park, Birchington, and in the iron framed dockyard buildings (from 1852) at Chatham and Sheerness. Another pioneering use of a new material was Erith Oil Works (1913-17) in reinforced concrete.

Modern frame buildings have a very ancient history in the structural use of timber. There are thousands of small and medium sized timber framed houses in Kent. From the fourteenth to the seventeenth centuries, these were almost always built of local oak, usually with infillings of lath and plaster, but eighteenth and early nineteenth century timber cottages have frames of imported pitchpine (plate 21). Wooden shingles, also originally oak, were sometimes used especially on church spires (fig. 67 and 69).

CHURCHES

The most prominent rural buildings before the advent of obtrusive factories and farm silos and still the most attractive are the parish churches. Particular churches may give character to a whole district, like Aldington and Egerton, high on the Greensand ridge. Even the towers of some urban churches, such as Lydd, Ashford, Tenterden or Canterbury Cathedral itself, can be seen for miles across the surrounding countryside. Many attractive villages, such as Penshurst, Chiddingstone, Brenchley, Goudhurst, Chilham or Wye, are enhanced by their parish church. Others, such as the unique timber framed church at Fairfield on Romney Marsh, stand among fields remote from habitation.

The church is often the oldest building in the village. Indeed its history is often so long and complex that an elementary course in the history of architecture might be illustrated from a single building. A Norman original, rebuilt in the Early English period and later embellished with one or more Decorated windows and a Perpendicular tower, would sum up an oft-repeated pattern in the history of Kentish churches. This makes it difficult to write a simple account giving clear cut examples of each period.

A room with decorations appropriate to Christian worship is to be seen in the Roman villa at Lullingstone, while St. Martin's Church, Canterbury, probably originated in Roman times, being afterwards used by the Christian queen, Bertha, before St. Augustine came. The present seventh century chancel (fig. 87) incorporates much Roman material, as does the ruined church of St. Peter and St. Paul of about the same age which stands in the grounds of St. Augustine's Abbey nearby. Away from Canterbury considerable early Saxon work remains at Minster in Sheppey. Late Saxon churches can be seen at Lyminge, of about 960, and within Dover Castle where St. Mary in Castro (about 1000) is virtually complete, although much restored.

Norman work is abundant in Kent churches, except in the Weald. While the twelfth century south doorway at Barfreston commonly illustrates this period in guide books, it is church towers that most impress the wayfarer. The setting of Godmersham Church in the Stour gap north of Wye is a picture, with thick trees around and the Downs behind. Here the lower part of the flint church tower was

Fig. 65.
New Romney Church Tower.
Late Norman. The doorway on the right is below ground level from the silt deposited in the great flood of 1287.

probably built just before the Conquest, like the similar one at West Kingsdown. The much more bulky Norman tower of St. Mary's, Brook, illustrated in fig. 94, can be seen across the fields to the east of Wye. It is built of particularly large, unknapped flints, but otherwise has some resemblance to the nearly contemporary towers at Leeds, Lympne and Sturry. St. Clement's, Sandwich, has a much more sophisticated Norman tower embellished with blind, ornamental arcades, as is the elaborate west front of Rochester Cathedral. One of the most impressive towers in Kent (shown in fig. 65) is the late Norman one (about 1160) at New Romney which is enhanced by its splendid large clock. The most famous ecclesiastical building of this period is, of course, the Choir of Canterbury Cathedral (1175-1220), but this represents a development in height and in delicacy of shafts and carving beyond the Norman style. Humbler echoes of this 'Transitional' style in the rural scene are to be found at Selling, Stockbury and St. Nicholas at Wade.

Fig. 66.
Goodnestone Church Tower. *A typical Perpendicular west tower with a corner stair turret.*

The Choir of Rochester Cathedral, completed in 1227, ushered in the full Early English style. Woodchurch, Westwell and Stone are among the best village churches of this period, but the interiors are more impressive and homogeneous than the exteriors. The deeply buttressed chancel at Hythe, with its unusual processional way now stacked with skulls, better exemplifies the outward appearance of thirteenth century architecture. Monkton-in-Thanet has a typical tower of the period.

At the end of the thirteenth century St. Mary's, Chartham, introduced to Kent the Decorated style, still relatively plain but with larger windows, here using the so-called Kentish tracery with characteristic diverging cusps. Another innovation at this period was the use of squared black flints, well seen in the church towers at Herne and St.-Nicholas-at-Wade. Squaring the flints made possible interesting patterns of stripes of chequer work, by alternation with pale dressed stone, as seen at Higham, Cliffe (plate 19) and Strood. Whole churches of the Decorated style are rare in the county. Southfleet is one, and so for the most part is Meopham.

The glorious nave of Canterbury Cathedral was begun as a renovation of the Norman structure in 1378 and completed in the Perpendicular style in 1410. The best complete parish church of this style in Kent is the oft-photographed All Saints, Maidstone. The cloth industry brought people to the Weald at this time and prosperity enough to pay for the building of fine Perpendicular churches at Cranbrook and Headcorn.

Perpendicular towers, often attached to earlier buildings (fig. 66), are a ubiquitous feature of the Kentish scene and about 90 of them exist. The south-west and central (Bell Harry) towers (fig. 68) of Canterbury are not typical, although there are other crossing towers at Ashford, Ash-next-Canterbury and Folkestone. Almost all the rest are at the west end of their churches and have staircase turrets at one corner and two projecting buttresses supporting each of the remaining three. The massive tower of St. James's, Egerton is one of the most prominent, and is built of the ragstone on which it is founded. Chilham has another typical but good example. The noble tower at All Saints, Lydd, 40 m high, and that of St. Mildred's, Tenterden (fig. 93), with its four big pinnacles, are very much out of the ordinary.

Equally noteworthy are several of the mediaeval spires, which are of timber covered with wooden shingles. Examples are at Upchurch and Bexley (fig. 69). That at Willesborough was rebuilt in 1865 retaining the odd indented shape. The detached wooden belfry (fig. 67) at Brookland is unique. Originating in the eleventh and twelfth centuries as an open rectangular framework for a single alarm bell to warn of floods and invasions, it was reconstructed about 1450 as a

Fig. 67.
Brookland Belfry.

Fig. 68.
Canterbury Cathedral.
As it was about 50 years ago. To the right of the central (Bell Harry) tower is the 12th Century choir, to the left the late 15th Century nave ending in the SW Tower. The NW Tower (behind) is 19th Century.

weatherboarded building with a frame supporting several bells. The few seventeenth century churches in Kent are Gothic. Eighteenth century churches are mainly urban and the best are classical like St. Lawrence, Mereworth with its steeple copied from that of St. Martin in the Fields. There are several plain but elegant Georgian chapels, for example at Tenterden and Maidstone (Unitarian), Sandwich (United Reformed) and Canterbury (Methodist).

The Gothic revival came early to Kent. A crown-like spire of 1799 dominates the town of Faversham, while a whole village church was built at Lower Hardres in 1832 using the Early English style. Soon after, Augustus Pugin made Gothic churches fashionable, with St. Augustine's Roman Catholic Church at Ramsgate, as his *pièce de résistance*. The prosperity of organized Christianity in the nineteenth century has left so many church buildings that the slimmer resources of today are embarrassed. Another unfortunate result is that modern churches are few. Their emphasis, as at St. Matthew, Wigmore (1965), is on light and nearness of the congregation to the action. Repair and restoration of the churches of the past is a continuing problem. Fortunately, the imprecations of William Morris and the Society for the Protection of Ancient Buildings, which he founded to combat both the excessive 'scraping' of mediaeval buildings and their demolition, have led to a more careful approach to restoration.

Fig. 69.
Bexley Church Spire. *Wooden frame, shingled. John Wesley preached in this church in 1749.*

HOUSES

While nearly all churches and many castles are open sometimes to the public, small houses hardly ever are, and only a small proportion of larger ones. It seemed best in this account to give greater prominence to accessible houses, and to indicate (A) those that are regularly open and (B) those that open occasionally or can probably be seen by arrangement, (C) inaccessible houses and (G) those with grounds open occasionally.

Roman Villas

The sites of about 40 country houses of the Roman period are shown on fig. 7. Although some are larger (e.g. Eccles), none are finer or more accessible than that of Lullingstone (A), now under the care of the Department of the Environment.

Its flint and mortar walls are still over two metres high in places. Other parts of the buildings were made of timber, and pantiled roofs covered them all, while hypocausts for heating and tessellated floors testify to a comfortable interior. An instructive reconstruction of the original appearance of the villa appears in the guidebook. Painted plaster walls with Christian motives occur at Lullingstone, and more elaborate decoration still in the so-called Painted House at Dover.

Mediaeval Stone Houses

Saxon houses were wooden; the charred framework of one of the eighth century has recently been found at Dover. Many early mediaeval stone domestic buildings are associated with castles or with religious houses, but even in the unfortified manor house life was essentially communal and revolved round the hall. In some early examples the hall is on the first floor, somewhat more secure from enemies, vermin and damp. The remains of a house consisting of a first-floor hall (or solar) and kitchen of the early twelfth century can be seen inside Eynsford Castle (A). More complete is the hall of Eastbridge Hospital (A), in St. Peter's Street, Canterbury. It was built about 1180 by one Edward, son of Odbold, presumably to house the very earliest Canterbury pilgrims. The hall is of stone with a vaulted roof, and is at first floor level with an undercroft beneath. The Department of the Environment has rescued a rather similar stone first floor hall of the early thirteenth century at Temple Manor (A), Strood, and also own the remains of a small country house of about 1290 in Old Soar (A), Plaxtol. Here the hall, which has largely been replaced by an eighteenth century house, was at ground level. A private living room (solar) survives and a chapel, both at first floor level.

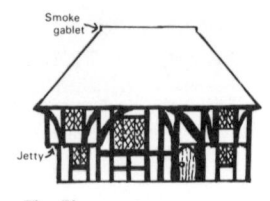

Fig. 70
Typical Wealden House.
Showing 'Kentish framing', timbers relatively few, large and well braced.

Most of the houses of this period were entirely of wood. An idea of their construction can be gained from Nurstead Court (B, about 1320), near Meopham, which has walls of knapped flints only 3½ m high, from which rises a steeply pitched roof, supported by aisles and crown posts (fig. 79). It is very similar to contemporary barns except that the ends were two storied, showing it is a precursor of the 'Wealden house'.

The hall at Nurstead has been partly demolished and partly split into rooms, but the much grander hall of Penshurst Place (A), is preserved in all its glory. It was built by Sir John de Pulteney, a wealthy London merchant, about 1341. The hall is 12 m wide and is spanned by a fine crown post roof. A stone staircase enabled Sir John and his wife to retire to a first floor solar. His servants slept in the hall around a central hearth. There was no chimney, and the hole in the roof has since been blocked.

Of the same period is the hall of Ightham Mote (A), which fortunately is not only entire, but has also remained a living room. Here a fireplace was added, with the date 1583 on the iron fireback, and later an overmantel and panelling by the eminent Victorian designer, Norman Shaw. Ightham Mote is a gem, still in an almost mediaeval setting with woods around and water filling the moat.

Timber Framed Houses 1300-1650

Kent contains literally thousands of old timber-framed houses, their oak beams in many cases obscured by cladding (often tiles) or by later additions. Only in the last few years has this heritage been studied, notably by Kenneth Gravett and Stuart Rigold, and new discoveries are continually being made. The houses described in this category are of medium size, built by yeoman farmers, or other citizens of moderate means.

Fourteenth and fifteenth century timbered houses originally had halls open to the roof, with two storied sections at one or both ends. Usually, but not always, Kentish examples are covered by a single hipped roof (fig. 70), of generous size. The first floor rooms and their supporting joists generally project a little way towards the front and sometimes to the side also. This overhang is called a jetty. At the so-called 'low' end of the hall were rooms for the storage of food and drink (buttery and milk-house) over which was an upper chamber, which might be used as a store or as a bedroom (fig. 71). At this period normal chimneys were not general and cooking fires, being dangerous, were relegated to a separate outhouse. For heating there would have been a central hearth in the hall, at the 'low' end of which were doors on opposite sides of the house. Grander halls had screens to check draughts, hence 'screens passage'. Some early hall houses had only one two storied end, but usually there was another at the 'high table' end of the hall, giving a parlour below and

Fig. 71.
Plan of typical Wealden House.

Fig. 72.
Priest's House, Small Hythe. *Showing 'close studding', timbers relatively numerous, narrow and parallel.*

bedroom above. When both ends are jettied, the hall appears recessed and this form has been called the 'Wealden House'. There are hundreds in Kent and Sussex, most especially around Maidstone, so that the term 'Wealden house' is perhaps somewhat misleading. Examples easily visible externally are on the A20 at Larkfield and on the A229 at Sandling (plate 20). These earlier houses have thick, widely spaced timbers, often with the curved braces (fig. 70), characteristic of 'Kentish framing'. Their roofs usually show a 'smoke gablet', now filled.

Big changes took place around 1500. Brick became a common material, so chimneys could replace a bare roof opening in wooden houses, and it was safe to have the kitchen in the main building rather than in an outhouse. Moreover halls open to the roof now seemed cheerless, and in smaller houses were invariably divided at first floor level to give more rooms of cosier dimensions. This happened at Eyhorne Manor (A), Hollingbourne, built in the early fifteenth century, where the visitor may see the history of alterations and additions illustrated by models. A narrow section of the original hall has been walled off as a 'smoke bay' in which hams could be hung. Conversely when Stoneacre (B) at Otham was restored and extended in 1921 the hall was reopened to its crown post roof. Pattyndene Manor (B), Goudhurst is of transitional style, a 'Wealden' hallhouse but with the narrow closely spaced timbers typical of the sixteenth century. In fact it was built about 1470, and was later owned by King Henry VIII's standard bearer.

In contrast to the three just mentioned which are now comfortable modern homes, Bayleaf, the Wealden house from Bough Beech now rebuilt at the Wealden and Downland Museum, near Chichester, has been restored to its original state (about 1450), complete with wattle and mud infilling.

Just as existing homes were modified after 1500, so new timber framed houses no longer had halls and the overhanging first-floor 'jetty' now extended right along the front. Examples are Smallhythe Place (A), Ellen Terry's house near Tenterden, and the adjoining Priest's house (fig. 72). In such houses 'Kentish framing' is replaced by 'close studding', the first dated example in Kent being in the hall of Wye College (B, about 1447). Roofs became lighter, using trusses with two vertical 'queen posts' (fig. 80). Large brick chimneys are a prominent feature. At this period the wool industry brought prosperity and new houses to the Wealden townships such as Headcorn, Smarden, Biddenden and Goudhurst. Standen (C), Weavers Court (C) and Castweazel Manor (C) represent the period around Biddenden.

In towns timber framed houses were often built on narrow plots end on to the road, showing a gable. There are a number in Canterbury and one in Charing, where there is also a splendid sixteenth century butcher's shop. Another urban form is three storied and jettied twice. Examples can be seen in Canterbury, Sandwich, Tonbridge, and at Faversham, where the pride of the imaginatively restored Abbey Street is Arden House (C), built about 1540 for Thomas Arden, who was later murdered there.

By 1600 timbered houses were becoming much more sophisticated. Shaped chimneys and bay windows came in, as for example at Yew Trees (C), Wye, of about 1605. About the same time gabled fronts became common, three symmetrical gables as at the Old Vicarage (B), also at Wye, or just two as at Honywood (C), of 1621, at Lenham. Frognal (C), at Teynham has as many as four gables in a row, and is dated 1668. Urban examples are common, especially in Canterbury (e.g. St. Dunstan's Street).

Large Houses from 1450

Penshurst Place (1341) had substantial walls around it, but a century

Plate 20
Wealden house at Sandling, near Maidstone. Probably fifteenth century, but with later windows, chimneys and side and rear extensions.

later the battlements of Knole were little more than decoration. So emerges the era of the large unfortified mansion. Houses of great size are built for display as well as use, and it is a reflection of changing values that the rich were building mansions rather than churches or religious establishments such as monasteries or hospitals. The most magnificent were usually built by national or metropolitan magnates rather than local landlords, and represent wealth brought into the county from outside.

House plans change completely as needs for comfort and privacy were met by abandoning the Great Hall in favour of numbers of smaller rooms, each with a separate fireplace, and entailing wings or courtyard arrangements. If the house becomes an expression of the owner's wealth or good taste, style and indeed fashion become important. The increasing sophistication of society is shown by these fashions being cosmopolitan and, from about 1600, presided over by architects. These stylistic characters distinguish large houses from the smaller ones erected by local builders which constitute so-called 'vernacular architecture'.

Large houses of the fifteenth century are represented by Archbishop Bourchier's ragstone palace at Knole (A), built in the 1460s, but incorporating some pre-existing buildings. With its seven courtyards, Knole is a far cry from the simple hall house, although it still retains a great hall with a musicians' gallery. The King's Palace at Eltham (B), must have been even more magnificent, but not much survives apart from the fine hammer-beamed hall of 1479. The oldest surviving Kentish mansion built of brick is Wickham Court (B), about 1470 near Bromley, now part of the buildings of Coloma College.

Elizabethan houses may also be of stone or brick. Boughton Monchelsea Place (A), standing on the Ragstone Ridge, is appropriately built of stone. Dating from about 1570, it has the

Fig. 73.
Knole
A magnificent ragstone palace built at Sevenoaks in the 1460's by Archbishop Bouchier, remodelled by Thomas Sackville, about 1605.

characteristic mullioned and transomed windows, but also battlements added in 1819. The older part of Cobham Hall (A) is a splendid Elizabethan building (1580-1602) in rose red brick, its wings ending in characteristic turrets. Penshurst Place (A) also has an Elizabethan portion (1575) in red brick, with a characteristic amenity of the period—a long gallery, found also at Cobham and Knole.

The red brick Jacobean house at Chilham (G) built in 1616 has an ingenious plan occupying five sides of a hexagon. Its brickwork, however, is plain compared with Broome Park (C), near Barham, built in 1638 with many tall chimneys and shaped pedimented gables (fig. 74), giving a very Dutch appearance. Shaped gables were added to Knole (figs. 73 and 74) at Thomas Sackville's rebuilding about 1605, and are a paramount feature of Godinton (A, 1628) near Ashford.

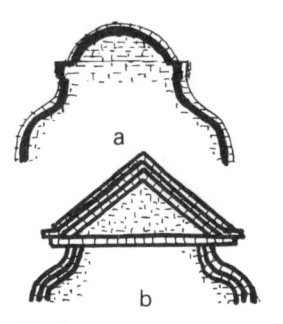

Fig. 74.
Gables
(a) *shaped gable added to Knole about 1605.*
(b) *'Dutch' gable from Broome Park, Barham, 1638.*

A mid-seventeenth century feature was to incorporate pilasters into the brickwork of the facade. A very famous example is Lees Court (C), south of Faversham, another is Restoration House (B), at Rochester, where Charles II stayed on the night before his formal restoration. At this time, however, Inigo Jones had already initiated the style with rectangular elevations and windows we now call Georgian. St. Clere (C), Kemsing, is a very early example from about 1630, and so is Chevening Park (C) now made available to Prince Charles, following an admirable restoration.

The typical 'William and Mary' house with a plain rectangular shape in brick, enlivened by an elaborate central door-case or porch and surmounted by a cornice and a hipped roof with attic dormers also begins earlier than its name implies. Hall Place (A) Bexley, of about 1650, Eltham Lodge (C, 1662) and Owletts (A), Cobham, of 1684, are examples. Squerries Court (A), Westerham, and Bradbourne (B), part of East Malling Research Station, are larger and have a pediment. The brickwork of Bradbourne is especially fine.

The classical revival comes abruptly in Mereworth Castle (G), a straight copy (1723) of a villa by the Italian architect, Palladio. It is square, with four porticoes of Ionic pillars and a large dome. With Coombe Bank (C, about 1730), at Sundridge, the style had become more domesticated, while at Godmersham Park (G, 1732) the exterior is comparatively plain. The interior is rich, a feature of somewhat later houses associated with Robert Adam such as Mersham-le-Hatch (B, 1762) and Brasted Place (B, 1785). Externally Mersham is plain, but Brasted Place has a pillared and pedimented portico in the Palladian fashion. There are many good smaller Georgian houses, such as Barming Place (B, 1768) and Howletts (G, 1790) at Bekesbourne.

Later houses revive a variety of earlier styles. The tower of Hadlow Castle (C, 1840) is 52 m high and appears magnificently Gothic (fig. 75) until one learns of the brick beneath the rendering. The Reptons did not need to cover the excellent brickwork of their additions to Cobham Hall (A, 1812-18). The use of a Tudor style was appropriate and successful here, but uninspired imitation could become dreary as at Preston Hall (C) a massive stone Jacobean pile of 1850, seen from the M20 near Aylesford. One Victorian architect supremely mastered the craft of building mansions in the Tudor style and worked for much of his life in Kent. George Devey began by making extensions to Penshurst Place (A), continuing with Betteshanger House (C, 1861), St. Alban's Court, Nonington (B, 1864), now a College of Education, and largest of all, Hall Place, Leigh (G and see Chapter 8).

Red House, Bexley (C), built by Philip Webb, for William Morris in 1859-60, is a relatively small, asymmetrical house, with its outward shape largely determined by the rooms within. Tudor and Georgian features can be discerned, but in its freedom Red House is a new beginning, to be followed by many middle class houses over the next 60 years. Large houses virtually died with the first World War; Great Maytham (A, 1909) at Rolvenden, neo-Georgian by Lutyens, is one of the last.

Fig. 75.
Hadlow Castle Tower
Built by George Taylor for Walter May about 1838-1840. Much of the house itself has been demolished but the 52 m high tower is a prominent landmark.

Small Houses

Saxon huts and early mediaeval cottages no longer survive, although reconstructions can be seen at the Wealden and Downland Museum near Chichester. The oldest original building there is a small house from Bough Beech, Kent, called Winkhurst, which is probably late fourteenth century. Although tiny, it is a miniature hall house. The hall occupies the entire ground floor, but extends to the rafters for only half the length of the house. The other 'bay' has a bedroom on the upper floor. Other houses of a similar sort, for example, Frogholt at Newington near Folkestone which is early fourteenth century and thatched, and Southdown Cottage, Nonington where the central open hall is less than 4 m square, are complicated by later additions. Single storey mediaeval timbered houses must also have existed. The Priests House (perhaps about 1500), adjoining the churchyard gate at Great Chart, is one of the earliest survivors.

An early sixteenth century cottage often had only two rooms, a hall and a parlour cum bedroom, although garrets might be used for extra bedrooms or storage. A central chimney gave fireplaces in both rooms, that in the hall adapted for cooking with hooks and perhaps an oven. From about 1570 separate kitchens became usual, sometimes in an extension at the rear called a cove or outshot covered by a continuation of the main roof known as a 'cat slide'. An early seventeenth century innovation is a separate wash house. Many early seventeenth century cottages have two stories, with two rooms on each, served by a central chimney with four flues.

During the seventeenth century the older type of timber framing was gradually superseded, even for small houses. In North and East Kent the new material was brick, or, occasionally, flint with brick dressings. The houses are plain, but in East Kent 'Dutch' gables are not uncommon, especially in the seventeenth century. In the Weald and Romney Marsh wooden framed houses (plate 21) continued from the seventeenth right up to the early nineteenth century, but the frame was wholly concealed and usually of pine. Soft wood weather boarding painted white (not tarred as in Essex) or else tile hanging covered the frame. Occasionally, particularly in the

Plate 21
White, weatherboarded cottage with (to right) *village sign showing the Biddenden Maids (Siamese twins who lived 1500-34).*

Tenterden area, stonework was simulated in wood (plate 28).

With the late eighteenth century towns grew rapidly. Speculative builders built whole streets of terraced houses for poorer people, while somewhat more well-to-do-houses were also rather stereotyped, being often taken from standard pattern books. Throughout the nineteenth century slate imported from North Wales was a common roofing material, although tiles were never wholly superseded and bricks continued to be local: pale yellow 'London stocks' along the North Coast, and red in the Weald. Quite humble houses were built of ragstone in early nineteenth century Maidstone, and only in the twentieth did pink 'Fletton' bricks from Bedfordshire and Northamptonshire become universal. In the rural scene the nineteenth century was the age when numerous cottages, sometimes almost whole villages (Chapter 7), were built by great landlords often in a characteristic style, the Derings with 'lucky' curled windows (fig. 76), the Tokes with Dutch gables.

Fig. 76.
Dering 'Lucky' Window. *From the Swan Inn, Little Chart, near Surrenden Dering, burnt down in 1952 but once the seat of the Dering family. It is said that a Dering escaped from the Roundheads through such a window. The design was used everywhere on the estate.*

Modern houses too are usually designed *en masse*, and one must judge an estate or development as a whole. An early example is New Town, built next to their railway works in Ashford by the South Eastern Railway Company from about 1850, with cottages, in blocks of six with shaped gables as well as plain terraces, and surrounding a sort of village green. New Town was an unusual environment for Victorian workmen. It still looks half its real age, especially now it is being refurbished. A planned mining village like Aylesham (1926-7) is a lineal descendant. Even in the more remote country areas groups of modern farm cottages or of council houses are a ubiquitous feature: not all are obnoxious, and some continue local traditions of weather boarding and tile hanging. The proliferation of housing estates on the London fringe, around railway stations and along the coast has swamped other landscape features over areas which are very extensive even if rather more confined than elsewhere in the Home Counties. Certain large developers have put a distinctive stamp on particular areas, as with New Ideal Homesteads in north Sidcup and between Hayes and West Wickham, and the London County Council around St. Paul's Cray. Viewed from Shooters Hill the London boroughs of Greenwich, Bexley and Bromley retain a pleasing number of trees. In Chislehurst, Petts Wood, Orpington and around Sevenoaks the retention of mature trees and winding lanes gives a more attractive type of suburbia than the more regimented rows of houses characteristic of Bexleyheath and Welling.

Some modern estates are expansions of villages. Wye shows three good examples. The East Ashford R.D.C. created a large new village green, overlooked by the Parish Church, and grouped attractive brick houses around it. Later bungalows for old people in Little Chequers also border a square green, and adjoin an attractive new residential home for the elderly. Nearby Chequers Park (fig. 77) a private development (1961-68), has attempted by communal landscaping in front of the houses and a single joint television aerial to escape some of the visual impact of individualism. ·

New Ash Green, initiated by Span and Eric Lyons and Partners, takes communal landscaping even further, perhaps too far. However, the groups of short two story terraces are not unattractive and by minimizing use of land will enable the retention of many trees and thus make the smallest possible demand visually as well as territorially on the surrounding attractive countryside.

Fig. 77.
House in Chequers Park, Wye.
The appearance of the estate echoes local building traditions, including tile hanging and cladding with white painted wooden boards.

PARKS AND GARDENS

Kent has been richly endowed with gardens from Norman times onwards, an endowment made more diverse by the great variety of soil types which may be found even within relatively small areas.

No doubt Roman villas had gardens, but the earliest garden remains surviving in Kent belonged to monasteries. Half of the infirmary cloister immediately north of Canterbury Cathedral is shown as a herbarium on a plan of about 1165, and beyond the walls were orchards, a vineyard and a garden with a large mulberry tree under which the murderers of Becket threw off their cloaks. The modern garden at Boxley Abbey is a successor to that in which the monks 'pleasured much in odoriferous savours, since they had converted corn and grain rents of the monastery into gilliflowers and roses', according to Henry VIII's Commissioners. Fishponds, of which remains survive at the Friars, Aylesford, were a common feature.

Kings and great nobles fenced in deer parks from Norman times onwards. Middle Park near Eltham is a reminder of one walled round in 1315. Knole Park, Sevenoaks, which still has deer in it, was enclosed by Archbishop Bourchier in 1456 and was 373 ha in extent.

In Tudor times the gardens of large houses were usually walled. At Knole the garden wall is of ragstone; the gardens here were laid out for Henry VIII in 1543. Remains of other Elizabethan gardens are to be found at Northbourne Court, near Deal and Roydon Hall, East Peckham.

A good example of an eighteenth century garden can be seen at Chilham Castle where terraces with a bowling green and clipped yews were laid out in 1631. The surrounding park belongs to the next period when the aim was to create artificially an idealized landscape of natural appearance, often with a lake. Launcelot ('Capability') Brown (1716-83), the most famous landscape designer of this period, was at Chilham in 1777 and, while designing stabling, lodges and greenhouses, was probably also responsible for impounding the lake and planting trees, although subsequent planting has blurred the clarity of his scheme. Danson Park near Bexley Heath, also with a lake, is another example of his work (about 1761), but has become, as a public park, rather threadbare. Leeds Castle grounds, probably laid out by Brown, are almost perfectly preserved, and early nineteenth century building has completed an incomparable 'Gothic' landscape.

Fig. 78. Garden of Chilham Castle. *Laid out in 1631. Brick steps with giant balls, an urn and a sundial.*

A feature of this period was the construction of buildings and other architectural park ornaments for the sake of their appearance. An early example in Kent is the Palladian style belvedere at Waldershare (1725-7). There are two small classical temples of the eighteenth century at Godmersham (fig. 17), in which Jane Austen doubtless sat. At Chiddingstone a massive urn (1780) stands beside the tree-lined lake, while at Knole there is a Gothic folly called the Birdhouse, built in 1761, with some mock ruins attached. The park of Mereworth Castle even houses an eighteenth century triumphal arch.

Humphry Repton (1752-1818) can be regarded as Capability Brown's successor. He laid out the grounds of Holwood House, Keston, for William Pitt the younger. One of his most ambitious schemes was at Sundridge Park, near Bromley, where the grounds are now a golf course. He lowered a hillside 10 m to achieve a felicitous placing for the house. Repton recorded his plans in so called Red Books, making one for Cobham Hall in 1790, where he went on working until his death. Cobham Park contains magnificent trees, especially chestnuts and ashes, and is embellished by a fine mausoleum now itself buried in a wood. The latest example of the deliberate creation of a romantic landscape was at Scotney (1837), but here the ruins of castle and mansion are real, with the new house skilfully fitted in. During the late seventeenth and eighteenth centuries orangeries were very popular and a fine example exists at Belmont dated 1790. In 1777 hothouses were built at Knole to grow pineapples.

Victorian tastes were much more varied than Georgian. George Devey (1820-86) was essentially an architect, but from 1850-60 worked at Penshurst Place, not only building a lodge, a gateway and cottages in the Tudor style but recreating the formal gardens shown on Kip's engraving of Penshurst dated 1720. Other enthusiasms of the Victorian era included rock gardens, shrubberies, wild gardens and collections of specimen trees, for example Sandling Park, near Hythe. Italian style gardens were also popular, complete with statues, pillars and urns. At Hever Castle, W. W. Astor created a garden, regardless of cost, around 1905. It is said 2,000 men were employed. There are really three gardens: an informal English garden around the castle, with water lilies in the moat, clipped yews, daffodils and herbaceous plants, and also a wooded garden. The formal Italian garden is one of the most elaborate of twentieth century gardens with abundant genuine classical statuary, sarcophagi and pillars, together with topiary and fountains.

Fig. 79. Construction of a barn at Brook. *Early roof timbering using a single large vertical crown post.*

Many twentieth century gardens in Kent take up one of the three themes, exemplified at Hever. Sissinghurst Castle gardens created by Victoria Sackville-West and her husband, Sir Harold Nicholson, are a catena of traditional English gardens, the Cottage Garden, a Spring Garden, a Rose Garden, a Herb Garden, a White Garden and a Purple Border. Sandling Park is a magnificent woodland garden with magnolias, primulas, azaleas and especially rhododendrons. Godinton, near Ashford, has gardens remodelled by Sir Reginald Blomfield about 1902 in the formal manner. Bedgebury Pinetum was begun in 1924 so that the national collection of conifers could escape the sooty atmosphere of Kew. The gardens of Crittenden House, Matfield, created since 1955 by Mr. B. P. Thompsett, are specially designed to minimize the heavy cost of upkeep so characteristic of earlier gardens, but also to be suitable for illuminations at night. The same criteria have often guided the planning of public gardens, especially in seaside places, examples being the clifftop gardens at Broadstairs and Folkestone.

FARM BUILDINGS

Agriculture in Kent was prosperous from early times, and this has resulted in a rich heritage of buildings, now being rapidly depleted, partly because they are inappropriate to modern agriculture, partly through urban extension and partly as a result of fires, often started by vandals.

The most substantial building in a mediaeval farmstead in arable areas such as North and East Kent, was the barn. Threshing by flail was a time consuming task, a man would take more than a week to thresh a ton of wheat, and it required a large dry floor space and through draughts for winnowing let in through passage bays with big

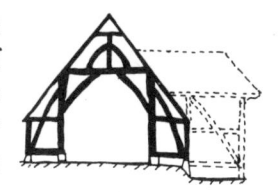

Fig. 80. Construction of barn at Teynham. *Later roof timbering using a pair of vertical queen posts.*

doors on both sides. Kent barns are nearly always of timber, the stone ones at St. Radegund's Abbey, near Dover, Westenhanger and Boxley are exceptional. Generally they are 'aisled', before about 1500 with 'crown post' roofs (fig. 79) from about 1500 to about 1650 with 'queen post' roofs (fig. 80) and after 1650 with angled struts. The earliest surviving examples (about 1300) are at Frindsbury Manor and Littlebourne Court, but the best opportunity of examining one, probably of about 1375, is at the Wye College Agricultural Museum at Court Lodge, Brook (plate 29). The big waggon porches were added about 1500. Barns were often in pairs, one for wheat, one for oats and barley, as at Faversham Abbey and Willesborough Court. It is good to note that occasionally new uses are being found for these splendid buildings, for example a hall at Charing and a garden centre at Bybrook, near Ashford.

Other mediaeval farm buildings have seldom survived, but dovecotes are an exception. These were a perquisite of the Lord of the Manor, providing him with fresh meat in winter at the expense of his tenant's crops. Surviving dovecotes are of stone or brick with niches for up to 600 birds, as, for example, at Leeds Castle. During the eighteenth century the prevailing material for new farm buildings gradually became brick rather than timber, especially in the more prosperous east and north and on the estates of improving landlords, where favoured steadings including the 'home farm' were often rebuilt as a courtyard of red brick buildings including barns, stables, cowhouses, piggeries, a cart lodge and sometimes oast houses. In 1786 a threshing machine of modern type was invented, used in the barn and powered by men or animals at first, but from the 1820s sometimes by a stationary steam-engine still occasionally evidenced by a disused chimney. By the mid nineteenth century portable steam engines and 'threshing boxes' were general, and barns lost their function. They have often survived, as general purpose stores or converted to other uses.

From 1870 agriculture declined, and existing buildings were increasingly patched with corrugated iron, unpainted as it was cheaper to let it rust away. New buildings were few, but Dutch barns became common and most have been prefabricated since 1880, at first in steel and corrugated iron. From about 1930 the general use of asbestos cement sheets began, pioneered in Kent by the 'Uralite' works near Higham. More recently 'Atcost' of Paddock Wood made modular buildings with steel or reinforced concrete frames popular. Since 1945 buildings for intensive pig and poultry production have become common, and combine harvesting has necessitated grain driers. Silage has partly replaced hay. The first tower silo in England was built on Wye College Farm in 1901, but modern ones generally date from after 1960.

OASTS

Oast houses are a characteristic feature of the Kentish landscape, their abundance reflecting the need to dry hops from a former multitude of small gardens.

The earliest description of an oast house in 1574, is of a small oblong building, about 6 by 3 m, with a brick kiln fuelled by charcoal under a slatted floor in the middle, and space on one side to load and on the other to cool the hops. A good draught is important, and a traditional white painted wooden cowl was often added later. Early rectangular oasts (seventeenth and early eighteenth centuries) exist at Woodchurch and in Charing Palace and a variant with two kilns at Bough Beech (plate 22).

The conventional kiln with a sloping roof surmounted by a cowl was introduced in the late eighteenth century. At first they were square and rather small (about 3.7 m wide). A separate oblong forebuilding (stowage) was provided for loading and cooling, and

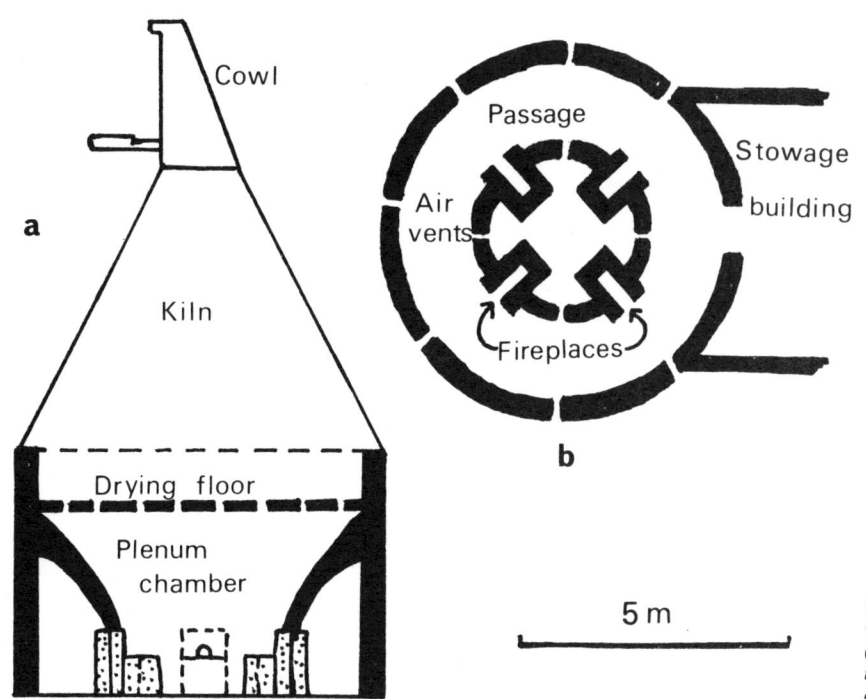

Fig. 81
Oast House
(a) section and (b) plan of a typical 19th century round oast house (Brook).

often served a group of kilns. An attractive set of six occurs at Swarling Farm, Petham (about 1780) and the type is also seen at Sissinghurst Castle. Where coal was used as a fuel an enclosed 'cockle' stove was preferred, with an external chimney. Later it was found that anthracite could be burned in open fireplaces.

The round oast house began to appear after 1800 under the misapprehension that the heat was more evenly distributed. They were bigger (5–6.2 m in diameter) and often had multiple fireplaces. An example, of 1815, can be examined at the Agricultural Museum of Wye College at Court Lodge, Brook. A section is shown in fig. 81. This was called a 'hopper' kiln, and the inverted cone really did distribute the draught more evenly. Most round kilns were built between 1850 and 1900. This was the era when the area under hops was at its peak, more than four times its present extent. Thus large groups of kilns were often needed, such as those at Sheerland, Pluckley, where the black horses of the Dering family embellish the vanes of the cowls.

From about 1900 it was realized that square kilns were fully satisfactory; they were widely built to larger dimensions (6 m rather than 3.7 m) than the eighteenth century square kilns, and are sometimes slated whereas earlier oasts were always tiled. Fans

Plate 23
Similar round oast with cowl replaced by fan ventilation. Hop pockets are being loaded into a pair of early twentieth century square oasts. Spring Grove, Wye.

Plate 24
New style Oast House, East Peckham.

Plate 22
At Somerden, Bough Beech, an early eighteenth century rectangular oast with two cowls is joined by a common stowage to a nineteenth century round oast.

Plate 23.

Plate 24.

began to be introduced, and became general by 1930. Some oast houses were converted, while newer buildings had louvered openings instead of cowls (plate 23).

Oil fuel was first used in 1933. Modern oasts are unromantic barn-like structures once again (plate 24), so that their general appearance has come full circle. The traditional structures are redundant, but conversion into distinctive homes has been encouraged by planning policy.

WINDMILLS

Wind and water mills were formerly the commonest industrial buildings of the countryside. Over 400 windmills have existed in Kent and about the same number of water mills. Windmills are more prominent in the landscape, but this makes them all the more vulnerable to the forces of nature. 226 were shown on early nineteenth century maps, and about 100 still turned in 1900. Now only 15 still have some remains of sails and there are about ten more lacking sails but with some other machinery. None now work commercially.

Fig. 82.
Rolvenden Windmill.
A typical post mill with roundhouse.

There are two main types of windmill. In the post mill the entire body with all its machinery is pivoted on the top of a large post (fig. 82). In the tower mill only the cap moves the sails as they are turned into the wind, while the body with the machinery remains fixed (fig. 83).

The earliest dated windmill in Kent (1295) was a stone tower mill within Dover Castle, but most mediaeval windmills were post mills. Only the post and its supports remain of Town Mill, Smarden, which dates from the seventeenth century. It was built on a mound, the better to catch the wind in flat country. Here the bearing on which the body of the mill was pivoted can be seen on the top of the post. The 'open trestle' post mill in which the post and its supports are uncovered is normally the earliest form, but the open trestle mill at Chillenden, south of Wingham, is anomalously the latest post mill in Kent (1868). Chillenden Mill, which worked until about 1950, now belongs to the County Council and is open to visitors. The machinery, however, is neither complete nor typical. There are other post mills at Keston (1716), Wittersham (1781) and Rolvenden, all of which have the substructure enclosed in a brick roundhouse. Rolvenden Mill (seventeenth or eighteenth century) has been restored complete with the earlier so called 'common' sails which were spread with sailcloth. Most Kent windmills have the later shuttered sails.

The smock mill, a wooden tower mill, is the type most typical of Kent, where about 250 have existed at some time. They are weatherboarded, octagonal in plan and rest on a brick base (fig. 83). Tarred black mills outnumbered painted white mills in the proportion of three to one. The earliest Kentish examples appear in the early eighteenth century and were low, commonly of three storeys, having no 'stage' or gallery and little base so that the sails almost reached the ground. The cap was turned by an endless chain hanging from a wheel.

From the late eighteenth century the typical smockmill was tall, with a base one to three storeys high, surmounted by a four storey wooden body in most cases. A wooden stage was built round the mill, often level with the top of the base, from which the sails could be adjusted. The cap was turned into the wind by a device fixed behind it resembling a small auxiliary windmill and known as a fantail. Earlier smock mills were often modernized by being jacked up while a brick base was built under them; a fantail was generally added. This happened at Herne, a black mill still worked by auxiliary power, having last used the wind in 1952. Herne Mill was originally built in 1781 by John Holman, the most famous of Kent millwrights. The Canterbury firm he established could still build a traditional white smock mill in 1929 (at St. Margaret's Bay), to generate electricity. Cranbrook mill, built in 1814, is the finest remaining white smock mill in Kent, and the tallest in England. It is 22 m to the ridge of the cap, with four floors above the stage and three floors and a basement below. The sails span 21 m from tip to tip. It last worked by wind in 1950, and was thoroughly restored eight years later. Sandwich has another white mill with machinery in good order. The white mills at Willesborough and Woodchurch are not in good condition. The County Council has restored the black smock mills at West Kingsdown and Meopham. The latter was built in 1801 and is unusual in being hexagonal in plan. The County Council has also decided to maintain Stelling Minnis Mill, a slender black smock mill which ceased working in 1971, the last commercial windmill to use the wind in Kent. Draper's Mill, Margate, is another black smock mill which has been restored to working order.

St. Martin's Mill, at Canterbury, is the only brick tower mill in the county to retain sail stocks. Stanford Mill, built in 1857, was worked by engine until recently although its sails had gone.

Most windmills were for grinding corn, but there were also sawmills and pumping mills. The tower of one, for water supply, survives near the M2 south of Faversham, as does a small drainage

Fig. 83.
Cranbrook Windmill.
The finest example of a smock mill in Britain.

mill at Stodmarsh.

WATERMILLS

When the Domesday Survey was made in 1086, 352 mills were recorded in Kent. None of these are likely to be windmills, some were no doubt powered by animals, but most were watermills. The great majority of these sites had mills working up to the eighteenth and nineteenth centuries. 137 watermills are shown on early nineteenth century maps of Kent, as compared with 226 windmills. Very little use is now made of water power, but modern industrial enterprises have grown up around some mills and others have been converted into houses. A few watermills have been restored to working order. A notable large example is at Crabble near Dover, which is open to the public, as is the smaller but delightful Swanton Mill, Mersham. At Haxted, on the border of Kent and Surrey near Edenbridge, is a watermill museum. Other mills at Wateringbury and Chilham are being reconstructed. Part of a gunpowder mill has also been preserved—Home Works, Faversham—including a water wheel, gears and grinding stones dating from the eighteenth and nineteenth centuries.

Fig. 84.
Westwell Watermill.
Showing overshot water wheel, the most efficient type.

Most water power was applied to the corn milling industry, but when the Wealden cloth industry was flourishing many mills turned to the fulling of cloth, first in the Wealden area, but later elsewhere in the county. Water mills were also associated with the Wealden iron industry, as the hammer forges were water powered. In the course of time the cloth and iron industries decayed, but in their place, also requiring water power, came the paper industry. This sequence of events can be illustrated from the valley of the Len and its tributaries, where there were 26 watermills, including one of the earliest in Britain of which there are substantial remains. This mill, built of ragstone probably in the early thirteenth century, is attached to the barbican of Leeds Castle. Chegworth Mill, near Harrietsham, is a complete water-powered corn mill, one of the few still workable in south-east England. Turkey Mill, lower down the stream on the outskirts of Maidstone, was converted from fulling to paper making about 1700. Fulling mills were more suitable for conversion than corn mills, for some of the equipment such as the vertical stampers, previously used for pounding the cloth, could be adapted to macerate the rags in preparation for final pulping. For most of its history Turkey Mill has been associated with the Whatman family, whose paper remains a world-famous product of the highest quality. There are remains of a smaller water-powered paper mill in private grounds at Otham. No waterwheel, shafts or gear remain, but much of the mill fabric is still in place, and allows a visual reconstruction from the 'wet-end' to the old machine bed at the 'dry-end'. Also near Maidstone is the Loose stream, which is so steeply graded that it supported 13 mills in 5 km. Many were paper mills. The earliest paper mill in Kent was on the Darent at Dartford (1588), and later at Eynsford (1646) and Shoreham (1690). One of the best surviving Darent mills is at Farningham, a corn mill.

There were at least 25 watermills on the Great Stour and its tributaries, and there are four more on the Little Stour, such as the picturesque weather-boarded mill at Wickhambreux. Most were undershot, using a flow of large volume, but small fall like those at Wye and Chilham. Upstream where the fall is greater, some were overshot, as at Westwell (fig. 84). At Chartham a turbine was used latterly. A particularly interesting site is that of the 'wind, steam and water mill' at Kennington. The steam mill building is joined to the brick base of the smock windmill. On the other side of the private road, once crossed by a footbridge, stands the watermill with the mill house next door. Even this rustic symbiosis with steam power proved uneconomic, and the trade was moved in 1890 to Pledge's Victoria Mill beside the railway station in Ashford. Thus with the spread of steam-power and the growing tendency to concentrate all industries in larger units the water-wheels of Kent gradually became silent.

Plate 25
Furnace Pond, Cowden. Before and during the Civil War this tranquil scene rang with the manufacture of armaments. A defective gun and many cannon balls have been dug up near the furnace site, which stood in Kent although the waterwheel that powered the bellows was in Sussex. The sluice which controlled the flow to the wheel is seen on the far side of the pond.

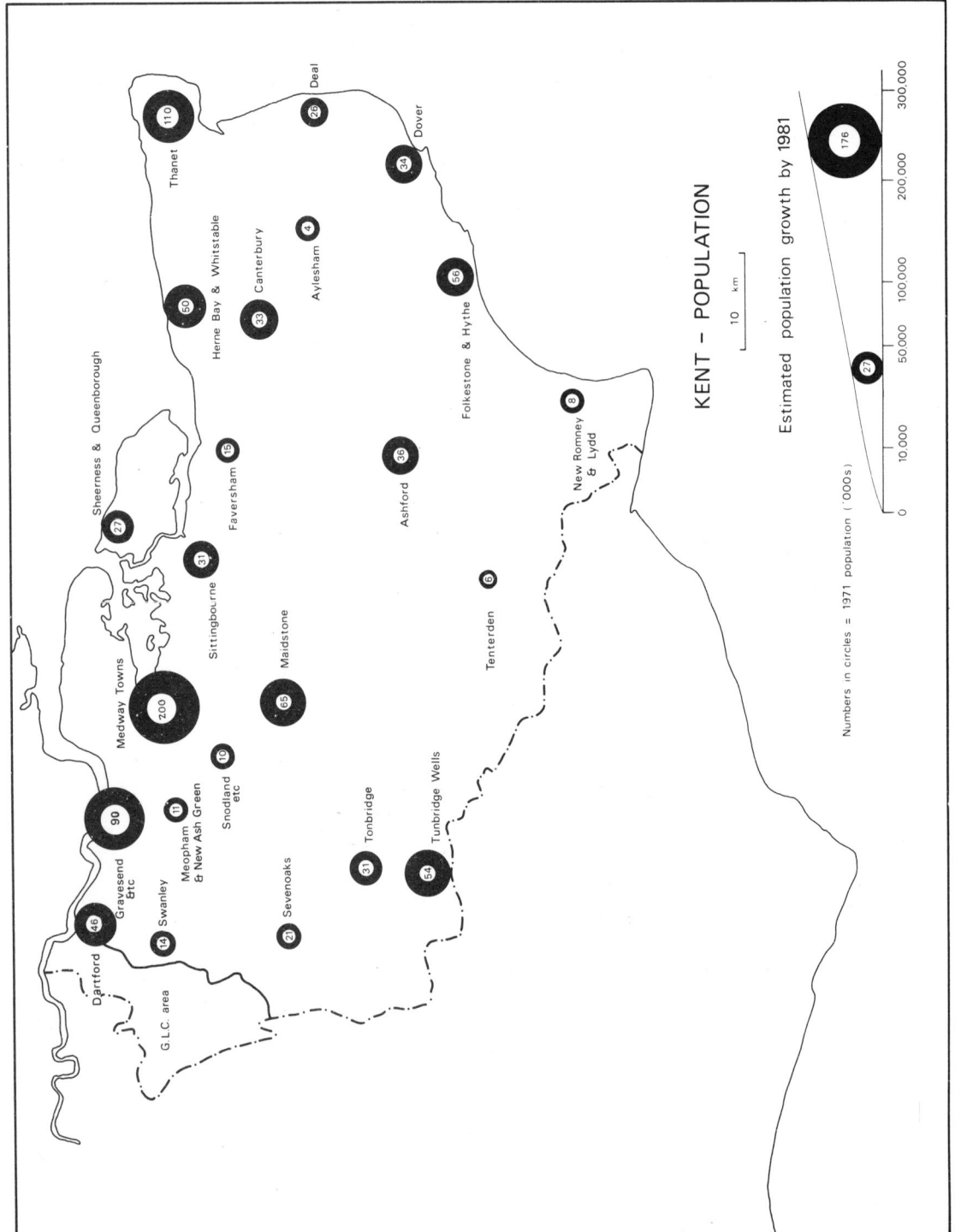

Fig. 85. Kent: Population of Towns.

Towns and Villages   7

In 1971 about two-thirds of Kent's 1,399,463 people had their homes in the 26 towns of more than 10,000 inhabitants. Twenty-four of these were urban centres a century ago (fig. 18) so that modern townscapes, no less than villages, are often fascinating mixtures of buildings old and new, and each place cherishes its own traditions and loyalties. Some counties are dominated by a single town, but Kent boasts two capitals, Canterbury and Maidstone, as well as several other centres of comparable or greater population and range of facilities.

This chapter is not a gazetteer, and thus some towns of substantial size or historical interest have had to be omitted. Conversely two towns, Canterbury and Tenterden, and two villages, Brook and Leigh, have been selected for more detailed consideration.

TOWNS AND CITIES

Canterbury

Although surprisingly small even today (33,000 in 1971) Canterbury is Kent's only city of international eminence, the focus of Anglican Christianity. By happy coincidence Canterbury was probably established during the lifetime of Jesus Christ, albeit by the Cantii, one of the Belgic tribes under the suzerainty of Cunobelin. Remains of this period lie beneath the shops of St George's Street.

By whichever route Romans crossed the Straits of Dover, they reached Canterbury on their way to London or beyond (fig. 7). So here was the capital of Kent, Durovernum Cantiacorum, one of the major towns of Roman Britain. Its extent was virtually identical with mediaeval Canterbury (fig. 86), for the foundations of the walls originally built around AD 280 were reused in Norman times. Except for Ridingate the entrances were changed, but the Roman

'Kent: The Garden of England'

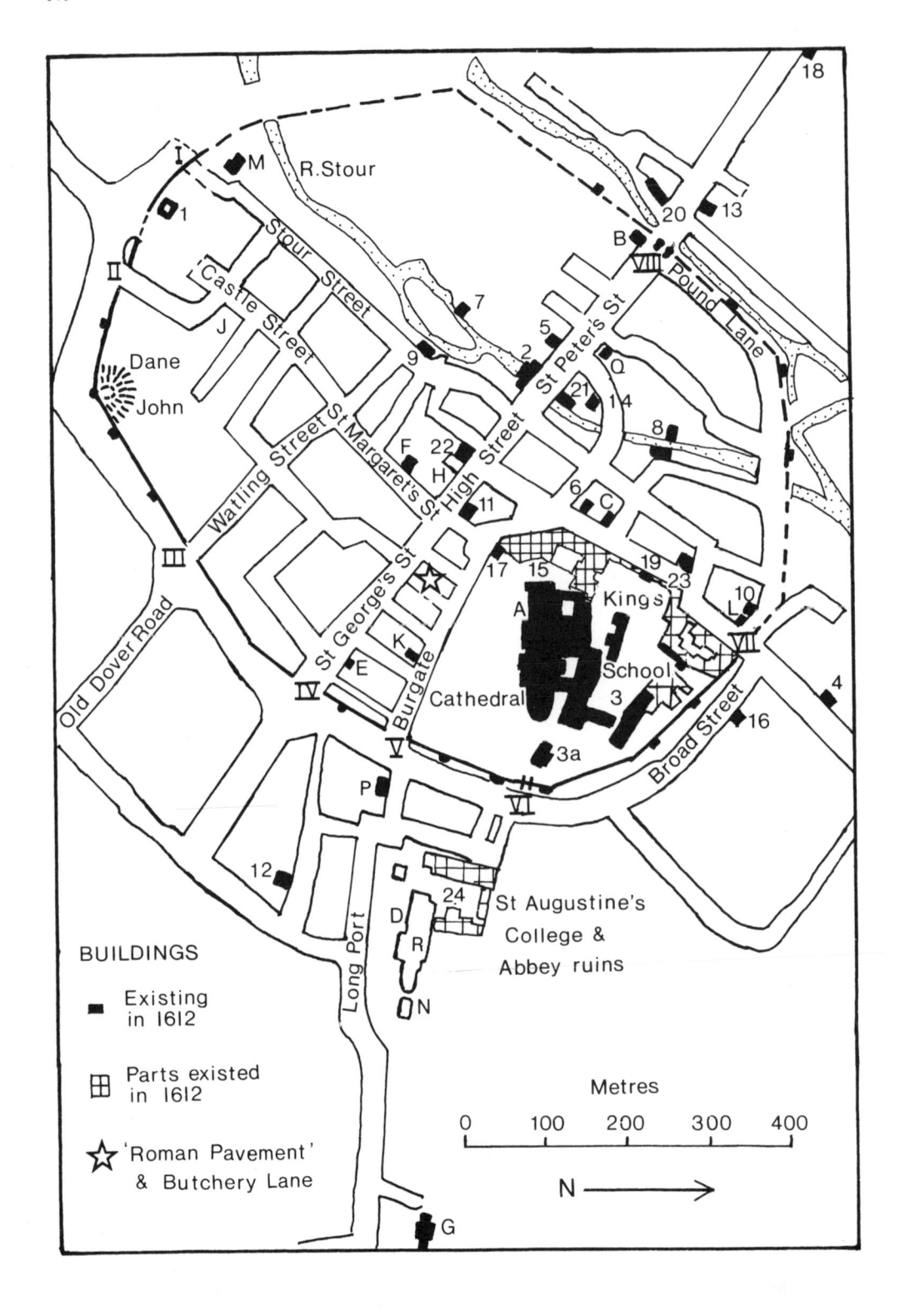

Worth Gate is marked by a plaque near the Wincheap roundabout, while Queningate has survived in the present wall as a blocked arch less than 3 m wide. The remains of Roman Canterbury lie several metres below present ground level, but after wartime bombing some excavations were carried out, and a tessellated pavement found off Butchery Lane has been preserved in a basement museum. The most impressive building must have been the massive stone theatre, looking like a semi-circular version of the Colosseum. Its ruins lingered on till Norman times, and the foundations can still be seen by visitors to Slatter's Restaurant in St Margaret's Street. The public baths were nearby, while the remains of another bathhouse underlie the present Woolworths store. The public hall and the Forum, with its gravelled courtyard, were situated where the County Hotel and the shops of High Street now stand. Near Whitehall Road a children's paddling pool marks the site of a Roman fountain into which hundreds of coins were thrown for luck.

Fig. 86.
Canterbury before 1612 (Speed's map).
Date or century of surviving features in brackets.

Gates
I Worthgate, II Wincheapgate, III Ridingate, IV Newingate, V Burgate, VI Queningate, VII Northgate, VIII Westgate (1381).

Churches
A, Cathedral (12th century and later). B, Holy Cross (1380). C, St. Alphege (13th and 15th). D, St. Augustine (11th, ruins). E, St. George (12th and 15th, tower only). F, St. Margaret (14th and 19th). G, St. Martin (7th and later). H, St. Mary Bredman (site). J, St. Mary de Castro (site). K, St. Mary Magdalene (1502, tower only). L, St. Mary Northgate (mediaeval and 19th). M, St. Mildred (Saxon to 16th). N, St. Pancras (7th, foundations). P, St. Paul (13th and 19th). Q, St. Peter (13th). R, St. Peter and St. Paul (7th, foundations).

Other Buildings
1, Castle (12th and 14th). 2, Eastbridge Hospital (12th and later). 3, Christchurch Priory (12th and later) including 3a Meister Omer's (13th, 14th and 19th). 4, St. John the Baptist's Hospital (12th and later). 5, Cogan's House (circa 1200 and later). 6, Tudor House (13th, 15th and 17th). 7, Greyfriars (13th and later). 8, Blackfriars (13th and 14th). 9, Poor Priests' Hospital (14th). 10, Hall House in Church Lane (14th). 11, Chequer of the Hope (14th). 12, 44 Ivy Lane (14th). 13, Falstaff Inn (15th). 14, All Saints' Court (15th). 15, Archbishop's Palace (15th and 19th). 16, 70 Broad Street (15th). 17, Christchurch Gate (1517). 18, Gate of Place House (16th). 19, Parker's Gate (16th). 20, Westgate Grove (16th). 21, The Weavers (16th). 22, Queen Elizabeth's Guest Chamber (16th and 17th). 23, Sir John Boys' House (circa 1600). 24, St. Augustine's College (19th, gatehouses 14th).

A more substantial continuation of Roman use concerns St Martin's Church (G in fig. 86) which was already 'ancient' when Bede wrote about 730. The walls of the western half of the chancel (fig. 87) may well have heard mass said by St Augustine. He also built the church of St Peter and St Paul (R in fig. 86) whose remains may still be seen among the ruins of the Abbey he founded. In later Saxon times Abbot Wulfric extended it with a magnificent rotunda (1047-59), whose demolition in the course of rebuilding by the Norman conquerors was a great loss to posterity.

Fig. 87.
Chancel of St. Martin's Church, Canterbury. *The left hand part is early Saxon, and incorporates Roman work.*

Of Norman Canterbury much more survives, a remarkably complete account of it has been pieced together by Dr W. G. Urry. It was dominated by the Cathedral, rebuilt after being burnt to the ground in 1067. The massive, gloomy nave built around 1075 under Archbishop Lanfranc has gone, but much of the crypt and outer walls of the choir erected by Priors Ernulf and Conrad (1107-30) survive. The monastery attached, Christchurch Priory (3 in fig. 86) was remarkably large, even for 140 monks. Lanfranc's Dormitory (about 1080) and Prior Ernulf's 80 m long Infirmary (about 1100) form massive ruins, but the Chapter House (1304) and cloisters (1390-1411) remain complete. The Strangers' Hall, lodgings for guests built about 1150, is still in use as King's School Library and has a most attractive staircase covered by a porch. Other fragments, such as the block of 1303 which originally housed the bakehouse, brewhouse and granary, and 'Meister Omer's' (3a) a guest hall of 1399 with one of the widest fireplaces (6.6 m) in England, are also used by King's School.

Archbishop Lanfranc was a kindly man and founded St John's Hospital just outside Northgate in 1085, and at an appropriately greater distance a leper hospital at Harbledown, where the adjacent Norman church largely survives. Both institutions are still almshouses, as is the late twelfth century Eastbridge Hospital (2) where the refectory hall has a remarkable wall painting of Christ and the four evangelists. Visiting Eastbridge Hospital, one steps down into the past almost a metre below the present pavement. Of twelfth and thirteenth century domestic buildings several cellars survive, a good example is under Boots shop, and two much modified stone houses: Cogan's House (5) and Tudor House (6). The latter was only refronted in Henry VIII's time, having been built as the parsonage of St Alphege's Church in about 1250.

A ditch around the city was mentioned in Domesday and walls in 1140, having gates shown in fig. 86. The Castle (1) was built about 1080, and became a prison about 1200. It has been derelict for 600 years, latterly serving as a coke store for the gas works. The Dane John mound, possibly originally a tumulus, may once have carried a stockade. The present stone embellishment dates from the creation of the gardens in 1790-1803. The roads shown on fig. 86 are those of Speed's map of 1612. With a few additions they survive today, and subtracting Guildhall Street the same system existed by 1200, when Canterbury already had a population of 2,000 and more than 200 shops. These prospered as a result of a tragedy, which in worldly terms was the best thing that ever happened in mediaeval Canterbury—the murder of Archbishop Becket in 1170. Numerous pilgrims were quickly drawn to Canterbury, their gait on horse back has given us our word 'to canter'. They were housed at inns, such as Chequer of the Hope (11) and Falstaff Inn (13). Friars also came in to minister to these religious tourists. Franciscans to the Grey Friars (7) in 1224 and Dominicans to the Black Friars (8) in 1237.

Fig. 88.
The Murder of Becket
Becket is murdered by Fitz Urse, while another knight wounds the cross-bearer.

A fire in 1174 opened the way to remodel the Cathedral to house Becket's tomb. The choir was rebuilt to a design by William of Sens, who imported from France many features that have been called 'Early English'. After William of Sens had been crippled in an accident, 'William the Englishman' built Holy Trinity chapel for Becket's shrine, and magnificent stained glass windows were installed. At present these are being restored with other parts of the Cathedral at great cost, hopefully to last another 800 years.

It is more difficult to raise money to preserve the numerous other churches. Mediaeval Canterbury had about 20, many of which have already disappeared or been converted to other uses. Small and unpretentious, they resemble village churches and generally have a hall-like nave with a crown post roof and aisles on both sides. St Alphege (C), St Mildred (M), St Margaret (F), St Dunstan, outside Westgate, St Paul (P) and St Peter (Q) are surviving examples. Chapels also existed over the Westgate (VIII), over Newingate (IV) and against the wall near Northgate (L). In about 1380-1400 Archbishop Sudbury rebuilt much of the wall, providing new bastions which can be seen in Pound Lane and incorporated in Tower House, Westgate Gardens. He also rebuilt the Westgate in 1379, with 18 loopholes for guns, one of the earliest buildings to be so equipped. It became a prison, and survived the destruction of the other remaining gates in 1769-1825. To replace the chapel over the old Westgate Holy Cross church (B) was built nearby.

At the very same time (1378) it was decided to rebuild the nave of the Cathedral to a design of Henry Yevele in the Perpendicular style. Its interior is magnificent. The south-west tower followed about

1424 and the central (Bell Harry) tower in 1494-1503. Built by John Wastell, who later finished Kings College chapel, Cambridge, Bell Harry resembles the dome of St Paul's Cathedral in having a hidden core of brick. It is the crowning glory of Canterbury Cathedral, especially as seen from a distance (plate 26).

From the fourteenth century to the seventeenth many timber framed buildings were constructed, which are still a characteristic element in the Canterbury townscape. Their development is described in Chapter 6, but can easily be illustrated in Canterbury. Of the fourteenth century, there are two 'Wealden' hall houses (10 and 12), built in rural fashion long side to the road. All Saints Court (14) is a simple fifteenth century timbered house with a single continuous jetty. Sixteenth century houses tend to be more elaborately decorated, and to have three stories with two jetties. Examples are the Weavers (21) and Queen Elizabeth's Guest Chamber (22). In the late sixteenth and early seventeenth centuries came timbered houses with double jetties topped by gables facing the street, as in Westgate Grove (20) and the House of Agnes in St Dunstan's Street.

Elaborate gatehouses are another characteristic of the same

Plate 26
Canterbury cathedral (Bell Harry tower on right). Wartime bombing devastated the area in the foreground. The Longmarket redevelopment overlies Roman foundations, with a tessellated pavement accessible in a basement.

epoch. St Augustine's Abbey (24) had two, of the fourteenth century, now part of St Augustine's College. Christchurch Gate, again of stone, was built in 1517 and makes a magnificent entrance to the Cathedral Close. Later Tudor gateways are of brick, such as Roper's gate (18) which led to the now demolished Place House, once the home of Sir Thomas More's daughter, and Parker's Gate (19) which led to the palace (15) of the Elizabethan archbishop.

The Reformation led to the dismantling of the monastic institutions, which were already in decline. But although Henry VIII took much he left the Cathedral adequately staffed and provided an endowment to maintain King's School with two masters and 50 scholars. The Civil War too led to much excitement, and some destruction. Iconoclasts 'rattled old Becket's glassy bones' by breaking windows and statues in the Cathedral, while the south-western quarter of the walls was demolished to make the city indefensible.

The Georgian period added a good number of new or refronted houses, an austere classical Sessions House and prison and a plain but elegant Methodist Church. The Victorian era brought considerable expansion beyond the walls and several institutional buildings of note. St Augustine's College (1848) for Anglican theological training, is a conscious attempt by the Gothic revival architect William Butterfield and his patron A. J. Beresford-Hope to recreate a monastic environment. St Edmund's School, also in formidable Gothic, has been described as the finest Victorian school in Kent, its fortress-like ragstone making an interesting contrast with the homely red brick of Kent College on the other side of the Whitstable Road. The Beaney Institute (Library and Museum) in High Street is an impressive late Victorian attempt to conform to the half-timbering of olde-world Canterbury.

The heavy bombing of 1942 left the Cathedral miraculously unscathed, but just to the south of it flattened an area 500 metres across. The rebuilding ranges from safe neo-Georgian north of Burgate to the imaginative Longmarket shopping area (plate 26) and an uncouth multistorey car park. The new ring road is sensibly placed just beyond newly-restored city walls. On a windy height to the north the University of Kent has gained much space for its impressive buildings at the cost of losing any close visual relationship to the city.

Maidstone

The modern capital of Kent, Maidstone, was a small town in

mediaeval times, developed at an important crossing of the Medway. Only the area around All Saints' Church retains the atmosphere of this period, with remains of a fourteenth century riverside palace of the Archbishops of Canterbury remodelled as a house in Elizabethan times. The Archbishop's stables, with its accommodation for grooms and coachmen on the first floor, appropriately houses a carriage museum. Nearby Archbishop Courtenay founded a college of 24 priests in 1395, rebuilding All Saints' in the Perpendicular style and providing collegiate buildings around a courtyard, of which an impressive gate tower and the Master's House survive.

Maidstone received a charter as a borough in 1548, and the fine Town Hall in High Street, dates from 1763. Behind this, Bank Street is still almost entirely of buildings that existed then, mostly timber framed and including some splendid pargetting, dated 1611 (plate 27). Since the early nineteenth century Maidstone's most notable function has been that of County Town. Until recently this focused on the square outside the East Station, where the original Shire Hall of 1824 can be glimpsed through the main archway. It is now the Sessions House, and behind is the Prison built in 1810-17. Of the prison only the high ragstone wall is normally seen by law-abiding citizens, and even this is partly masked by the early twentieth

Plate 27
Decorated plasterwork (pargetting) dated 1611, on timber frame building in Bank Street, Maidstone.

century County Hall. Today most departments of the County Council have moved up the Sandling Road to the grounds of Springfield, a Victorian mansion now dwarfed by fine buildings which represent a disquieting post-war growth of bureaucracy.

In the centre of the town contrasts of scale are much more painful. Pre-war Maidstone had narrow streets of three storied buildings, and a good mixture of local ragstone and brick. Eleven storey office blocks, however well designed, crush the remains of old Maidstone. Many older buildings have already been destroyed, and those that survive look sadly anachronistic. Even the characteristic smell of brewing has gone, an industry once the mainstay of the town.

The Medway Towns

Fig. 89.
John Fisher (1469-1535). *One of the most famous bishops of Rochester, consecrated in 1504, he was executed by Henry VIII for refusing to acknowledge the King as head of the Church of England, and canonised by Pope Pius XI in 1935.*

An alien geographer would expect the capital of Kent to occupy the lowest bridging point of its largest river, the Medway. His expectations would be correct to the extent that Rochester, Strood, Chatham and Gillingham already formed the largest conurbation in Kent at the 1801 census, mustering 23,000 inhabitants and reached 200,000 in 1971. Rochester was a walled city in Roman times and acquired a bishop in 604, just seven years after Canterbury which it came in some ways to resemble. Thus, in Norman times an impressive Castle (fig. 10), a Cathedral and adjacent priory were built, while buildings near the Cathedral now house another King's School. The rise of Chatham, is linked to the Naval Dockyard, established in about 1550. Today one cannot tell where Rochester ends and Chatham begins, but the once fortified chalk escarpment known as Chatham Lines marks off the nineteenth century developments of Brompton and Gillingham. The river also gives a sense of space and isolates Strood, the western bridgehead, and the erstwhile village of Frindsbury, both immensely expanded but retaining fragments of mediaeval churches and manorial buildings, the thirteenth century Temple Manor House at Strood and an immense fourteenth century barn at Frindsbury.

The M2 motorway has made a sharp southern boundary to the whole conurbation and has left most room for expansion up the well wooded dry valleys around Walderslade, Hempstead and Wigmore. The tide of houses has not entirely obscured this attractive landscape, and a worthwhile centre for Walderslade has been formed between 1958 and 1967, including a church, parish hall, public library, schools and old people's housing. Rainham has also been swallowed, but it is to be hoped that the conurbation will not be allowed to extend further east over some of the finest land in Kent.

It remains odd that we speak of the Medway Towns and not of the city of greater Rochester, which by historical precedent should give its name to the entire conurbation. The reason is probably the nature of the hinterland with its steep sided dry valleys which confined growth, so that first Chatham and then Gillingham became too large to be ignored.

Seaside Towns

Kent is a maritime county, and even if the industries around the Thames and Medway estuaries and the ports are described in other chapters, some space must be found for seaside resorts. The earliest major seaside resorts in Kent were Margate and Ramsgate, which were originally reached from London by sailing boats, the 'Margate hoys'. A Margate resident, Benjamin Beale, invented the 'bathing machine' in 1753, a covered wagon from which to enter the sea in

Fig. 90.
A Bathing Machine *Invented at Margate in 1753. It allowed people to enter the sea in complete privacy.*

complete privacy. The Royal Sea Bathing Hospital (fig. 91), founded in 1791, testifies to the supposed health-giving value of immersion, or even of drinking sea water. The Georgian town centre (Cecil Square, Hawley Square), its entertainments represented by the Theatre Royal and the Shell Grotto, is several hundred metres from the sea, and even Victorian Cliftonville stands a little back. Extreme preoccupation with the sea front is modern, and seasonal at that, for winter gales and sleet lash shuttered shops and amusement galleries as life ebbs back into the sheltered older part of the town. Ramsgate expanded slightly later in Regency and Victorian times, and is somewhat smaller than Margate. It is less exclusively a seaside resort, and so retains more life in winter. The harbour is more sheltered and much more active than Margate's, specializing in yachting and the import of cars. Broadstairs emerged in the early nineteenth century from a fishing hamlet to a minor resort, beloved by Dickens (fig. 19). Now many people take holidays abroad, leaving the Thanet resorts to be supported by day visitors from London and an increasing number of retired residents encouraged by the dry climate and relatively low property prices. Margate, Ramsgate and Broadstairs are now a single conurbation, both in geography and administration.

Deal was bigger than either Margate or Ramsgate in 1800, when it was a valuable roadstead for sailing vessels anchored or becalmed in The Downs, the sheltered waters inside the Goodwin Sands. The fishermen and bumboat owners of Old Deal built their cottages in a strip along the coast, unlike Margate. Since the advent of steam, ships have ceased to linger and Deal has grown slowly, handicapped by inconvenient railway connections and an exposed pebbly beach.

Fig. 91.
The Royal Sea Bathing Hospital, Margate.

Folkestone, conversely, owes its status as a resort to the advent of the South Eastern Railway, and the solidity of its Victorian and Edwardian buildings still testify to its popularity in those eras.

Despite a false start in 1830, Herne Bay was late in developing. Again it was essentially dependent on the railway although a pier was built, more than a kilometre long, to reach deep water at low tide. Railway electrification in 1955-9 has brought Herne Bay into the commuter belt, and recent development has made it continuous with Whitstable along the coast and inland has enveloped the older village of Herne.

The motor car now threatens the possibility that the whole Kent coast will become one urban strip, industrial west of Sheerness and residential beyond. Groups of expensive houses near St Margaret's at Cliffe and by the golf courses of Sandwich Bay, humbler bungalows from Sheppey to Lydd-on-Sea, holiday camps at Dymchurch and St Mary's Bay and caravan sites at Graveney, Reculver and elsewhere have combined to fill in most of the gaps which still existed in the early twentieth century.

Tunbridge Wells

Kent has only one major inland resort, Tunbridge Wells. The iron-rich 'chalybeate' waters, discovered about 1610 by Lord North while passing through a lonely wood, became popular after a six week's visit by Queen Henrietta Maria, wife of Charles I. Loyalties die hard, and to this day the parish church dedication is to 'King Charles the Martyr'. Nearby in the Pantiles the atmosphere of the Georgian spa survives, and one can still drink the water, which has an unpleasant enough taste to persuade the drinker of its good effects. In reality these may have arisen from a reduced thirst for alcoholic beverages.

Elsewhere the environment is spacious, and owes much to the underlying Tunbridge Wells sandstone. The infertile soils led to the survival of much uncultivated land in the vicinity, enlivened by picturesque natural outcrops such as the Toad Rock. Most of the nineteenth century buildings of the town centre are built of this reasonably durable but easily squared yellowish grey stone. They make it clear to the visitor that even if the 'spa' declined at the end of the eighteenth century Royal Tunbridge Wells has remained a genteel address ever since.

Fig. 92. South Eastern Railway Locomotive *'Little Sharp'* class 2-4-0 No. 131. Built at Ashford 1859.

Ashford

Some Kentish inland towns have good road and rail connections, such as Dartford, Sevenoaks, Tonbridge and Sittingbourne. These have experienced rapid expansion during both the nineteenth and twentieth centuries, and none more so than Ashford.

In pre-railway days Ashford was barely large enough to warrant the name of town: the population in 1801 was only 2,600 even if Willesborough was included. Nevertheless the High Street and the small passages to the south had an urban feel, as had the large church with its central tower. After the arrival of the South Eastern Railway, Newtown, a planned settlement around a green, was built near its locomotive works, and the town itself expanded considerably. Since the second World War the peripheral villages of Kennington and Willesborough have expanded into suburbs and a large number of houses, mainly municipally owned, have been built to the south of the town, including the London overspill estate of Stanhope. Light industry also developed, and latterly large office blocks, particularly the Charter Consolidated building, have dwarfed the previously dominant tower of the Parish Church. Ashford increased in population by 37 per cent between 1961 and 1971. In response to the resulting congestion Ashford has cut a swathe round its centre for a new inner ring road. It has the unenviable distinction of being one of the smallest towns included in a recent survey of destructive urban developments. An example is North Street, worth a separate paragraph in the Buildings of England volume in 1969, but now hacked through by two new roads within a hundred metres of one another.

Tenterden

In contrast to Ashford, places like Cranbrook, Tenterden, New

Romney and Lydd have remained 'off the beaten track'. The best opportunity to see a small Kentish market town almost as it existed in the late eighteenth century is at Tenterden. Georgian Tenterden was a single street about two kilometres long, occupying the summit of a ridge which reaches its highest point (68 m) exactly at St Mildred's Church (fig. 93), whose splendid tower, a further 38 m high, dominated the town then as now. Westwards from the church the High Street has wide grass verges, at that time used as a market. The trees were planted in 1871, while the stone gatehouse to Heronden Hall, now an effective terminal feature, is also Victorian. The Georgian High Street was part of a turnpike road from Cranbrook to New Romney, then the only routes of any pretensions leading from the town (fig. 13).

The whole street still looks Georgian today, but only at the two ends are the buildings genuinely of eighteenth century origin, the central part is mediaeval in Georgian dress. To escape taxation only a minority are of brick. Tile hanging, mathematical tiles and woodwork imitating stone blocks (plate 28), all play their part, both in genuine Georgian houses and in hiding timbered buildings. Mediaeval Tenterden, with its wharf at Smallhythe a modest 'limb'

Plate 28
At the eastern end of Tenterden High Street, Georgian style buildings are covered with tiles and woodwork, sometimes imitating stone.

of the Cinque Ports, was already a substantial village, the reputed birthplace of William Caxton, the first English printer. Fortunately, the Tudor Rose tea room escaped cladding to give a glimpse of mediaeval Tenterden. It has 'close-studded' timbers, but originally had a central hall and jetties only at the two ends, a combination dating it to the late fifteenth century. In the sixteenth century the open hall had a floor put across it, and at the same time the jetty was made continuous.

Opposite is the Town Hall of 1790, well restored with the aid of the Tenterden Trust. An openable venetian window gives access to a fine balcony. The mayor's parlour was once actually part of the Woolpack Hotel next door, one of the many inns which are a feature of Tenterden. In contrast there are several non-conformist chapels, the oldest, the Old Meeting House, almost unchanged since 1746. It looks just like a cottage outwardly, but inside still has the magnificent pulpit with an inlaid sounding board from which Joseph Priestley, the discoverer of oxygen, preached to a congregation including the American visitor Benjamin Franklin. Some of the numerous congregations of Georgian days were ultimately interred in the barrel vaulted brick tombs which are an intriguing feature of the graveyard behind the chapel.

By the eighteenth century the woollen manufactures which had been the economic mainstay of Tenterden in mediaeval times were defunct, as were the miniature river ports of Reading Street and Smallhythe. Tenterden lived on as a minor regional centre and market town. Its industries used agricultural products, a tannery, a brewery and wind and water driven corn mills, but only the disused Ashbourne watermill remains. A manufacturing chemist, which in Georgian times produced veterinary and other medicines still survives as a retail pharmacy in a building of mediaeval origin a few metres west of the church. Actual working farms existed in the High Street, and one still does with its much patched timbered barn, just east of the Town Hall.

Benjamin Franklin would recognize Tenterden if he revisited it after two centuries, even if much of the Georgian appearance is only a façade, concealing ramshackle older cottages or modern reconstructions or adaptations. Moreover it looks well kept, smart white paint setting off the rich red of tiles and bricks. For this no doubt national and local authorities through planning legislation and designation as a conservation area are partly responsible, but individual owners and the Tenterden Trust have contributed even more.

Fig. 93.
Tenterden Church tower. *Built between 1450 and 1500, the top later carried an Armada beacon. There are eight bells, said to be the best peal in Kent. The tenor bell weighs one and a half tonnes.*

VILLAGES

The settlement pattern of Kent north of the Hythe Beds escarpment dates from Anglo Saxon times, and most of the present villages in North and East Kent are mentioned among the 300 Kentish manors in Domesday Book (fig. 8). In the Weald most of the villages were established in the twelfth and thirteenth centuries as woodland was cleared. The distribution in both cases is the same: a fairly regular scatter 2 to 5 km apart with the precise site often determined by water supply. The spacing is determined by the need to walk to the fields, often leading draft animals. Since defence was not generally an important consideration, these early villages were not tightly clustered, and there were also a good number of isolated farmsteads from an early date.

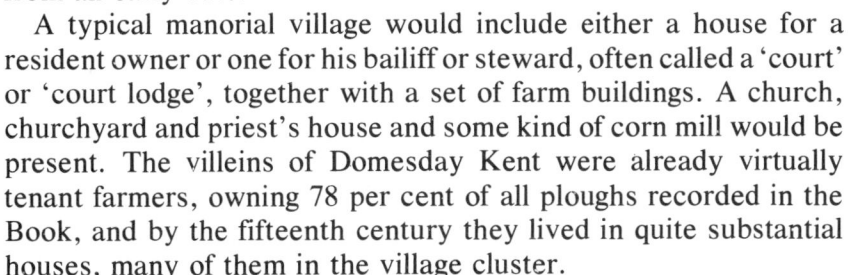

Fig. 94.
Brook Church Tower. *Although like a keep there is no evidence of a defensive function.*

A typical manorial village would include either a house for a resident owner or one for his bailiff or steward, often called a 'court' or 'court lodge', together with a set of farm buildings. A church, churchyard and priest's house and some kind of corn mill would be present. The villeins of Domesday Kent were already virtually tenant farmers, owning 78 per cent of all ploughs recorded in the Book, and by the fifteenth century they lived in quite substantial houses, many of them in the village cluster.

A volume could easily be devoted to the mediaeval villages of Kent, but one example, Brook, near Ashford, must suffice, chosen because its core survives reasonably unaltered and accessible to visitors. The village of Brook, is a mediaeval manorial village which has never been influenced by a locally resident magnate. Essentially it is a single street of houses and gardens 2 km long which leaves the ancient trackway following the foot of the North Downs near the Devil's Kneading Trough (plate 2), crosses the stream which gives the village its name and passes over a knoll called Spelders Hill. The old core of the village comprises St Mary's Church, built about 1100, and substantially unaltered, Court Lodge, a mediaeval timber-framed house, and adjacent farm buildings, including a large timber-framed barn (plate 29) now containing Wye College's Museum of agricultural implements. Three scarp-foot springs feed the stream, and before the chalk aquifer was pumped it was copious enough to work a small overshot watermill belonging to the manor. Even now it sometimes causes flooding in the village.

Half the agricultural land of Domesday Kent belonged to the church. Brook was owned from Saxon times by Christ Church, the monastery attached to Canterbury Cathedral. Originally rented out, it was probably taken in hand by the vigorous prior Ernulf

(1096–1107), who is thought to have built the church with its massive tower (fig. 94). Brook church seems large for so tiny a village. However, Christ Church had great resources, owning 34 manors in Kent and 22 others elsewhere, yielding a total of over £1,000 per annum, a fabulous sum in present money. The visitor to Brook church should not miss the unusual chapel on the first floor of the tower, where a twelfth century painting of Christ blessing can be seen. In the chamber above, the bell frame and two of the three bells date from the fourteenth century. The church itself has extensive thirteenth century wall paintings.

For two and a half centuries after Ernulf's time the manor was administered by the priors of Christ Church through a bailiff who would have lived at the predecessor of the present Court Lodge. This is the usual name in Kent for the administrative centre of an ecclesiastical manor, the place where the manorial court would have met. The Black Death in 1348–9 wrought little havoc in the abbey, only four monks died, but it produced a great labour shortage which made it difficult to run many scattered manors. From 1374 Court Lodge was taken over by a lay farmer. The great barn is believed to date from about this time, the two large porches having been added about 1500. The original manor house may have stood a few metres further east where there are remains of a moated enclosure, the

Plate 29
Fourteenth century barn at Brook, now the Agricultural Museum of Wye College.

present house is possibly fifteenth century. There was a hall, originally open to its crown post roof, and a separately roofed two storey solar end. At the other end, three doors led to the pantry, kitchen and buttery with a further chamber above. Around the sixteenth century, the hall was divided by inserting a floor, and the present massive chimney breast was erected. Thus the original plan and later history resemble a typical 'Wealden' timbered house (fig. 71), although several details are unusual. The adjoining oast house (fig. 81) was built in 1815 and used for a few years only. The soils of Court Lodge Farm are not well suited to hops.

Today there are about a hundred houses in Brook. A recent inventory suggests that the building of ten of them was initiated in the sixteenth century or earlier, ten in the seventeenth and eighteenth centuries, nine belong to the nineteenth century and 19 to between 1900 and 1940. Fifty-seven are of post-war construction, including a small group of council houses. Although it may appear from this that the village has greatly expanded, planning constraints have ensured that the new houses complete the street and do not spread widely. Brook is still a small village with a population of 245 in 1961 and 286 in 1971. Brook has links with neighbouring Wye with which it shares a parish priest, but it has a community life of its own, although the village hall has been burnt down and not yet replaced.

There is a small but lively Baptist Church, a post office, a shop, a primary school and an inn, the 'Honest Miller'. Miller or no, there is no mill, both the watermill and the black smock windmill on Spelders Hill having gone. The forge is disused, so that there is now no industrial activity and only two active farms actually within the parish. Brook is now a residential entity only, and few of its inhabitants work in the village.

Brook has no 'big house' but many villages have developed under the influence of a resident landlord. Some of the great estates of lay magnates originated in mediaeval times, and others were formed when church lands were sold after the Reformation. As Kent is near London successful merchants and politicians often acquired estates, particularly in West Kent. Thus resources from outside the agricultural economy of Kent were injected into the county, but only in certain places and at particular periods. The effect of these injections can easily be seen today. It may be negative, for extension of the buildings and park of a great house sometimes suffocated a nearby village. The church alone would remain, embedded in the park, virtually a private chapel for the squire's family and their sumptuous tombs. In East Kent Waldershare and Knowlton are examples, in West Kent, Lullingstone. Eastwell near Ashford is the saddest of all, showing how vulnerable the appurtenances of the gentry have become in an era of social change. Eastwell Park was an eighteenth century mansion belonging to the Earls of Winchelsea. It has been demolished and only more recent and subsidiary buildings remain including a fine nineteenth century gatehouse in flint and stone. The deerpark was 20 km in circumference, and includes an interestingly scalloped part of the North Downs scarp from which views extending from the Thames Estuary to Dungeness can be obtained. This is now unspoiled farmland, but Eastwell church has had a sorrier fate. It collapsed in 1951 and became a ruin which did not justify rebuilding as nobody lives nearby. The magnificent monuments were sheltered for a time in a mean brick hut, but were removed in 1968 to the Victoria and Albert Museum. Near the church at the edge of the Park's large artificial lake, is the last relic of the village, also derelict. This is Lake House, a most unusual stone house of the late thirteenth century with a hall on the first floor.

Normally, however, the village benefited from an enlightened desire of 'the rich man in his castle' to do something for 'the poor man at his gate', or at least for his tenants and retainers. Instead of a medley of buildings, some shabby and some smart, such as characterizes a village in the ownership of many individuals, the 'estate village' has pretentious buildings, often designed to a pattern and uniformly well kept, at least until recently. An example is Great Chart, where the red brick and Dutch gables of the cottages reflect the architecture of Godinton, home of their landlords, the Tokes.

The 'estate village' is specially characteristic of south west Kent, examples being Chevening, Leigh, Penshurst, Chiddingstone, Hever and Groombridge. The dates of the buildings range from the sixteenth and seventeenth centuries at Chiddingstone, where ownership passed from the Streatfeilds to the National Trust, to the early twentieth century at Hever as developed by the Astors. The great period was the nineteenth century and the most notable architect, especially at Penshurst and Leigh, was George Devey. Leigh is a very interesting, if unspectacular, example of the type. It owes its present form almost entirely to Samuel Morley, MP (fig. 96), a textile manufacturer with works in London and the Nottingham area. Having found the area attractive while still residing in London he bought Hall Place in 1870. Although the Elizabethan house was part of the attraction, he found it in poor order and had it demolished. The rebuilding, still in the Tudor style, was Devey's most expensive mansion. Though Hall Place remains

Fig. 95.
Brass of John, Lord Cobham, died 1408.
He is offering a church, symbolising his building an extension to Cobham Church. He also founded a College, now converted into almshouses.

Fig. 96.
Samuel Morley, MP (1809-1886).
of Hall Place, Leigh, near Tonbridge.

in the mid-twentieth century a nobleman's seat, of Lord Hollenden, it was far too big and the northern half has been pulled down. Samuel Morley also expanded the grounds from 30 ha to a deer park of 100 ha with a gateway and lodge at each end. While providing for his own comfort, he was also extremely generous in his support of social and religious causes and he left ample evidence of this during his sixteen years as squire of Leigh.

Leigh is situated on the dank Low Weald plain, not far from the Medway, so it is not surprising that Morley's first task in the village was a new drainage system, followed by a new water supply: a well and pump supplying four fountains in the village and a granite trough for dogs and horses. He extended the village green, put a road round it and paths across it, planting it with trees. Now it has become the home of a very active cricket club (plate 30) with a new and splendid pavilion, not one whit Victorian. At intervals during his time at Hall Place, Morley built cottages in the village in what seemed to his architects, Devey and later Sir Ernest George, an appropriate half-timbered style. He provided allotments and presented prizes for cottage gardens, giving his gardener *carte blanche* to supply trees and shrubs free of charge. It would please him to know that Leigh won the Kent Best Kept Village title in 1971. Samuel Morley was a free-churchman and built an undenominational chapel which is still in use, although the Sunday School block is now the village hall. Yet he was also on most friendly terms with the vicar and paid

Plate 30
Cricket on the green at Leigh, showing late nineteenth century estate cottages and church tower which, though not mediaeval, has the battlements and corner turret typical of Kent.

wholly for a new Church Infant School, and for a new vicarage in part. He gave a retirement home in Leigh (Park Cottage) to Dr Robert Moffat, the pioneer missionary to Southern Africa who was David Livingstone's father-in-law. With justification, Samuel Morley's biographer wrote 'he found a neglected village, and, as the gradual work of years, he transformed it into one of the neatest and prettiest in the country'.

Until quite recent times existing villages accommodated relatively few newcomers of modest means, nor could all the rising generation always find homes. Some moved to the towns, but a few managed to establish cottages or even small-holdings on waste or common land. Hothfield Common, west of Ashford, and not legally a common, has a well documented history of encroachment, but often entirely new villages were gradually formed: Wrotham Heath, Lenham and Charing Heaths, Barming Heath, Brasted Chart, Stelling Minnis, Rhodes Minnis and Challock Lees are a few examples. In those listed the remnant of open land was enclosed by Act of Parliament between 1750 and 1866, except for Stelling Minnis and Challock Lees where it still remains. Such 'wasteland villages' have distinctive features to this day. While the houses vary much in age they are all small and include few prosperous farms and normally no gentleman's seat. They lack a parish church of any antiquity, and the gap was nearly always filled by a non-conformist chapel, usually Methodist. Lenham Heath is a good example (fig. 97) where the Methodist chapel was once a stronghold. In Borough Green it is not the Parish Church but the Baptist Chapel that is the oldest place of worship, is centrally placed and has a large graveyard. Windmills were also common in such places. The value of sites for watermills was appreciated from an early date, but an aspiring business man of small means might find a cheap and unobstructed site for a windmill on the heath. Stelling Minnis mill is a good surviving example, while the windmill base on Lenham Heath (now a house) still shows how it was raised one and a half storeys when hedges were introduced round about.

Recently a few settlements of village size have been built for industrial or purely residential purposes. Apart from ribbon development along main roads or near the coast these were mainly linked to specific employers such as coal mines in East Kent (Hersden, Aylesham, Elvington) factories (Kemsley near Sittingbourne), or military installations (Chattenden near Strood). It could be argued that these are small townships, as villages exist to service agriculture. This was true in the past, but now most villages are redundant in their agricultural function. Farms are larger and employ only a small fraction of their former staff. Many farm workers live in tied cottages on the farm and not in the villages. Motor transport makes the close spacing of villages an anachronism, and their service function to agriculture is now an incidental activity of a few market towns. In parts of the United States villages were made of wood and disappeared as they became redundant. In Britain, our houses of brick and stone were too solid to disappear and too attractive as an environment for living to be abandoned. The new villagers, ofter retired folk or commuters, have taken over the loyalties and conservative attitudes of their agricultural predecessors with zeal, and using the machinery of town and country planning to the full can often inhibit developments and especially commercial and industrial developments that might enable the village to be reborn as a self-contained community with opportunities of local employment. Nevertheless, with the exception of a few on the urban fringe, Kent's villages are being preserved reasonably intact, and for this we and our successors should be grateful.

Fig. 97.
Methodist chapel at Lenham Heath.
The Primitive Methodists began to hold meetings nearby in 1850. Among the leaders were the seven brothers Dinnick, who all became ministers in the denomination. The Rev. Timothy Dinnick's name is on a foundation stone of the chapel, built in 1870.

'Kent: The Garden of England'

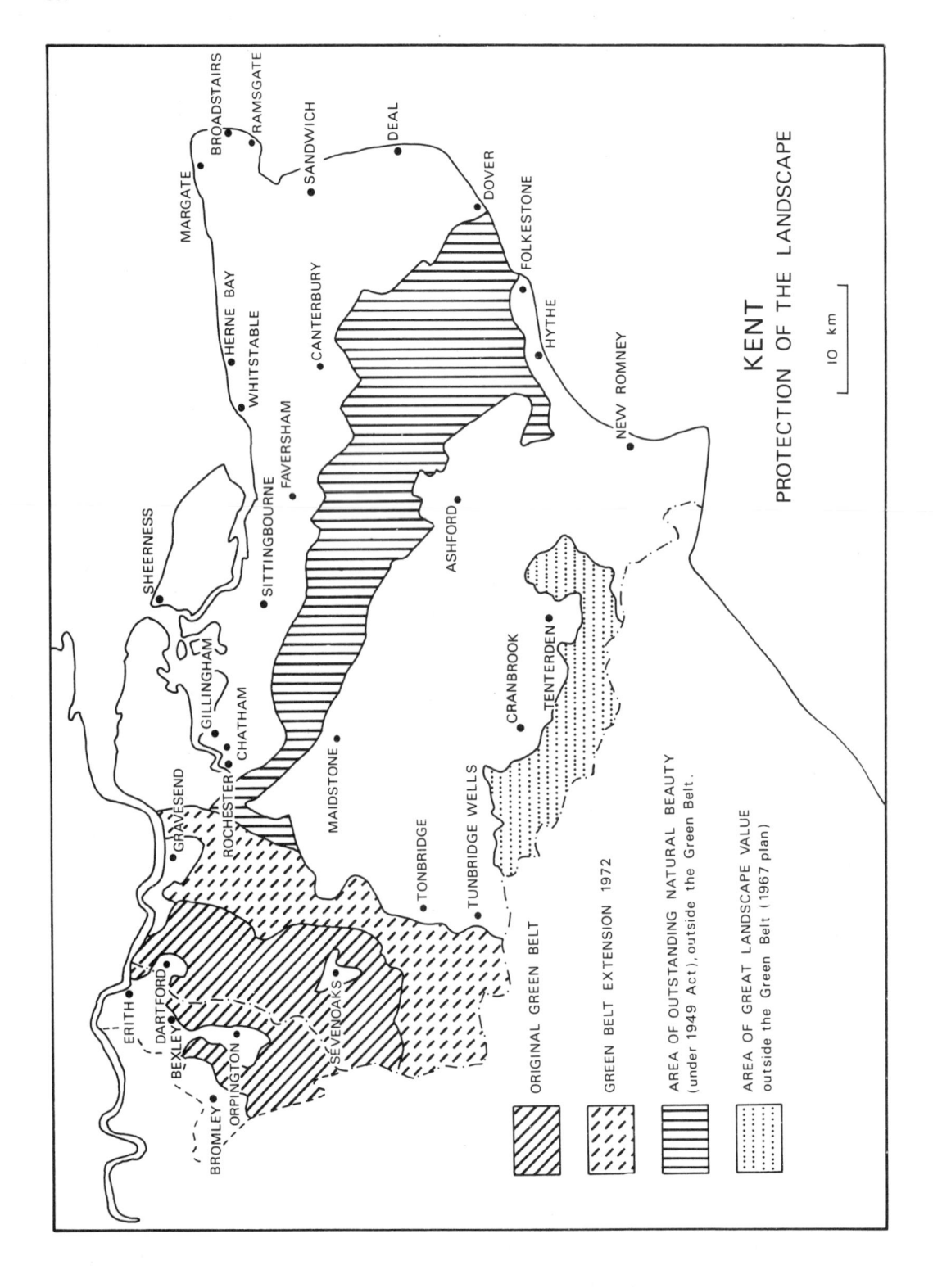

Kent Now and Tomorrow   8

The population within the ancient boundaries of Kent has increased more than ten-fold since 1800 and this increase continues. Smaller families need more houses per thousand of population. Greater material prosperity has increased the power to consume resources and to alter the environment, while many traditional checks and balances have been removed by social changes and rapid transport. Had these forces had free rein the landscape of Kent would have been changed beyond recognition, and for most of us the county would have become a very unpleasant place in which to live. Private enterprise remains the predominant motive power for change in the landscape but, with the important exception of agricultural technology has often been stifled or diverted by town and country planning. So pervasive is the influence of the planner that it is easy to forget the novelty of its emergence, essentially since 1947.

Negative planning has sought to protect valuable features of the landscape, both in economic terms, particularly high quality agricultural land and resources of sand, gravel and water, and in terms of environmental quality, such as noteworthy buildings or areas of natural beauty or scientific interest. Moderating the growth of London has been another objective, furthered by the establishment of a Green Belt on its periphery in which urban development is discouraged, a discouragement extended in some measure to all housing which is mainly for commuters. The protected zones resulting from these policies are shown in fig. 98 and when the areas of good agricultural land (fig. 46) are added it is apparent that only a few areas, notably the Isle of Sheppey and a tract west and south of Ashford, are free from general restrictions. Even then other discouraging factors, such as the inaccessibility of Sheppey and the attractiveness of certain Wealden villages, need to be weighed.

Planning has a positive aspect in encouraging desirable developments. Thus provision must be made for some population

Fig. 98.
Protection of the Kent Landscapes
Showing Green Belt and designated areas of Outstanding Natural Beauty and Great Landscape Value.

growth. Ashford has been indicated as a possible nucleus for a major town, and some expansion suggested for the Sheppey townships, Maidstone and Dover. Road construction is a particularly influential aspect of planning. With the Channel Tunnel and its high speed rail link in limbo, Kent roads are having to serve heavy traffic to and from the cross-channel ferries, and as a result priority is being given to the completion of the M20 from Swanley to Folkestone.

In town and village centres the need to conserve and indeed rehabilitate not simply individual buildings but whole areas that form a visual unity is being appreciated. A considerable number of statutory conservation areas now exist, and the imaginative scheme applied to Abbey Street, Faversham is an example of comprehensive improvement that should be widely copied.

In the countryside many smaller houses and cottages have been splendidly restored by unprompted private enterprise. The area round Smarden and Biddenden affords fine examples, together with many converted oast-houses. The oddity of an oast-house with windows is preferable to dereliction or demolition. With so many tumbledown cottages upgraded to 'period houses of character', however, it becomes sadly difficult for local people of humble means to find homes. Moreover local employment opportunities are shrinking as farms need less labour and small industrial units, such as brickworks, are closed, so that villages are ceasing to be socially balanced communities.

Social factors are difficult to measure and to plan, and the most valuable social virtue is loyalty. Loyalty to a town or village makes it worthwhile to struggle to improve its life and facilities, and such a loyalty shared redoubles the bonds of neighbourliness. It means time is gladly given to community organizations and local government. Loyalty also means interest in a place or an area, covering every aspect of its geography and history. It is no accident that the Kent Council of Social Service has a very active Local History Committee. The Kent Archaeological Society is one of the oldest and strongest county societies. More general interests are covered by the Association of Men of Kent and Kentish Men. The loyalty to Kent of most of its inhabitants is very deep, so that any division or amalgamation of the county during local government changes would have led to a great sense of outrage and the loss of much goodwill. The purpose of this book is the exact opposite, by a review of the distinctive or particularly valuable features of our county to increase not only the appreciation of visitors but the proper pride of Kentish people.

BIBLIOGRAPHY

A full bibliography would be extremely voluminous, so the list below concentrates on relatively recent books. It includes few articles, but many more can be found in the reference lists of *The Rural Landscape of Kent* by S. G. McRae and C. P. Burnham (published by Wye College in 1973 and now out of print). On historical themes, including buildings, the reader is referred to *The History of Kent: a select bibliography* by F. W. Jessup (K.C.C., Maidstone, 1966) and to *Archaeologia Cantiana,* the Journal of the Kent Archaeological Society, a selection of papers from which has been edited by M. Roake and J. Whyman as *Essays in Kentish History* (Frank Cass, 1973). *The Kent Bibliography,* a full list of public library holdings to March 1973, compiled by G. Bennett and edited by W. Bergess and C. Earl, was published by the London and Home Counties Branch of the Library Association in 1977. This contains references to many local histories of individual towns and villages, which are with a few exceptions omitted from the list which follows. In this list, publication place is London, if not stated otherwise.

GENERAL

Burke, J. *Discovering Britain: South East England,* Faber, 1975.
Church, R. *Kent,* Hale, 1967.
Coleman, A. M. and Lukehurst, C. T. *British Landscapes through Maps: 10—East Kent,* Geographical Association, Sheffield, 1967.
Crouch, M. *Kent,* second edition, Batsford, 1967.
Crouch, M. *The Cream of Kent,* Arthur Cassell, Sheerness, 1973.
Furley, R. *A History of the Weald of Kent,* J. R. Smith, 1874.
Goodsall, R. H. *The Kentish Stour,* Cassell, London, 1953.
Goodsall, R. H. *The Medway and its Tributaries,* 1955, republished E.P., Wakefield, 1970.
Hasted, E. *History and Topographical Survey of the County of Kent, 1797-1801,* republished E.P., Wakefield, in 12 vols, 1972.
Higham, R. *Kent,* Batsford, 1974.
Hughes, P. *Kent: A Shell Guide,* Faber, 1969.
Jennett, S. *The Pilgrims' Way from Winchester to Canterbury,* Cassell, London, 1971.

McRae, S. G. and Burnham, C. P. *The Rural Landscape of Kent,* Wye College, 1973.
Mee, A. *The King's England: Kent,* Hodder and Stoughton, revised edition, 1969.
Melling, E. (editor) *Kentish Sources* (a series of archival excerpts), K.C.C., Maidstone, 1965 onwards.
Millward, R. and Robinson, A. *Landscapes of Britain: South-East England—Thamesside and the Weald,* Macmillan, 1971.
Millward, R. and Robinson, A. *Landscapes of Britain: South-East England—The Channel Coastlands,* Macmillan, 1973.
Murray, W. J. C. *Romney Marsh,* Hale, second edition, 1972.
Pyatt, F. C. *Chalkways of South and South-East England,* David and Charles, Newton Abbot, 1974.
Spence, K. *The Companion Guide to Kent and Sussex,* Collins, 1973.
Stamp, L. D. *Report of the Land Utilisation Survey of Britain, Part 85— Kent,* Geographical Publications, Bude, 1943.
Victoria County History of Kent, 3 vols, 1908-32, reprinted Dawson, 1974.
White, J. T. *The South East, Down and Weald: Kent, Surrey and Sussex,* Eyre Methuen, 1977.
Wooldridge, S. W. and Goldring, F. *The Weald,* Collins, 1953.
Wright, C. J. *A Guide to the Pilgrims' Way and North Downs Way,* Constable, 1971.

GEOLOGY AND LANDSCAPE

Allen, P. *Geologists' Association Guide No 24: Geology of the Central Weald: The Hastings Beds,* Geologists' Association, 1960 (excursion routes).
Gallois, R. W. *British Regional Geology: The Wealden District,* fourth edition, H.M.S.O., 1965 (refers to maps, memoirs and other works).
Geological Survey *Memoirs* (exist for all Kent except the Faversham area).
Kirkaldy, J. F. *Geologists' Association Guide No. 29: Geology of the Weald,* Geologists' Association, 1967.
Maizels, J. K. *Geology in Kent and East Sussex,* Canterbury Museum, 1975.
Pitcher, W. S., Peake, N. B., Carreck, J. N., Kirkaldy, J. F. and Hancock, J. M. *Geologists' Association Guide No. 30B: The London Region (South of the Thames),* Geologists' Association, 1967.
Philosophical Transactions of the Royal Society, vol 272A (1972) (contains several papers concerned with the subsidence of south-eastern England).
Proceedings of the Geologists' Association, vol 86, pt 4 (1975). (contains a collection of papers on the geology of the Weald and related topics).
Sherlock, R. L. *British Regional Geology: London and the Thames Valley,* third edition, H.M.S.O., 1960.
Topley, W. *The Geology of the Weald,* Memoir Geological Suvey, 1855.
Wooldridge, S. W. and Linton, D. L. *Structure, Surface and Drainage in South-East England,* Philip, 1955.

FARMER'S LANDSCAPE

Avery, B. W. 'Soil Classification in the Soil Survey of England and Wales', *Journal of Soil Science,* vol. 24 (1973), 324-338.
Bagenal, N. B. and Furneaux, B. S. *Fruit-growing Areas on the Hastings Beds in Kent,* Ministry of Agriculture and Fisheries Bulletin No. 141, H.M.S.O., 1949.
Bibby, J. S. and Mackney, D. *Land Use Capability Classification,* Soil Survey Technical Monograph No. 1, Soil Survey of England and Wales, Harpenden, 1969.
Burgess, A. H. *Hops,* Hill, 1964.
East Malling Research Station *Annual Reports.*
Fordham, S. J. and Green. R. D. *Soils in Kent 2, Sheet TR35 (Deal),* Soil Survey Record, Soil Survey of England and Wales, Harpenden, 1973.
Fordham, S. J. and Green, R. D. *Soils in Kent 3, Sheet TQ86 (Rainham),* Soil Survey Record, Soil Survey of England and Wales, Harpenden, 1976.
Garrad, G. H. *A Survey of the Agriculture of Kent,* Royal Agricultural Society of England, 1954.

Green R. D., *Soils of Romney Marsh* Bulletin, Soil Survey of England and Wales, Harpenden, 1968.
Green, R. D. and Fordham, S. J. *Soils in Kent 1, Sheet TR04 (Ashford)* Soil Survey Record, Soil Survey of England and Wales, Harpenden, 1973.
Green, R. D. and Fordham, S. J. *Soils of Kent* Bulletin, Soil Survey of England and Wales, Harpenden (in preparation).
Hall, A. D. and Russell, E. J. *A Report on the Agriculture and Soils of Kent, Surrey and Sussex,* H.M.S.O., 1911.
Harrison, A. A. 'A Discussion of the Temperatures of Inland Kent with Particular Reference to Night Minima in the Lowlands', *Meteorological Magazine,* vol. 100 (1971), 97-111.
Lee, L. L. 'The Possibilities of an International System for the Classification of Soils', *Journal of the Southeastern Agricultural College,* vol 28 (1931), 65-114 (summarises early work by S. G. Brade-Birks and B. S. Furneaux).
McRae, S. G. and Burnham, C. P. 'The Soils of the Weald', *Proceedings of the Geologists' Association,* vol 86 (1975), 593-610.
Meteorological Office *Climatological Atlas of the British Isles,* H.M.S.O., 1952.

WILDLIFE IN THE LANDSCAPE

Barrington, C. A. *Forestry in the Weald,* Forestry Commission Booklet, No. 22, H.M.S.O., 1968.
Chalmers-Hunt, J. M. *The Butterflies and Moths of Kent,* three volumes, Entomologists' Record, 1960-73.
Collis, M. and others *Environmental Studies at Hothfield,* K.C.C., Maidstone, 1972.
Department of the Environment *Report on a River Pollution Survey of England and Wales, 1970,* vol 1, H.M.S.O., 1971.
Durman, R. *Bird Observatories in Britain and Ireland,* Poyser, Berkhamsted, 1976 (includes Dungeness, etc.)
Forestry Commission *Forest Walks in Kent,* H.M.S.O., 1973.
Gillham, E. H. and Homes, R. C. *The Birds of the North Kent Marshes,* Collins, 1950.
Hanbury, F. J. and Marshall, E. S. *Flora of Kent,* Hanbury, 1899.
Harrison, J. *Wildfowl of the North Kent Marshes,* Wildfowlers' Association of Britain and Ireland, Chester, 1971.
Harrison, J. M. *The Birds of Kent,* Witherby, 1953.
Louseley, J. E. *Wild Flowers of Chalk and Limestone,* Collins, 1969.
Macdonald, Sir M. and partners *River Stour study, vol. 4 Biology and Chemistry,* Kent River Authority, Maidstone, 1973.
Manning, S. A. *The Naturalist in South-East England,* David and Charles, Newton Abbot, 1974.
Morgan, G. H. and Spain A. (editors) *A Symposium on Hothfield Local Nature Reserve,* Transactions of the Kent Field Club, vol. 5, pt 3 (1975).
Nature Conservancy *The Nature Conservancy in Kent,* Wye, 1970 (also publish guides to individual National Nature Reserves).
Nature Conservancy *Wildlife Conservation in the North Kent Marshes,* Wye, 1971.
Pollard, E., Hooper, M. D. and Moore, N. W. *Hedges,* Collins, 1974.
Rose, F. 'The East Kent Fens' *Journal of Ecology,* vol. 38 (1950), 292-302 (Ham Fen).
Salisbury, E. J. *Downs and Dunes, Their Plant Life and its Environment,* Bell, 1952.
Salisbury, E. J. *Weeds and Aliens,* Collins, 1961.
Tansley, A. G. *The British Islands and their Vegetation,* University Press, Cambridge, 1939.
Wells, T. C. E. 'Botanical Aspects of the Conservation and Management of Chalk Grasslands', *Biological Conservation,* vol. 2 (1969), 36-44.
Wilson, M. 'Plant Distribution in the Woods of Northeast Kent' *Annals of Botany,* vol. 25 (1911), 857-902.

LANDSCAPES OF THE PAST

Banister, J. *A Synopsis of Husbandry,* G. G. Robinson, 1799 (eighteenth century agriculture).
Barton, S. *Castles in Britain,* Lyle Publications, Galashiels, 1973.

Bignell, A. *Hopping Down in Kent,* Hale, London, 1977.
Boorman, H. R. P. *Hell's Corner, 1940. Kent becomes the Battlefield of Britain,* Kent Messenger, Maidstone, 1942.
Boys, J. *General View of the Agriculture of the County of Kent,* third edition, Board of Agriculture, 1805.
Brentnall, M. *The Cinque Ports and Romney Marsh,* Gifford, 1972.
Bushell, T. A. *Barracuda Guide to County History,: 1—Kent.* Barracuda, Chesham, 1976 (a chronology, sometimes uncritical).
Camden, W. *Britannia: Kent.* R. Gough's revised edition, 1789, reprinted Hutchinson, 1977.
Chalklin, C. W. *Seventeenth Century Kent,* Longmans, 1965 (valuable, especially on industries).
Cobbett, W. *Rural Rides in the Counties of Surrey, Kent, etc., during the years 1821-32. . .* 2 vols, Reeves and Turner, 1893.
Crouch, M. and Bergess, W. *Victorian and Edwardian Kent from Old Photographs,* Batsford, 1974.
Daly, A. *History of the Isle of Sheppey,* 1904, reprinted Arthur Cassell, Sheerness, 1975.
Darby, H. C. and Campbell, E. M. J. *The Domesday Geography of South-East England,* University Press, Cambridge, 1962.
Dyer, J. *Southern England: An Archaeological Guide,* Faber, 1973.
Everitt, A. M. *The Community of Kent and the Great Rebellion, 1640-60,* University Press, Leicester, 1966.
Everitt, A. M. 'The making of the agrarian landscape of Kent', *Archaeologia Cantiana,* vol 92 (1976), 1-31.
Everitt, A. M. *The Making of the Kent Landscape,* Hodder (in preparation).
Evison, V. I. *The Fifth Century Invasions South of the Thames,* Athlone Press, 1965.
Glover, J. *The Place Names of Kent,* Batsford, 1976.
Hadfield, C. *Canals of South and South-East England,* David and Charles, Newton Abbot, 1969.
Hinings, E. *History, People and Places of the Cinque Ports,* Spurbooks, Bourne End, 1975.
Hoskins, W. G. *The Making of the English Landscape,* Hodder and Stoughton, 1955.
Ireland, W. H. *A Treasury of Kent Prints,* Arthur Cassell, Sheerness, 1972 (the illustrations from a book of 1818-31).
Jenkins, F. *Men of Kent before the Romans. Cantium in the Early Iron Age,* Canterbury Archaeological Society, 1962 (authoritative booklet).
Jessup, F. W. *Kent History Illustrated,* K.C.C., Maidstone, 1966 (valuable series of maps).
Jessup, F. W. *A History of Kent,* Phillimore, Chichester, 1974 (the most reliable comprehensive work).
Jessup, R. F. and Jessup, F. W. *The Cinque Ports,* Batsford, 1952.
Johnson, S. *The Roman Forts of the Saxon Shore,* Elek, 1976.
Kidner, R. W. *The South-Eastern and Chatham Railway,* Oakwood Press, Lingfield, 1963.
Kidner, R. W. *A History of the Southern Railway,* 2 vols, Ian Allen, Shepperton, 1964.
Lambarde, W. *A Perambulation of Kent,* 1570, reprinted Adams and Dart, Bath, 1970.
Margary, I. D. *Roman Roads in Britain,* third edition, Phoenix House, 1973.
Melling, E. *History of the Kent County Council,* K.C.C., Maidstone, 1975.
Sammes, E. *Discovering Regional Archaeology: South Eastern England,* Shire Publications, Aylesbury, 1973 (a booklet guide for visits).
Smith, R. A. L. *Canterbury Cathedral Priory. A Study in Monastic Administration,* University Press, Cambridge, 1969 (includes mediaeval agriculture).
Sutcliffe, S. *Martello Towers,* David and Charles, Newton Abbot, 1972.
Veale, E. W. P. *Gateway to the Continent: a History of Cross-Channel Transport,* Ian Allen, Shepperton, 1955.
Vine, P. A. *The Royal Military Canal,* David and Charles, Newton Abbot, 1972.
Waechter, J. A. 'Swanscombe 1968'. *Proceedings of the Royal Anthropological Institute,* (1968), 53-58.
Witney, K. P. *The Jutish Forest. A Study of the Weald of Kent from 450 to 1380 AD,* Athlone Press, 1976.
Wright, C. J. *Kent through the Years,* Batsford, 1975.

INDUSTRIES

Balston, T. *James Whatman, Father and Son*, Methuen, 1957.

Crossley, D. *The Bewl Valley Ironworks, Kent, c 1300-1730*, Royal Archaeological Institute, 1975.

Hewitt, E. M. 'Industries' *Victoria County History*, vol 3 (1932), 371-435.

Lovett, G. V. 'The Development of the Kent Coalfield' *Colliery Guardian*, vol 223 (1975), 510-515.

Planning Officers *Kent County Structure Plan Section 9B, Mineral Extraction in Kent*, K.C.C., Maidstone, 1975.

Preston, J. M. *Industrial Medway: A Historical Survey*, The Author, 162 Borstal Road, Rochester, 1977 (19th and early 20th centuries).

Shorter, A. H. *Paper mills and paper makers in England, 1495-1800*, Paper Publications Society, Hilversum, The Netherlands, 1957.

Straker, E. *Wealden Iron*, 1931, reprinted David and Charles, Newton Abbot, 1969.

Sweeting, G. S. 'Wealden Iron Ore and the History of its Industry' *Proceedings of the Geologists' Association*, vol 55 (1944), 1-20.

BUILDINGS IN THE LANDSCAPE

ABC Historic Publications *Historic Houses, Castles and Gardens* (annual).

Barley, M. W. *The English Farmhouse and Cottage*, Routledge, 1961.

Boorman, H. R. P. and Torr, V. J. *Kent Churches*, Kent Messenger, Maidstone, 1954.

Brown, R. J. *Windmills of England*, Robert Hale, 1976 (recent information about 14 Kentish mills).

Clifton-Taylor, A. *The Pattern of English Building*, Batsford, 1972.

Finch, W. C. *Watermills and Windmills*, 1933, reprinted Arthur Cassell, Sheerness, 1976 (almost entirely about Kent).

Gravett, K. W. E. *Timber and Brick Building in Kent*, Phillimore, Chichester, 1971.

Gravett, K. W. E. 'Brookland Belfry', *Archaeologia Cantiana*, vol 89 (1974), 43-48.

Harvey, N. *A History of Farm Buildings*, David and Charles, Newton Abbot, 1970.

Hill, D. I. *Christ's Glorious Church*, S.P.C.K. 1976 (about Canterbury Cathedral).

Jackson, A. A. *Semi-detached London, Suburban Development, Life and Transport, 1900-1939*, Allen and Unwin, 1974.

Mason, R. T. *Framed Buildings of the Weald*, second edition, The Author, Handcross, 1970.

Meates, G. W. *Lullingstone Roman Villa*, Heinemann, 1965.

Melling, E. *Kentish Sources I: Some Kentish Houses*, K.C.C., Maidstone, 1965.

Mercer, E. *English Vernacular Houses*, H.M.S.O., 1975.

Newman, J. *The Buildings of England: Vol. 38 West Kent and the Weald*, and *Vol. 39, North East and East Kent*, Penguin, Harmondsworth, 1969.

Oswald, A. *Country Houses of Kent*, Country Life, 1933.

Prizeman, J. *Your House: The Outside View*, Hutchinson, 1975 (includes urban vernacular architecture).

Rigold, S. E. 'Some major Kentish Timber Barns', *Archaeologia Cantiana*, vol. 82 (1967) 1-30.

Rigold, S. E. 'Domestic Buildings, in *The Rural Landscape of Kent*, (S. G. McRae and C. P. Burnham, editors), 184-190, Wye College, 1973.

Sackville-West, V. *Knole and the Sackvilles*, Drummond, 1947.

Spain, R. J. 'The Len Water-mills, *Archaeologia Cantiana*, vol. 82 (1967), 32-104.

Thompson, F. C. 'Hop Oasts', *Journal of Kent Local History*, No. 6 (March 1978), 2-4.

Wailes, R. *The English Windmill*, Routledge, 1967 (includes a detailed description of Cranbrook mill).

West, J. *The Windmills of Kent*, Charles Skilton, 1973.

West, T. *The Timber-frame House in England*, David and Charles, Newton Abbot, 1971.

White, J. T. *The Parklands of Kent*, Arthur Cassell, Sheerness, 1975.

Wright, T. W. *The Gardens of Kent, Surrey and Sussex*, Batsford, 1978.

TOWNS AND VILLAGES

Ashford Local History Group *Ashford's Past at Present,* Ashford, 1976.
Bentwich, H. C. *History of Sandwich in Kent,* The Author, Sandwich, 1971.
Bignell, A. *Kent Villages,* Robert Hale, 1975.
Bishop, C. H. *Folkestone: The Story of a Town,* Invicta Press, Ashford, 1973.
Boorman, H. R. P. *Ashford's Progress: the development of an important town* (mostly pictures, including some of villages within the borough), Kent Messenger, Maidstone, 1977.
Boorman, H. R. P. *Pictures of Maidstone,* Kent Messenger, Maidstone, 1965.
Boyle, J. *Portrait of Canterbury,* Hale, 1974.
Cantacusino, S. and others *Canterbury* (City Buildings Series), Studio Vista, 1970.
Church, D. *Cuxton—A Kentish Village,* Arthur Cassell, Sheerness, 1976.
Church, R. *Portrait of Canterbury,* Hutchinson, 1968.
Crouch, M. *Canterbury,* Longmans, 1970.
Davis, T. *Tunbridge Wells: The Gentle Aspect,* Phillimore, 1976.
Duggan, A. *Thomas Becket of Canterbury,* Faber, 1967.
Dunlop, Sir, J. K. *The Pleasant Town of Sevenoaks. A History,* The Author, Sevenoaks, 1964.
Frere, S. S. *Roman Canterbury: the City of Durovernum,* Canterbury Excavation Committee, 1962.
Hill, D. I. *The Ancient Hospitals and Almshouses of Canterbury,* Canterbury Archaeological Society, 1969.
Hodder, E. *The Life of Samuel Morley,* Hodder, 1887 (the 'improving' landlord of Leigh, near Tonbridge).
Jacob, E. *The History of the Town and Port of Faversham,* Arthur Cassell, Sheerness (1774, reprinted with additions 1974).
Measom, G. *The Official Illustrated Guide to the South Eastern Railway and its branches including the North Kent and Greenwich Lines,* 1858, reprinted E & W Books, 1970.
Royal Archaeological Institute *Programme of the Summer Meeting at Canterbury, 1969* (also printed in Archaeological Journal, vol. 126 (1970) includes valuable accounts of Brook, Canterbury, Chatham, Dover, Faversham and Sandwich).
Savidge, A. *Royal Tunbridge Wells,* Midas Books, Speldhurst, 1975.
Seymour, J. *The Companion Guide to the Coast of South East England,* Collins, 1975.
Smith, F. F. *A History of Rochester,* Hallewell, Rochester, 1928, reprinted 1976.
Urry, W. *Canterbury under the Angevin Kings,* Athlone Press, 1967 (twelfth to fourteenth centuries).

KENT, NOW AND TOMORROW

Buchanan, C. and Partners *Ashford Study. Consultants' Proposals for Designation,* H.M.S.O., 1967.
County Planning Officers *Towards a Structure Plan for Kent: The Main Issues,* K.C.C., Maidstone, 1975.
Thomas, D. *London's Green Belt,* Faber, 1970.

INDEX OF PLACE NAMES

Figures in parenthesis eg (TR 23) refer to the 10km National Grid square in which the locality is situated, shown on the endpapers. The annotation 'f' denotes one, 'ff' two or more following pages.

Abbot's Cliff (TR 23) 23
Addington (TQ 65) 2
Aldington (TR 03) 114
Allington (TQ 75) 12, 113
Andredsweald (Forest of) 6
Appledore (TQ 92) 76, 99, 113, Fig. 32
Ash (near Sandwich) (TR 25) 71, 116
Ashford (TR 04) xviii, 15f, 18, 23, 26, 36, 91, 107, 113, 116, 123, 129f, 137, 150, 156, 161f, Figs. 42, 57, 85, 92
Aylesford (TQ 75) xviii, 2, 124, 127
Aylesham (TR 25) 126, 159, Fig. 85

Barfreston (TR 24) 114
Barham (TR 25) 99
Barham Downs (TR 25) xvii
Barming (TQ 75) 124
Barming Heath (TQ 75) 158
Beckenham (TQ 36) 24, 40
Bedgebury (Goudhurst) (TQ 73) 48, 82, 89, 99, 129
Bekesbourne (TR 15) 124
Belmont (Throwley) (TQ 95) 128
Benenden (TQ 83) 99
Bethersden (TQ 94) 7, 34, 83, 111
Betteshanger (TR 35) 20, 91, 106, 124
Beult, river 18, 34, 61
Bexley (TQ 47) xvi, 24, 40, 99, 116, 123f, 126, Fig. 69
Bexleyheath (TQ 47) 126, 128
Bicknor (TQ 85) 112
Biddenden (TQ 83) 7, 120f, 162, Plate 21
Bigberry (Canterbury) (TR 15) 2, 3
Biggin Hill (TQ 45) 27, 75
Birchington (TR 36) 28, 44, 113
Blean (TR 16) 40, 75, 78, 97, 99
Bobbing (TQ 86) 6
Borough Green (TQ 65) 28, 159
Bough Beech (TQ 44) 93, 99f, 120, 124, 131, Plate 22
Boughton Aluph (TR 04) Plate 12
Boughton Monchelsea (TQ 74) 99, 122
Boxley (TQ 75)
Bradbourne (East Malling) (TQ 75) 123
Brasted (TQ 45) 99, 123
Brasted Chart (TQ 45) 158

Bredhurst (TQ 76) 99
Brenchley (TQ 64) 71, 99, 114
Brenley Corner (TR 05) 28
Bridge (TR 15) 7
Broadstairs (TR 36) 26, 129, 148f, Fig. 19
Brogdale (Faversham) (TR 05) 59
Bromley (TQ 46) xvi, 16, 24, 40, 122, 126, 128, Figs. 13, 18
Brompton (TQ 76) 147
Brook (TR 04) 115, 130, 132, 153f, Figs. 79, 81, 94, Plates 2, 29
Brookland (TQ 92) 116, Figs. 32, 67
Broome Park (Barham) (TR 24) 123, Fig. 74b
Burham (TQ 76) 90, 99
Bybrook (Ashford) (TR 04) 130

Canterbury (TR 15) xvif, 2ff, 6, 8, 12ff, 16, 18, 20, 22ff, 27, 47, 61, 74, 91f, 101f, 112ff, 121, 127, 135, 139ff, 153f, Figs. 1, 7, 8, 9, 13, 57, 68, 85-88, Plates 13, 26
Challock Lees (TR 05) 99, 158
Charing (TQ 94) 102, 121, 130f
Charing Heath (TQ 94), 74, 91, 158
Chart (see also Great and Little Chart) (TQ 94) 7
Chartham (TR 15) 115, 137
Chartham Hatch (TR 15) 99
Chartwell (Westerham) (TQ 45) 27, 99
Chatham (TR 15) xvii, 2, 13, 16, 19f, 22, 80, 101, 113, 147f, Figs. 13, 18
Chattenden (TQ 77) 159
Chegworth (Harrietsham) (TQ 85) 136
Chelsfield (TQ 46) 7
Chevening (TQ 45) 123, 156
Chiddingstone (TQ 54) 99, 114, 128, 156
Chilham (TQ 05) 2, 12, 61, 93, 114, 116, 123, 127f, 136f, Fig. 78
Chillenden (Goodnestone) (TR 25) 134
Chislehurst (TQ 46) 24, 99, 126
Chislet (TR 26) 91, 106
Cliffe (TQ 77) 99, 106, 112, 115, Plate 19

169

Cliftonville (Margate) (TR 37) 148
Cobham (TQ 66) 123f, 128, Fig. 95
Cowden (TQ 44) 93, Plate 25
Crabble (Dover) (TR 34) 136
Cranbrook (TQ 73) 11, 115, 135, 150f, Figs. 13, 83
Cray, river 2, 3
Cuxton (TQ 76) 99

Danson Park (Bexleyheath) (TQ 47) 128
Darent, river xvii, 2f, 6, 38, 43, 102, 137
Dartford (TQ 57) xvii, 14, 28, 109f, 137, 150, Figs. 13, 18, 85
Deal (TR 35) 3, 13, 18, 50, 74, 89, 127, 149, Figs. 12, 13, 18, 85
Dent de Lion (Margate) (TR 36) 112
Deptford (TQ 37) 13, 22f, 71, 80, 101, Fig. 13
Devil's Kneading Trough (Brook) (TR 04) 48, Plate 2
Doddington (TQ 95) 112
Dover (TR 34) xviii, 4, 8, 10ff, 16, 18, 23, 26, 28, 37, 74, 97, 109, 114, 118, 134, 136, 162, Figs. 6, 8, 13, 18, 85, Plates, 4, 6
Dowels (Appledore) (TQ 92) 76
Downe (TQ 46) 99
Dungeness (TR 01) 44, 56, 90, 94, 96f, 99, 109f, 156, Figs. 32, 60, Plate 18
Dunkirk (TR 05) 54
Dymchurch (TR 12) 19, 149, Fig. 32

East Farleigh (TQ 75) 18, Fig. 14
East Malling (TQ 75) 57, 71, 123
East Peckham (TQ 64) 127, Plate 24
East Stour, river 41, 93
East Sutton (TQ 84), 8
Eastwell (TR 04) 156
Ebbsfleet (TR 36) 6
Eccles (TQ 76) 117, Fig. 7
Eden, river 92
Edenbridge (TQ 44) 136
Egerton (TQ 94) 8, 114, 116
Egypt Bay (St Mary's Hoo) (TQ 77) 89
Eltham (TQ 47) xvi, 122f, 127
Elvington (Eythorne) (TR 25) 159
Erith (TQ 57) 24, 113
Eynsford (TQ 56) 12, 118, 137

Fairfield (Romney Marsh) (TQ 92) 114, Fig. 32
Farnborough (TQ 46) 16, 28
Farningham (TQ 56) 28, 137
Faversham (TR 06) 12, 23, 28, 59, 61, 104, 107, 117, 121, 123, 130, 135f, 162, Figs 13, 85

Folkestone (TR 23) 3, 10f, 14, 16, 19, 26, 34, 36f, 97, 108, 116, 129, 149, 162, Figs 7, 13, 15, 85
Folkestone Warren (TR 23) 23, 37, 97, 99, Plate 5
Fordwich (TR 15) 18, Figs 8, 13
Frindsbury (TQ 76) 113, 147

Garlinge (Margate) (TR 36) 112
Gillingham (TR 76) 20, 61, 147f
Godinton (Ashford) (TQ 94) 123, 129, 156, Fig. 42
Godmersham (TR 05) 21, 112, 114, 123, 128, Fig. 17
Goodnestone (TR 25) Fig. 66
Goodwin Sands (TR 45) 149
Goudhurst (TQ 73) 7, 53, 114, 120
Grain (TQ 87) 55, 95, 109f
Graveney (TR 06) 55, 149
Gravesend (TQ 67) xvii, 13, 16, 18ff, 26, 40, 108f, Figs. 13, 18, 85
Great Chart (TQ 94) 124, 156
Greenhithe (TQ 57) 7
Greensand Ridge 11, 35, 40, 42, 48, 54, 62, 78, 153, Figs. 31, 35
Greenwich (TQ 37) xvi, xvii, 22f, Fig. 13
Groombridge (TQ 53) 156

Hadlow (TQ 64) 34, 61, 124, Fig. 75
Halling (TQ 76) 104
Ham Fen (TR 35) 89, 99f
Ham Street Woods (TR 03) 80, 97, 99
Harbledown (TR 15) 99
Hardres (TR 15) 22
Harrietsham (TQ 85) 7, 102
Hawkenbury Bog (Tunbridge Wells) (TW 53) 89, 99f
Hawkhurst (TQ 73), 7, 99, Plate 14
Haxted (Edenbridge) (TQ 44) 136
Hayes (TQ 46) 126
Hayes Common (TQ 46) 2, 40
Headcorn (TQ 84) 115, 120
Hempstead (TQ 76), 147
Herne (TR 16) 115, 135, 149
Herne Bay (TR 16), 40, 44, 149, Fig. 85
Hersden (TR 16) 99, 159
Hever (TQ 44) 12, 129, 156, Fig. 11
Higham (TQ 77) 7, 115, 130
High Halden (TQ 93) 83
High Halstow (TQ 77), 89, 97, 99
High Rocks (Tunbridge Wells) (TQ 53) 2
Holborough (Snodland) (TQ 76) 104
Hollingbourne (TQ 85) 120
Homesdale 36
Hoo Peninsula 18, 40, 94
Horne's Place (Appledore) (TQ 93) 113

Horton Kirby (TQ 56) 20
Hothfield Common (TQ 94) 36, 54, 88, 99f, 158, Fig. 54
Hulberry (Lullingstone) (TQ 56) 2
Hythe (TR 13) 12, 16, 34, 40, 43, 109, 115, 129, Figs. 8, 13, 18

Ide Hill (Brasted) (TQ 45) 99
Ightham (TQ 55) 1f, 36, 54, 100, 118f

Julieberrie's Grave (Chilham) (TR 05) 2

Kemsing (TQ 55) 123
Kemsley (TQ 96) 159
Kennington (TR 04) 137, 150
Keston (TQ 46) 2, 128, 134
Keston Common (TQ 46) 40
Kingsferry Bridge (TQ 96) Fig. 20
Kingsnorth (Hoo) (TQ 87) 110
Kits Coty (Aylesford) (TQ 76) 2, Fig. 4
Knole (Sevenoaks) (TQ 55) 113, 122f, 127f, Figs. 73, 74a
Knowlton (TR 25) 155
Lamberhurst (TQ 63) 53, 99
Larkfield (TQ 75) 120
Leeds (TQ 85) 12f, 93, 115, 128, 130, 136
Lees Court (Sheldwich) (TR 05) 123
Leigh (TQ 37) 7, 93, 124, 156ff, Fig. 96, Plate 30
Len, river 74, 136
Lenham (TQ 85) 99, 109, 121
Lenham Heath (TQ 94) 74, 158f, Fig. 97
Leybourne (TQ 65) 99f
Littlebourne (TR 25) 130
Littlebrook (Dartford) (TQ 57) 110
Little Chart (TQ 94) 111, Figs. 7, 76
Littlestone (TR 02) 19
Little Stour, river 61, 92, 137
London xvif, 15f, 18ff, 22ff, 34f, 40, 56, 59, 61, 68, 71f, 102, 161
Loose stream (TQ 75) 137
Lower Halstow (TQ 85) 104
Lower Hardres (TR 15) 117
Luddesdown (TQ 66) 99
Lullingstone (TQ 56) 2, 48, 114, 117f, 156
Lydd (TR 02) 77, 96, 114, 116, 151
Lydd-on-Sea (TR 02) 149
Lyminge (TR 14) 38, 99, 114
Lympne (TR 13) 4, 115
Maidstone (TQ 75) xviii, 2f, 11, 14, 16, 18, 20, 22, 24, 27, 34ff, 57, 61f, 102ff, 107ff, 112f, 115, 117, 120, 126, 136, 139, 145ff, 162, Figs. 13, 85, Plates 15, 20, 27

Malling (see also East and West Malling) (TQ 65) 6
Manston (TR 36) 27
Marden (TQ 74) 34
Margate (TR 37) 22, 26, 47, 109, 135, 148f, Figs. 13, 90, 91
Marley (Lenham) (TQ 85) 109
Matfield (TQ 64) 129
Medway, river xvii, 2ff, 6, 18f, 23, 34, 36, 38, 43, 55f, 61, 75, 91ff, 102, Fig. 13
Medway Towns (TQ 76) 108, 147f, Fig. 85 (see also Rochester etc.)
Meopham (TQ 66) 115, 118, 135, Fig. 85
Mereworth (TQ 65) 88, 117, 123, 128
Mereworth Woods (TQ 65) 99
Mersham (TR 03) 123, 136
Middle Park (Eltham) (TQ 47) 127
Milton Creek (TQ 96) 91
Minster in Sheppey (TQ 97) 114
Minster in Thanet (TR 36) 2
Monkton (TR 26) 115
Murston (TQ 96) 99f

Naccolt (Wye) (TR 04) 89, 113
New Ash Green (TQ 66) 127, Fig 85
Newington (Folkestone) (TR 13) 124
New Romney (TR 02) 44, 77, 115, 151, Figs. 8, 13, 32, 65, 85
New Town (Ashford) (TR 04) 126, 150
Nonington (TR 25) 124
North Downs xiv, 2f, 7, 30, 37ff, 41f, 52, 54, 74, 78, 81, 84f, 114, 156, Figs. 31, 35, 51, Plate 2
North Downs' Way xvii, 3
Northbourne (TR 35) 127
Northfleet (TQ 67) 104, 106, 110, Fig. 31, Plate 16
Nurstead (TQ 66) 118

Oare (TR 06) 99
Oldbury Hill (Ightham) (TQ 55) 1f, 99, Fig. 5
Old Soar (Plaxtol) (TQ 65) 118
Orlestone (Ham Street) (TR 03) 99
Orpington (TQ 46) 24, 53, 126
Ospringe (TR 06) 99
Otford (TQ 55) Fig. 7
Otham (TQ 75) 120, 137

Paddock Wood (TQ 64) 61, 67, 107, 130
Pegwell Bay (TR 36) 39, 94f, 99, 107, Plate 3
Pembury (TQ 64) 16, 54
Penshurst (TQ 54) 114, 118, 121, 123f, 128, 156
Petham (TR 15) 132

Petts Wood (TQ 46) 99, 126
Pilgrims' Way 3, 38
Plaxtol (TQ 65) 118
Pluckley (TQ 94) 8, 132
Preston Hall (Aylesford) (TQ 75) 124

Queenborough (TQ 97) 13, Figs. 13, 85
Queendown Warren (Hartlip) (TQ 86) 99
Quex Park (Birchington) (TR 36) 113

Rainham (TQ 86) 50, 104, 147
Ramsgate (TR 36) 22, 26, 117, 148f, Figs. 13, 18
Reading Street (TQ 93), 152
Reculver (TR 26), 4, 149
Rhodes Minnis (TR 14) 158
Richborough (TR 36), 4, 26f, 88, 110
Riverhead (TQ 55) 109
Rochester (TQ 76) xvif, 4, 6, 8, 12f, 16, 26, 109, 115, 123, 147f, Figs. 10, 13, 18, 89
Rolvenden (TQ 83) 124, 134, Fig. 82
Romney (see also New Romney) (TR 02) 12, 22
Romney Marsh 3, 11, 20, 23, 43f, 50, 56, 71, 74ff, 83, 85, 93, 102, 114, 125, Figs. 32, 48
Rother, river 18, 23, 43f
Round Down Cliff (TR 23) 23
Royal Military Canal 19, 76, 99f, Fig. 13
Ruxley (TQ 47) 99f
Rye (TQ 92) (Sussex) xvii, 12, 18f, 43f, 77, Fig. 32

St Margaret's at Cliffe (St Margaret's Bay) (TR 34) 135, 149
St Mary's Bay (Dymchurch) (TR 02) 149
St Nicholas at Wade (TR 26) 115
St Paul's Cray (TQ 46) 126
Saltwood (TR 13) 10, 12
Sandgate (TR 23) 13
Sandhurst (TQ 72) Fig. 43
Sandling (Maidstone) (TQ 75) 120, Plate 20
Sandling Park (Hythe) (TR 13) 129
Sandown (Deal) (TR 35) 13, 18
Sandwich (TR 35) 7, 12, 14, 16, 18, 40f, 53, 59, 71, 101f, 108ff, 115, 117, 121, 135, Figs. 8, 13
Sandwich Bay (TR 35) 56, 96f, 99f, 149, Fig. 60
Scotney Castle (Lamberhurst) TQ 63) 111, 128
Seasalter (TR 06) Fig. 8
Selling (TR 05) 115

Sellinge (TR 03) 102
Sevenoaks (TQ 55) 16, 26, 35f, 54, 78, 91, 94, 99, 109, 126, 150, Figs. 13, 18, 85 (see also Knole)
Shakespeare Cliff (Dover) (TR 33) 23, 106
Sharsted (Doddington) (TQ 95) 82
Sheerness (TQ 97) 20, 22, 113, 149, Figs. 13, 18
Shell Ness (TR 06) 97, 100, Fig. 59
Sheppey, Isle of 28, 30, 40, 43, 75f, 86, 94f, 97, 99, 149, 161f
Shoreham (TQ 56) 137, Fig. 63
Sidcup (TQ 47) 24, 28, 126
Sissinghurst (TQ 73) 99, 129
Sittingbourne (TQ 96) 22, 26, 39, 80, 82, 107, 150, 159, Figs. 18, 85
Smallhythe (TQ 83) 18, 120, 151f, Fig. 72
Smarden (TQ 84) 120, 134, 162
Snodland (TQ 76) 26, 106, Fig. 85
Snowdown (Aylesham) (TR 25) 106
Southfleet (TQ 67) 115
Springhead (TQ 67) 4
Squerryes (Westerham) (TQ 45) 2, 123
Stanford (TR 13) 135
Staplehurst (TQ 74) 113
Stelling Minnis (TR 14) 135, 158f
Stockbury (TQ 86) 99, 115
Stodmarsh (TR 26) 94, 100, 136
Stone (Dartford) (TQ 57), 115
Strood (TQ 76) 23, 26, 28, 115, 118, 147, 159
Stour, Great, river xvii, 2f, 18, 23, 36, 38, 40, 43, 56, 74, 91ff, 102, 137, Fig. 57, Plate 2
Straits of Dover 43, 139
Sturry (TR 16) 115
Sundridge (TQ 45) 123
Sundridge Park (Bromley) (TQ 47) 128
Surrenden Dering (Pluckley) (TQ 94) 126
Sutton Valence (TQ 84) 8, 48
Swale, river 43, 56, 91, 94f, 99
Swanley (TQ 56) 71, 88, 162, Fig. 85
Swanscombe (TQ 67) xvi, 1, 99, 104, 106, Fig. 3

Teise, river 18, 61
Temple Ewell (TR 24) 99
Tenterden (TQ 83) 7, 15, 24, 114, 116f, 150ff, Figs. 8, 13, 85, 93, Plate 28
Teynham (TQ 96) 56, 104, 121, Fig. 80

Thames, river 3, 19, 43, 61, 72
Thames and Medway Canal 18, Fig. 13
Thames Estuary 20, 43, 55f, 94, 102, 156, Fig. 1
Thanet, Isle of 2f, 6f, 11, 16, 20, 23, 26, 28. 37ff, 43f, 52, 71f, 75, 87, Figs. 7, 85
Tilmanstone (TR 35) 106
Tolsford Hill (Lyminge) (TR 13) 13
Tonbridge (TQ 54) 2f, 16, 24, 26, 34, 46, 61, 99, 111, 121, 150. Figs. 13, 18, 85
Toys Hill (Westerham) (TQ 45) 35, 99
Trottiscliffe (TQ 66) 2
Tunbridge Wells (TQ 53) 2, 16, 26, 32, 89, 111, 149f, Figs. 13, 18, 85

Ulcombe (TQ 84) 8, 48
Upchurch (TQ 86) 116
Upnor (TQ 77) 13

Waldershare (TR 24) 128, 155
Walderslade (TQ 76) 147
Walmer (TR 35) 13, 18
Wantsum Marshes (TR 26) 43, 56, 75, Fig. 31
Wantsum, river 4
Wateringbury (TQ 65) 107, 136
Watling Street xvii, 4, 6, 15, 61
Weald, The xiv, 2ff, 8, 11, 14, 21, 30, 34, 38, 41f, 61ff, 75f, 78, 85f, 101, 104, 111, 114, 125, 153, 157, 161, Figs. 21, 31, Plate 1

Welling (TQ 47) 126
Westenhanger (TR 13) 130
Westerham (TQ 45) 2f, 19, 27 34ff, 99ff, 102, 123
Westerham Hill (TQ 45) 38
West Hythe (TR 13) 56, 96
West Kingsdown (TQ 56) 75, 115, 135
West Malling (TQ 65) 12, 27
Westwell (TQ 94) 115, 137, Fig. 137
West Wickham (TQ 36) 122, 126
Whitstable (TR 16) 11, 16, 19, 23, 94, 99, 149
Wickhambreux (TR 25) 137
Wigmore (TQ 76) 117, 137
Willesborough (TR 04) 116, 130, 135, 150
Wittersham (TQ 82) 134
Woodchurch (TQ 93) 115, 131, 135
Woolwich (TQ 47) 13, 22, 40, 102, Fig. 13
Wrotham Heath (TQ 65) 158
Wye (TR04) xviii, 18, 50, 55, 67, 71, 89, 92f, 97, 100, 114f, 120f, 126, 131, 137, 153, Figs. 7, 44, 57, 64, 77, Plates 8-11, 23
Wye Downs (TR 04) 48, 82, 84, 99f, Figs. 50-52

Yalding (TQ 65) 18, 34, 48, 61, 107
Yockletts Bank (Waltham) (TR 14) 99

INDEX OF SUBJECTS

Agriculture 2, 4, 11, 15, 20ff, 45ff, Fig. 16. (and see Fruit growing, Hop growing, Market gardening, Cattle, Sheep)
Barns 129f, 153, Figs. 79, 80, Plate 29
Bathing machines 148, Fig. 90
Battle of Britain xviii, 27
Beaker People 2
Belgae 3, 139
Black Death 154
Birds 80ff, 93ff, Figs. 49, 58, 62
Bogs 88f, 100, Fig. 54
Brewing 69, 107, 147, 152
Brickmaking 56, 79, 103, 112f
Bridges xvii, 18, Figs. 14, 20
Bronze Age 2
Building materials 111ff

Canals and navigable rivers 18, Fig. 13
Castles and Forts 2, 4, 10, 12, 13, 18ff, 89, 134, Figs. 5, 8, 10, 11, 12, 13, 15
Cathedrals, Canterbury 115f, 142ff, Fig. 68, Plate 26, Rochester 115, 147
Cattle 75ff
Cement making 56, 104, 106, Plate 16
Chalk xvii, 37ff, 90, 97, 103, 106, 112
Christianity xvi, 6, 8, 114ff, 139, 142ff
Churches, Parish, 12, 89, 112, 114ff, 142ff, 149ff, 153, 156, Figs. 63, 65, 66, 67, 69, 86, 87, 93, 94, 95, Plates 19, 30, Non-conformist 145, 152, 155, 157, 159, Fig. 97, Roman Catholic 117
Cinque Ports 12, Fig. 8, Plate 4
Climate 46ff
Clover, wild white or Kentish 83, Fig. 47
Coins xvi, Fig. 1
Colleges, Canterbury (St. Augustine's) 153, Maidstone 146, Wye 50, 71, 130, 132, Figs. 64, 79, Plates 8, 29
Cross channel traffic 28, 107

Dinosaur (Iguanodon) 32, 35, Fig. 24
Domesday Book 10, 153, Fig. 8
Dovecotes 130
Drainage, agricultural 55f, 76

Enclosure xvii, 11, 158
Engineering industries 108f

Erosion, coastal 40, 43, soil 2, 48
Farm buildings 129ff
Feudal system 8, 10
Flemings 14, 15
Flint 38, 40, 54, 112, 114f, Plate 19
Flint implements 1
Fossils 32, 34ff, Figs. 23, 24, 25, 26, 28, 29
Frost 47, 59
Fruit growing 15, 47, 52ff, 56ff, 127, Fig. 39, Plates 7, 8

Gardens 127ff, 143, Fig. 78
Geology xvii, 29ff, Figs 22-32, Plates 5, 16
Georgian period 15ff, 145, 151f, Fig. 13
Green Belt 160f, Fig. 98

Hedges 85f
Hill forts 2, Fig. 5
Hop growing 15, 26, 34, 48, 62ff, Figs. 40-44, Plates 9-13
Houses, general 117ff, timber framed 113f, 119ff, 124, 144, 151f, Figs. 70-72, Plates 20, 21
Huguenots 14

Ice Ages 1, 30, 38f, 42f
Inns 152, 155, Fig. 76
Insects 80, 84
Iron Age 2f, 139
Iron working, 4, 14, 101, Plate 25

Kingdom of Kent xiv, xvi, 6

Land quality xvii, 45, Fig. 46
Landscape Regions Fig. 21
Landslips 37, Plate 5
Lathes xviii
Long barrows 2, Fig. 4

Manors 10f, 153f
Market gardening 14, 71ff, Fig 45
Martello towers 19, Figs. 13, 15
Megaliths 2
Mesolithic period 1
Minerals: glauconite 34, gypsum Fig. 30, pyrite Fig. 27
Mineral extraction 101ff, 111ff, Plate 15
Monasteries and other religious houses 8, 12, 56, 89, 118, 122, 142ff, 145f, 153f, Fig. 8, 86
Murder, of Archbishop Becket 12, 143, Fig. 88, of Thomas Arden 121

Nature reserves 80, 82, 84, 88, 97ff, Fig 61

Neolithic Period 2, Fig. 4
Oast houses 68f, 131ff, 155, Fig. 81, Plates 22-24
Orchids 81f, 84, Figs. 50-52

Palaeolithic Period 1
Paper making 107, 136f, Plate 17
Pargetting 113, 146, Plate 27
Parks 127ff, 155ff, Figs. 17, 78
Place names xiv, 6f
Pollution of rivers 91f, Fig. 57
Population 15, 22, 24, 161, Figs. 13, 18, 85
Power stations 110, Plate 18

Ragstone 34f, 102f, 111f, 122, 146f, Fig. 10, Plate 15
Railways 23ff, 90, 149f, Figs. 18, 92, Plate 5
Rainfall 46f, Fig. 33
Redevelopment (of towns) 145, 147, 150
Revolts (*1381*) 11, 113 (*1450*) 11f, (*1830*) 22
Rivers 18, 41, 91ff, Fig. 57
Roads xvii, 4, 15ff, 28, 90, 150f, 162
Roman Period 3ff, 139ff, Figs. 6, 7

Saltmarshes 56, 95f, Fig. 59
Sand and gravel pits 36, 90f, 93f, 102
Saxon Period 6ff, 55, 114, 142, Fig. 87

Schools 145, 147, 155
Seaside resorts 26, 148f, Figs. 90, 91
Settlement pattern 4f, 7f, 29
Sheep 11, 74ff, 85, Fig. 48, Plate 7
Soils xvii, 3, 50ff, 70, Figs 34-38
Stuart Period 18f, 123, 149

Textile industries 14, 101, 136
Timber framing 129, Figs. 79, 80
  (and see Houses, timber framed)
Tokens, hop pickers' 68, Figs. 42-44, Plate 13
Towns 22, 24ff, 139ff, Figs. 13, 18, 85
Town halls 146, 152
Tudor Period 13ff, 145, Fig. 89

University of Kent 23, 145

Victorian Period 23ff, 124, Fig. 18
Villages, 153ff, 161f
Villas, Roman 4, 117f, Fig. 7

Wall paintings 142, 154
Wars, Civil (1642-9) 18, 145, World xviii, 26f, 88, 145
Watermills 92, 136f, 152f, Fig. 84, Plate 25
Weeds 87ff, Figs. 53, 56
Windmills 134ff, 155, Figs. 82, 83
Woodland 78ff

TQ4
TQ5
TQ6
TQ7
TQ8
7
6
5
4
3
2
Thames Estuary
River Thames
Erith
A282
DARTFORD TUNNEL
A207
Bexleyheath
Greenhithe
Cliffe
Lr. Stoke
Stoke
R. Medway
Eltham
A2
DARTFORD
Swanscombe
NorthFleet
GRAVESEND
A226
New Eltham
BEXLEY
Chalk
A266
Hoo
Mottingham
Sidcup
Wilmington
A2
Higham
Upshire
Wainscot
Upnor
Frindsbury
A2
BROMLEY
Chislehurst
Swanley
Sutton at Hone
Longfield
Strood
GILLINGHAM
Bickley
Swanley Junction
ROCHESTER
Lr. Rainham
Upchurch
Bromley Common
Farningham
Meopham
Cuxton
CHATHAM
A25
Orpington
Eynsford
New Ash Green
M2
Rainham
Newington
Chelsfield
A227
Halling
Wigmore
M2
Key Street
Farnborough
Green Street Grn.
A225
A20
M20
Walderslade
A21
Shoreham
Snodland
Stockbury
Bredgar
Biggin Hill
Otford
Wrotham
M20
Aylesford
M 25
Westerham Hill
Dunton Grn.
Ightham
W. Malling
A25
E. Malling
Detling
Seal
Offham
B2163
Riverhead
Borough Green
MAIDSTONE
M25
A25
A25
Sundridge
SEVENOAKS
B2016
Waterinbury
A26
Hollingbourne
Westerham
Mereworth
Leeds
Ide Hill
A21
Shipbourne
A227
Boughton Green
Sevenoaks Weald
A26
Yalding
Crockham Hill
Hadlow
Linton
B269
Four Elms
Hildenborough
Sutton Valence
Marlpit Hill
Leigh
B2027
A274
Bough Beech
TONBRIDGE
Collier Street
Edenbridge
B2017
Paddock Wood
Headcorn
Hever
B2026
Penshurst
B2015
B2162
Marden
Staplehurst
B2176
B2079
Smarden
B2188
Southborough
Matfield
B2160
A26
Horsmonden
A229
Cowden
Pembury
Curtisden Grn.
A264
TUNBRIDGE WELLS
A21
Biddenden
Ashurst
Goudhurst
A 262
Sissinghurst
Lamberhurst
Cranbrook
St. Michaels
A268
B2086
TENTERDEN
Benenden
Hawkhurst
Rolvenden
A268
Sandhurst
A28
Newenden
The County of KENT
Scale 0 1 2 3 4 5 Miles
Scale 0 1 2 3 4 5 6 7 8 9 10 Kilometres
© P.N.P. 1978
Map Drawing by Eric Martin
Note: The 10Km National Grid squares facilitate reference and to the sheets of 1:25,000 Ordnance Survey maps of the map first, e.g. Gravesend is in square TQ67.